Bill Clinton

As They Know Him

An Oral Biography

by David Gallen
with an introduction by Philip Martin

Gallen Publishing Group
New York

Preface

Optimism wavered when I first arrived in Little Rock on April 23, 1993, to begin researching a book project on America's new president, Bill Clinton. I didn't know anyone in town, and I foresaw mostly difficulties in finding willing interviewees. I parked my car on a deserted street. It was five o'clock in the afternoon, it was a weekday, and I was in the heart of downtown Little Rock, although I didn't know it. "Where's the downtown?" I asked the first person who walked by. "You're standing in it," she replied with a nod at the quiet street. "Well, then, where are all the people?" I asked. We looked off into the distance. A few blocks away a few people appeared. "These are them," she said. I thanked the woman for her time, but I thought to myself that I just might have a major problem here. As it turned out, I didn't. After that day I had no trouble finding people in Little Rock, most of whom were not only willing but often eager to share with me their perspectives on their former neighbor, boss, golf partner, political opponent or governor.

I spent four of the next six months in Little Rock. By November 2 I had traveled over much of Arkansas and interviewed more than 175 people, most of them in person. My phone interviews crisscrossed the country. This book belongs as much to the people who spoke to me as it does to me. Their thoughts and their voices provide the substance and the vitality. For the most part I simply listened, and listened, and listened.

I listened to friends of Bill Clinton; to staff members from Clinton's days as attorney general and governor for the state of Arkansas; to Arkansas state legislators as well as United States senators; to Clinton's political opponents and their strategists throughout his career in state politics; to Arkansas newspaper and magazine journalists who have been covering Clinton since his first run for office (for Congress) in 1974 as well as national correspondents and reporters who covered Clinton extensively throughout his 1992 presidential campaign; to radio and television journalists who have been following Clinton's career for eighteen years; to various other professionals who have known Clinton both on and off the stage of public life. I thank them all for their thoughts, their time, their generosity. I wish to thank them individually, too.

So I thank Clinton's friends: Judge Richard Arnold, Chris Ashby, Hazel Askew, Merlin Augustine, Kathleen Barnham, Woody Bassett, Nancy Bekavac, Paul Berry, Ellen Brantley, Sheila Bronfman, Tom Campbell, Lib Carlyle, Chuck Carroll, Patty Criner, Dale Drake, David Edwards, John Flake, Susan and Vic Fleming, George Frazier, Buddy Griffith, Mark Grobmyer, Bill and Merlee Harrison, Anne Henderson, Anne and Morriss Henry, Richard Herget, Judge Jack Holt, Edith Irons, Marlin Jackson, Phil Jamison, Robert Johnston, Jerry Jones, Brownie and Cal Ledbetter, David Leopoulos, Kathy McClanahan, Kay McClanahan, Myrna Martin, David Matthews, Starr Mitchell, Ark Monroe, Freddie and Reverend Victor Nixon, Walt Patterson, Donald Pogue, Margaret Polk, Hoyt Purvis, Joe Purvis, Skip Rutherford, Lottie Shackleford, Maurice Smith, Virgil Spurlin, Pat Storer, James Walters, Carl and Margaret Whillock, Lee Williams, Bill Wilson, Donna Wingfield, Professor Al Witte, and George Wright.

Clinton's former staff members: Kay Kelley Arnold, Bill Bowen, Sam Bratton, Winston Bryant, Bill Clarke, Jimmie Lou Fisher, Kathy Ford, Lee Jones, Mahlon Martin, Bobby Roberts, Craig Smith, Steve Smith, and Betsey Wright.

Current and former state legislators: Ben Allen, Jay Bradford, Preston Bynum, Charlie Cole Chaffin, Lloyd George, Max Howell, Myra Jones, Bill Lancaster, John Lipton, David Malone, John Miller, Knox Nelson, David Pryor (U.S. senator), and Nick Wilson.

Clinton's political opponents Orval Faubus, George Jernigan, Tom McRae, Sheffield Nelson, Frank White. And oppositional campaign advisors Darrell Glascock and Jerry Russell.

By and large the print and electronic media people both inside Arkansas and out of state were extremely cooperative and kind to me. I am grateful, I am appreciative. I extend my thanks to Arkansas newspaper journalists Paul Barton, Brenda Blagg, Phyllis Brandon, Max Brantley, John Brummett, Scott Charton, Bill Douglass,

Ernie Dumas, Joan Duffy, Jane Fullerton, Ed Gray, Paul Greenberg, Pat Harris, Maria Henson, Alyson Hoge, Phoebe Wall Howard, Jeff Katz, Terry Lemons, Mara Leveritt, Randy Lilleston, Gene Lyons, Philip Martin, Bob McCord, Carol Matlack, James Merriweather, Rex Nelson, Meredith Oakley, Mark Oswald, John Reed, Professor Roy Reed, Guy Reel, Doug Smith, John Robert Starr, Jeffrey Stinson, Bob Storer, Pam Strickland, Mike Trimble, Scott Van Laningham, and Bob Wells.

And to these national and out-of-state newspeople who covered the 1992 presidential campaign: Sidney Blumenthal, Chris Burrey, Eleanor Clift, Peter Goldman, John Hanchette, Tom Hannon, Gwen Ifill, John King, Sol Levine, Mark Miller, Adam Pertman, Gene Randall, Katharine "Kit" Seelye, and Juan Williams.

And to these current or former Arkansas radio and television journalists: Tom Atwood, Steve Barnes, Regina Blakely, Ron Blome, Herbie Byrd, Sonja Deaner, Mel Hanks, Anne Jansen, Alan Kelley, Gina Kurre, Pat Lynch, Mark Malcolm, Deborah Mathis, Amy Oliver, Andy Pearson, Bill Powell, Margaret Preston, Joe Quinn, Susan Rodman, Bill Sadler, and Bob Steele.

In addition I thank interviewees Professor Art English, Cliff Jackson, Greg Lathrop, Ernest and Zoe Oakleaf, and Professor Gary Wekkin.

Also, educator Charles Allen kindly allowed me the use of a series of interviews he conducted in 1991.

Over all, the people I met and spoke with in Arkansas redefined for me the meaning of southern hospitality. A few of them did even more, and I feel fortunate to have gotten to know them, to have enjoyed their company and to have benefited from their resourcefulness. I take special note, therefore, of Rex Nelson, political editor of the *Arkansas Democrat-Gazette,* who graciously paved the way for me in Little Rock by setting up my initial twenty or so interviews. He was also always available to answer the many questions I needed to ask, as were *Democrat-Gazette* columnists Philip Martin and Paul Greenberg. Especially helpful in providing me with leads to further interviews were Steve Barnes and Bob Steele, both of them veteran television journalists at KARK-TV. Sonja Deaner may be less of a veteran, but she was no less helpful and supportive.

I am also grateful to Andy Collins and his family. From day one, when I could not find downtown in what was then an unfamiliar city, they made me feel welcome and comfortable. Too, Andy generously allowed me the use of his office during my entire stay in Little Rock. I appreciate his many courtesies and I shall always value his friendship. Indeed, on those occasions in the eight weeks since I've left Little Rock that I miss particular people or some favorite place there, I feel good knowing that I have an open invitation to return and share an office on the eleventh floor of the Stephens Building on Center Street with friends.

It didn't all happen in Little Rock. This project would not yet be completed without the help of a few people in New York. For the past three years now I have been working on book projects with Peter Skutches. His considerable talents have never failed me. By November 8 I had accumulated ninety-seven hours of taped interviews—more than four thousand pages once they were transcribed—and I had five weeks to create and complete, say, a four hundred page manuscript. As they like to say in Arkansas, I was so low I could have played handball against a curbstone. By December 15 materials for the book had been extracted from several towering stacks of transcripts and had been shaped, in my opinion, into a very readable text. I couldn't have done it alone.

I also wish to thank Kate Gaffin, who had the patience and forbearance to transcribe all the tapes and later to type most of the manuscript, along with some assistance from Diana Wells and Raphaela Seroy. My thanks, too, to Anne Spivack for her fine work on the manuscript in the final editorial stretch.

David Gallen
January 6, 1994

Contents

Notes on a Boy President

"He had come a long way to this blue lawn, and his dream must have seemed so close that he could hardly fail to grasp it. He did not know it was already behind him, somewhere back in that vast obscurity beyond the city, where the dark fields of the republic rolled on under the night."

—F. Scott Fitzgerald, *The Great Gatsby*

From my backyard I can look through a thinning crop of autumnal gray trees and see the bathtub white dome of the state Capitol of Arkansas. It bears a passable resemblance to the national dome in Washington, a happy circumstance for moviemakers who need a surrogate to blow up or crash a helicopter into. Its caretaker, the Arkansas secretary of state—a rascal named Bill McCuen—is accommodating in such matters; he once allowed a washed-up linebacker named Brian Bozworth to spin a Harley-Davidson's tires across its polished floors while the cameras rolled. At Christmastime each year, McCuen has flashing lights strung across its cupola and converts it into a garish, rotating "Disco Dome." People come from all over the state, and, we suspect, Missouri and Oklahoma, to see what the Arkies have done up for Jesus's birthday. We are used to such abuse in Little Rock, we shrug off so much.

Until Bill Clinton came along, most people probably thought of Arkansas as a land of ignorant hillbillies, the realm of Li'l Abner and Daisy Mae and Snuffy Smith and Jed Clampett. True, ours is still a frontier state, raw and remote and sometimes less than civilized. True, if any state deserves to be called anti-intellectual, then

1

Arkansas is it. Too many of us think that dogs and guns and commerce are the only proper pursuits for men, that ideas and art are the province of the anemic and the weak.

Philip Roth has compared Arkansas to Israel, a country unto itself, surrounded by the Other. Of course in our case, the Other is the United States of America, the richest and most powerful nation on earth. And while we may not be so backward as we fear, there is a whiff of the Third World about our state.

Arkansas was what was left over after Missouri and Louisiana were chiseled out of the Louisiana Purchase and after Oklahoma was designated Indian Territory. Poor farmers with large families, little cash, and very few slaves settled these unwanted regions; as H. L. Mencken put it "the miasmatic jungles of Arkansas."

Yet, there is much of Arkansas that is beautiful, and more that is surprising. Our countryside is as pretty as any; up in the hills, rivers boil through spectacular, bluff-lined passes. The changing fall foliage rivals New England's.

Little Rock, Clinton's first capital, sits on the southern bank of the Arkansas River, where the flatlands of the Mississippi Delta meet the hills, very near the geographical center of the state. Our state's only real city, Little Rock, is more cultured and cosmopolitan than one might expect. There are a number of fine restaurants, some good book stores, and a ready supply of alert professionals who stock Jack Stephens's downtown bond house, the University of Arkansas for Medical Sciences, the various media outlets, state government, and the courts. For a town of its size—roughly 300,000 people live in the city or its suburbs—the theater is good and so is the local arts center.

Other towns hold diverse, and often painfully subtle charms. The mountain resort of Eureka Springs is a looney version of an artists' colony, lately infiltrated by country music Christians. Hot Springs, where Bill Clinton grew up, is a high camp cross between Las Vegas and Disneyland, smack in the middle of the Bible Belt, that in its glory days was a favorite retreat of the likes of Babe Ruth and Al Capone. Fayetteville is a remote and hilly college town, home of the beloved Arkansas Razorbacks. Pine Bluff, the state's second largest population center, once enjoyed the distinction of being named by Rand McNally as the worst place to live in the nation. (I say "enjoyed" because the subsequent attention paid to the city, as well as several semi-debunking reports on network news shows, actually had the result of enhancing Pine Bluff's reputation.) Texarkana, a border-straddling oddity in the extreme southwest corner of the state was the boyhood home of H. Ross Perot.

There is an amiable resourcefulness about most Arkansans; they are a good-humored people who can live well with the most modest of resources. They are the kind of people who have had to make do with what they could scrape together.

Arkansas has its billionaires—the late Sam Walton's children, the Stephens brothers, J. B. Hunt, and a Rockefeller—but the disparity between our very few rich and powerful and the mostly rural masses is uncomfortable. For four decades starting with World War II, the economy of Arkansas grew faster than the national average, still it has yet to catch up with the rest of the country in per capita income. The average Arkansan still makes about 25 percent less than the average American. We lead the country in the production of chickens and rice, but we have fewer natural resources than our neighbors and no major growing industry. The aluminum fields of the central part of the state are depleted, as are the timber lands of the east.

In terms of area, Arkansas is the smallest state between the Mississippi and the Pacific. In terms of population, it is the smallest southern state. Despite the undeniable progress that was accomplished during—and before—Bill Clinton's years as governor, Arkansas remains near the bottom of the states in terms of literacy rates and teacher salaries. We have fewer museums and libraries, and fewer books in the libraries we do have. Conversely, we lead the states in the incidence of venereal disease and unwed mothers; the infant mortality rate is inexcusable. For years, the unofficial state motto has been "Thank God for Mississippi."

Though Arkansas was part of the Confederacy, it is really not of the South. It is in the South, certainly; but not *of* the South. At the time of the War Between the States, only the cotton plantation country near the Mississippi River was completely settled. Even in the faded towns along the Mississippi, where today great slouching homes overlook public housing tracts, there is little of the sense of cloying ruin that permeates the real South. There is no real aristocracy here, no great founding families. There were no great robber barons, no great plantation owners. There are none of William Faulkner's Compsons here, only striving or bitter Snopeses, each scrambling for a place at the table. To be from Arkansas is to be turned away from the big house, to be designated redneck or trash.

This is not without its benefits. Until a few years ago the license plates on Arkansas cars announced we were living in the "Land of Opportunity." With no tight traditions, Arkansas has long honored the bright young person with creative ideas. Upward mobility is no myth here. It is said that anyone who can write a $1,000 check to a charity can become part of Little Rock society, invited to all manner of balls, soirees and fetes. In this regard, Arkansas has more of a western than southern sensibility—family counts for less than ability. Even our billionaires have modest roots—Sam Walton began his career running small-town dime stores; Jack Stephens and his late brother Witt built their fortunes from scratch.

Sometimes it seems the most southern thing about Arkansas is its people's habit of self-deprecation and instinct for shame; a pathology of melancholia and self-loathing that manifests itself as a kind of palpable inferiority complex. Arkansans reflexively assume anything of local origin to be second-rate, we mistrust the most innovative and original among us. Likewise, we often suspect the worst of ourselves; like all hell-fearing beings we continually question our motives and hold fast to guilt.

Because of this insecurity, this inappropriate defensiveness, we fear the harsh judgments of outlanders. Because we are from Arkansas, we have none of the advantages. We are quickly and deeply hurt, even when censure is offered constructively. We see offense where none is intended. To be from Arkansas is to simultaneously seek and scorn the approval of the Other.

Hope, Arkansas, in the southwestern corner of the state, is a fairly conventional American small town, perhaps poorer than most. While today, an outsider might have considerable difficulty distinguishing the working-class white neighborhoods from their black counterparts or in discovering a qualitative difference between the squalid trailers favored by "white trash" and the silverwood shotgun shacks of poor blacks, there are clear caste boundaries in this little town. The locals know which streets are which and generally keep to their own. Those still-extant boundaries were more pronounced and enforced in August 1946, when the boy who was to become Bill Clinton entered the milieu.

William Jefferson Blythe IV was born eleven months after the end of World War II and three months after his father, a salesman for a heavy equipment firm, was killed in a freakish one-car accident. (The elder Blythe, we now know, was a bit of a rounder and possibly a bigamist. After Clinton's inauguration, a man appeared claiming, apparently truthfully, to be the president's half-brother.)

Relatives say even now they can discern in the president the familiar tics of the father he never knew; they see it in the puppyish way he cocks his head, in his slender fingers, and easy smile.

Five months after his birth, Billy Blythe's mother Virginia turned the child over to her parents and returned to nursing school in Louisiana to gain certification as an anesthetist. This might account for at least a portion of young Blythe's precocity—he was, by all accounts, an exceptionally serious child. His grandparents, Elridge and Edith Cassidy, were uncommonly decent people. They ran a general store in a rural area near Hope that had a reputation as one of a very few places where black people could freely mingle with whites. The Cassidys would even extend credit to blacks and are remembered by some in Hope as rather self-righteous social liberals. The uglier phrase, which still has surprising currency in south Arkansas today, is "nigger lover." Billy Blythe heard the words frequently.

During a late night airplane flight from Texarkana to Little Rock during his 1990 gubernatorial campaign, Clinton spoke about his earliest childhood, and gave credit to his grandparents for forging his moral instinct. "I know how people are divided," he said. "I've seen it, I grew up with it. If there's anything I feel strongly about . . . it's that we can't let ourselves be torn apart like this."

When Billy was four years old, his mother returned. Three years later, she married Roger Clinton. The family moved to Hot Springs, where Roger took a job in his brother's Buick dealership. The union was not a completely happy one. Roger Clinton was an alcoholic who sometimes beat his wife and once fired off a handgun in the living room. Perhaps as a reaction to the turmoil at home, Billy Blythe threw himself into his school work, becoming a model student. He remembers engaging his mother—a voluble and opinionated woman—in sprightly conversations about the issues of the day.

Some have suggested that Virginia was pushing her son to develop his already apparent intellectual gifts, preparing him for a public life that would take him far beyond Hot Springs. In any event, Virginia and her clever eldest son spent many hours in the kitchen in earnest discussions that likely provided both of them with an escape from the domestic terror that would start with Roger's first glass of bourbon.

A familiar chapter in the Bill Clinton hagiography has the pre-teen Billy Blythe lecturing his mother on the inherent evil of American apartheid, and Bill Clinton has claimed that the Central

High School crisis of 1957, which occurred when he was eleven years old, was a significant event in the development of his intellectual character.

Two anecdotes from Billy Blythe's early teens mark him as a child of unusual sensitivity and courage. After Virginia divorced, and then quickly reconciled with Roger Clinton, fifteen-year-old Bill adopted his stepfather's surname in an effort to heal the fractured family. Then—following the incident in which Roger fired his pistol in the house—Bill took his mother and younger half-brother by the hand as he confronted his stepfather. "You will never hit either of them again," he said. "If you want them, you'll have to go through me." While Roger Clinton continued to drink, apparently the young man's warning had the desired effect—the violence at home ceased.

Years later, the half-brother who had held Bill Clinton's hand that fateful evening, Roger Clinton, Jr., would tell reporters that Bill was virtually a father to him while he was growing up. "He was always there," Roger said. "After my father died, he practically raised me and I adored him."

Meanwhile, Bill was becoming the perfect student, the sort of driven overachiever whom teachers love and classmates usually detest. But though Bill Clinton was not the most popular kid in school, neither was he a nerdy pariah. He seemed to have existed comfortably among the upper reaches of high school society, an exceptionally able and gifted kid determined to rise above his decidedly white trash roots. In high school, he was selected as a senator to Boy's Nation, an annual exercise in mock government sponsored by the American Legion. He traveled to Washington, where he met John F. Kennedy in a ceremony in the Rose Garden. That image, of the thin, bushy-headed boy in a white polo shirt with an oversized Legion crest, encumbered by the inevitable, unfortunate name tag, leaning into a handshake with the impossibly young, doomed president, surfaced during Clinton's 1992 presidential campaign, in both still photo and grainy film formats. It is a remarkable record—young Clinton seems to have pushed himself to the front of the crowd, there to be noticed, selected by the most glamorous American politician ever. There is something pushy and earnest in the face of that young man, something that was not lost on all his former high school and college classmates who now say they were certain Bill Clinton would one day become president.

Clinton himself marks that moment as the instant his political ambitions jelled. While he says he had earlier considered a career in music—his saxophone was good enough for the statewide scholastic honor band—or medicine, after experiencing the electric shock of brushing against JFK, he never thought of any career but public service.

He enrolled at Georgetown University largely to be in Washington, near the seat of power he hoped someday to occupy. While he was at Georgetown, Roger Clinton was dying of cancer at Duke University Hospital. For months, the twenty-year-old Clinton would make the drive from Washington to Durham, North Carolina, every weekend to visit his dying stepfather, the man who had created the domestic misery young Bill wanted so desperately to escape.

The rapprochement came on Easter weekend in 1966, as the two men attended services at Duke Chapel. Clinton later described the moment to Peter Applebome of the *New York Times*: "It was, God, beautiful. I think he knew I was coming down there just because I loved him. There was nothing else to fight over, nothing else to run from. It was a wonderful time in my life, and I think, his."

Then came Oxford, Clinton's Rhodes scholarship (an old joke has us Arkies misunderstanding it as a "Roads scholarship," and considering it a very fine practical diploma) and the subsequent deepening of his activism and putative vision of governance. It was here the machinations surrounding Clinton's avoidance of the draft took place, culminating in the remarkable, impassioned letter he sent to his ROTC Colonel Eugene Holmes, thanking him for "saving me from the draft." Although Clinton critics have used the letter as evidence that Clinton took extraordinary measures to escape military service in Vietnam, the letter was dated December 3, 1969, three months after Clinton received a very high lottery number. It is difficult to read the text of the letter without being moved and impressed by its thoughtful young author. In it, Clinton describes himself and his peers as "still loving their country but loathing the military, to which you and other good men have devoted years, lifetimes of the best service you could give."

It is at best simplistic, and more likely disingenuous, to read into those words a distaste for American servicemen. "Loathing the military" seems, in context, to refer to the ongoing actions in Vietnam, not to the "good men" who did serve. On the other hand, it is apparent that Bill Clinton—like many of the ablest young men of his generation—chose to use whatever sneaky means he could to avoid military service. In the practical, if not strictly legal sense, he did in fact dodge the draft. And it is equally clear that, when confronted with the evidence years later, he chose to dissemble and spin the facts, rather than to own up to doing what he did.

Bill Clinton did not return home and enroll in the ROTC program at the University of Arkansas as he promised Colonel Holmes he would. Instead he entered Yale Law School where he met and wooed and eventually moved in with Hillary Rodham, another middle-class striver from a comfortable Chicago suburb. Hillary Rodham was and is every bit Clinton's intellectual equal, and in her career as an activist attorney, she has consistently seemed less willing to compromise her principles for political reasons than the ever-pragmatic Clinton.

In 1972, Hillary and Bill worked together as he ran George McGovern's ill-fated presidential campaign in Texas. She then moved on to Washington, where she worked for the special impeachment investigation staff of the House Judiciary Commitee. When that job abruptly ended with the the resignation of Richard Nixon, Hillary joined Clinton back home in Arkansas. For a time, they both taught law in Fayetteville. They married in 1975, after Clinton had run an unsuccessful, but ultimately encouraging race for Congress against an entrenched Republican. But he was elected attorney general in 1976, and in 1979, he became, at thirty-two, the youngest governor in the country since the thirty-one-year-old Harold Stassen was elected in Minnesota in 1938.

Clinton's first term as governor resembles, in a way, his current presidency. He came in furious, with a program for every problem, and surrounded himself with a coterie of young, smart, and bearded reformers from out of state. It at times seemed like a calculated attempt at a southern Camelot, though it had its less-than-graceful episodes. For instance, to celebrate his inauguration, Clinton threw a huge rock-and-roll dance party, unfortunately themed, like a high school prom, "Denim and Diamonds." For good measure, near the end of the night, he joined the band on stage for a saxophone solo.

With his longish hair and uncommonly liberal—for Arkansas, at least—ideas, Clinton was a dashing figure, unafraid to pick fights with some of the state's most powerful interests. He argued with the state's timber companies and trucking interests, and anonymously coauthored a newspaper article that denounced Arkansas Power and Light Company's involvement in a nuclear power plant in Mississippi. Immediately, he set about fulfilling his campaign promise to upgrade the state's highway system by raising gasoline taxes and automobile licensing fees to finance road improvements. He also expressed misgivings about the state's death penalty— though he was careful to add that he thought capital punishment could be an effective deterrent to crime.

Democratic party insiders quickly recognized him as a potential star, and Clinton addressed the party convention in 1980, where he claimed to represent "a new generation of party leaders." His speech did not, however, foreshadow his "New Democrat" rhetoric of 1992 so much as look backward to the liberal idealism of Hubert Humphrey. "We have proved that our party is more sensitive than the Republicans' to equality and justice, to the poor and the dispossessed," he said. "But now we must prove that we offer more in the way of creative and realistic solutions to our economic and energy and environmental problems, and that we can have a vision that can withstand the erosion of special interest politics that is gripping our land."

But however high Bill Clinton's national stock had risen, at home many Arkansans took exception to his Ivy League kitchen cabinet, many of whom seemed to regard the Arkansas *hoi polloi* as backward hicks. Clinton's national ambitions seemed a little too obvious. But although the popular mythology has it that many Arkansans felt their governor and his wife—who at that time still called herself Hillary Rodham—had grown arrogant, and that they voted for his Republican opponent, a gregarious savings-and-loan executive named Frank White, merely in order to send Clinton a message, in reality, other factors played at least as large a role as Clinton's imperiousness.

This was also the year that witnessed the ascendancy of Ronald Reagan and country-western Republicanism in the South. Jimmy Carter faltered, and so did Bill Clinton. Now the youngest ex-governor in American history, Clinton retreated to the relative safety of his friend Bruce Lindsey's Little Rock law firm. A year after his defeat, he was running again. He went on television, apologized to the voters, and asked for another chance.

"I made a young man's mistake," he said on the eve of his comeback Democratic primary in 1982. "I had an agenda a mile long that you couldn't achieve in a four-year term. I was so busy doing what I wanted to do I didn't have time to correct mistakes."

There is no question that Clinton's 1980 setback radically altered his political style, that Frank White ripped the fearlessness from Bill Clinton. His defeat very easily could have been the end of a political career that Clinton had trained for like an athlete since his youth. Those who believe themselves to be close to Bill Clinton say that during much of 1981, he was depressed, fretting that his chosen trajectory might not be available. He returned to the public eye contrite, with his longish hair shorn, and without his carpetbagger advisers. He was suddenly a more incremental, moderate politician. Gone were any lagging doubts about the usefulness of the electric chair, gone were his vocal broadsides against the timber companies and other powerful interests. Hillary Rodham became Hillary Clinton. And, in 1982, Bill Clinton once again became governor of Arkansas.

He would remain governor until after he was elected president.

"There is the world of ideas and the world of practice," Matthew Arnold wrote. Government, the science of determining how a country's citizens will live, is ideally (though rarely) suspended in the juncture of these two spheres. Policy is best enacted by specialists but driven by visionaries. Even so, it is considered naive to argue for a vision of a good society unpolluted by partisan politics. Democratic government works only so long as an intellectual superego—a leader—is in place to harness the collective id of the masses. Demagogues, such as Wisconsin's Joe McCarthy, Mississippi's Theodore Bilbo, Louisiana's Huey Long, North Carolina's Jesse Helms, and Arkansas's own Orval Faubus arise when charismatic and cunning leaders neglect their moral duty and bend the mass whim to their own political ends.

After regaining the statehouse in 1982, Bill Clinton seemed determined never to repeat the mistakes of 1980. His new issues were, appropriately enough for a state in Arkansas's miserable economic condition, education and the development of new jobs. During the next eight years, Clinton would return to these issues again and again, while occasionally emphasizing utility reform, ethics in government, highway improvement, and even the environment. But he was much more measured than he was in his first term, as his teenage predilection for peacemaking seemed to reemerge—Clinton developed a passion for consensus-building, developing what my friend and former colleague Stephen Buel has called the "politics of agreement."

With his perennially boyish looks and easy smile, Clinton maintained Richard Corey's common touch while, for the most part, fighting the good fight against a know-nothing legislature. Although education reform is surely the safest issue a progressive southerner can champion, Clinton staked out the high ground. He also advocated an ambitious restructuring of the state's tax system. His education reform package passed in 1983, and his job training program passed in 1985. In 1988, he took a referendum to voters that set a code of ethics for legislators even though this last victory angered lawmakers and injured his ability to work with the legislature.

He even had a moment of startling moral clarity and courage. In 1984, when the state police came to Clinton and told him they had evidence that his half-brother Roger Clinton was selling cocaine, Clinton approved the sting that resulted in Roger's arrest and imprisonment.

Yet, such instances were becoming increasingly rare. There were, in the post-1980 Clinton, some troubling tendencies. He controlled his risks. As he was preparing to run for reelection in 1990, he made some murky pronouncements on issues such as capital punishment and flag-burning that seemed desperately cynical, designed not to cost him the yahoo vote. During a Democratic Leadership Conference, Clinton said that in order to compete with Republicans for the White House, Democrats had to "get on the right side of" such emotional issues as flag-burning—advice that seemed uncomfortably near endorsing situational demagoguery. Throughout the 1980s, Clinton ran his gubernatorial races not as a man determined to impress his vision upon a land he loves, but as a politician attempting to cling to a power base. Damaged by his 1980 defeat, Clinton turned skittish—it often seemed that he was willing to hedge his notion of virtue rather than risk rejection by the voters.

During 1986 and 1987, Clinton was chairman of the National Governors Association, a position that gave him rein to travel the country and gauge his support. Clinton made thirty-four trips to twenty-one states during his tenure, and he said later that his trips convinced him that he could run well. Most Arkansans expected their governor to announce that he would run for president. On July 14, 1987, Clinton stunned his supporters—and many journalists—by announcing in a press release that he would not run.

A hall had been rented for the next day, and the governor had scheduled a press conference. Ray Strother, a well known Democratic consultant, was already in town planning media strategy. There seems little question that Clinton was planning to make the race in 1988, and then, at the last possible moment, backed out.

There has always been speculation that the problems encountered by Senator Gary Hart of Colorado—forced out of the race following revelations of womanizing—had much to do with Clinton's decision. Suddenly, the rules were changed and any candidate could expect to have his private life scrutinized by an emboldened press.

"Mentally I was 100 percent committed to the race, but emotionally I wasn't," Clinton said at the time, denying that his decision was based on anything other than family considerations. He recalled the uncertainty of his own childhood and said he feared the effect the distractions and pressure of a national campaign would have on his then eight-year-old daughter Chelsea.

A year later, Clinton's national political fortunes seemed to plummet further when he delivered a stupefying thirty-three minute keynote speech at the 1988 Democratic National Convention in Atlanta. After becoming a national joke, Clinton showed two conflicting yet very genuine sides of his personality. First he whined, blaming his speech on the guidelines set forth by nominee Michael Dukakis's camp. Then he redeemed himself by going on the *Tonight Show with Johnny Carson,* and blowing a credible rendition of George Gershwin's "Summertime" on his saxophone.

I remember watching Clinton on the *Tonight Show* with two friends of his, both of whom were nervous and doubted the wisdom of Clinton's appearing on a show where he had become a running joke. But as I watched the easy-grinning governor on television, I experienced something of a revelation—I suddenly realized that Bill Clinton was indeed a person of destiny.

Even so, by the time the 1990 gubernatorial election rolled around, many Arkansans who, in other years would have supported Clinton, were wondering if his very longevity in office had not affected the state's welfare, by calcifying the power structure and creating a kind of imperial executive. There was widespread speculation that Clinton would not make the race in 1990, that he instead would concentrate on running for the presidency in 1992.

Among those who thought Clinton was vulnerable was the late Lee Atwater, the genius GOP campaign strategist and the architect of George Bush's rather nasty—and undeniably successful—1988 presidential campaign. Driven to some extent by his personal dislike for Clinton, Atwater recruited the then-Democratic congressman from Little Rock, a wild-eyed loose cannon named Tommy Robinson, to run as a Republican against Clinton. Robinson, a former sheriff and Clinton appointee, was best known for his reckless willingness to say anything about anyone. Atwater and other GOP strategists thought that even if Clinton could survive what would surely be a vicious mud-slinging attack by Robinson, his reputation would be so sullied that any national ambitions would have to be, once again, postponed.

Here in Arkansas we anticipated a bloodbath, that Robinson would accuse Clinton not only of womanizing, but possibly of miscegenation, fathering bastards, drug abuse, or even worse— Robinson was the most colorful kind of southern demagogue; whenever convenient, he could conflate rumor and innuendo into charges that, however unsubstantiated, could not be ignored.

In fact, when Clinton reluctantly announced he was, in fact, to run for governor in 1990, he said his chief reason for making the campaign was to save the state from the "black shadow" of Tommy Robinson. Clinton averred that no other Democrat could defeat the popular former sheriff, and he may have been right. But when the smoke cleared in the GOP primary, it was Sheffield Nelson, another former Clinton ally gone over to the Republicans who had vanquished Robinson. Clinton—after promising to serve his full four-year term as governor, a promise that seemed to preclude his running for president in 1992—easily handled Nelson in the general election.

It was during this 1990 campaign that I would write, in *Spectrum*, a departed Little Rock alternative newspaper, perhaps the most embarrassing words of my career:

> He is the Sun King and if you look too long at him you will be blind, your senses flooded with his gold-spined brilliance. As e.e. cummings might have said of him, *Jesus he is a handsome man* ... despite his too big head and hands and feet and his roomy, rheumy, allergy-ridden nose. There must be some elemental undercurrent here that generates envy in other men, not just the musk of power but something pheromonic. Since it is not polite to compare your governor to Mussolini, or even Huey Long, then let's say he is like one of those Kennedy boys, or that rare thing, a soulful politician.
>
> Bill Clinton has a common touch, a dangerous charisma and a sense of his own mortality. At forty-four, he is running for governor for the sixth time, though men like Clinton and Joe DiMaggio seem to glide more than run.

In some respects it is difficult to stand by such language, but that is the kind of response Clinton evokes in people. His personal skills are extraordinary, and are trivialized by television. Bill Clinton can make you think you are the smartest, most insightful person in the world even as he dazzles you with his own command of facts and figures. He can deliver just the right dose of simulated intimacy; for instance, once he told me that despite all outward appearances, he was very nervous when he appeared on the *Tonight Show*. "I remember Joe Cocker was on there with me," Clinton confided. "I wanted to play with him but I was too scared to ask—he had a wildass band." As difficult as it may be to imagine Bill Clinton intimidated by a rock star's bass player, when the anecdote is relayed by the current president, it charms and flatters.

To understand Clinton, one must understand Arkansas. And to understand Arkansas, one must understand Central High and its residual guilt. For some of us in Arkansas, Bill Clinton still stands as our best hope for redemption. Others of us think his anguish and spirit have shrunken, and that he is as hollow as he is gifted.

Beneath that dome that hovers over my backyard, in the sepulchral, marble-spread stillness of the state Capitol, there resides an ugly monument. In 1990, with some stealth and without the benefit of public money, supporters and friends of Orval E. Faubus installed in a hallway off the second floor rotunda a brown bronze bust of the obstructionist architect of the 1957 Central High School crisis.

An enigmatic, sphinx-like smile cracks the erstwhile six-term governor's frozen aspect. The effect is further confused by the nearly touching, sad cast of its eyes. This is a statue that seems not to know whether to laugh or weep. Though even the model does not thoroughly approve of the knurled and creased likeness, complaining that Winthrop Rockefeller's bust is "much better," it is one of only three busts as yet placed in the Capitol and, as such, it must be regarded as high tribute.

To the out-of-state visitor, as well as to many lifelong residents, the bust might suggest an ugliness more insidious than unhandsomeness. It must seem strange recognition to bestow on the most infamous Arkansan, a man best known for his defiance of federal law.

For Faubus, of course, is the governor who ordered the Arkansas

National Guard to seize Little Rock's Central High School in an effort to prevent nine black students from enrolling there. It was Faubus who, in August 1958, shepherded through the state legislature a bill that established a "legal basis to close schools forced to integrate and transfer public funds to private schools."

On September 27, 1958, Little Rock voters elected to do just that, and the public schools remained closed for the entire 1958-59 school year. Only after the U.S. Circuit Court of Appeals for the Eighth Circuit ruled the closing law unconstitutional, and the business elite of the city mobilized, leading to the election of three desegregation candidates to the school board in May 1959 did the high school reopen—with limited integration.

While there is evidence that Faubus became a segregationist hero more from political opportunism that pathology, his actions helped throw the schools of Little Rock into a still extant cycle of turmoil and bad faith, with economic and social ramifications that cost the state at least as much as the estimated $123 million settlement. Faubus converted one of the ugliest and most ignorant strains of the American character into political capital; he exploited racial mistrust and dread in order to secure a political base.

While the maneuvers of politicians such as Faubus and Alabama's George Wallace might seem silly and perverse to the great majority of Americans today, one might wonder whether things have really changed so much in the intervening years. Racism is one of the most persistent and potent undercurrents of civilization; only since the end of World War II has America found it necessary to officially expunge the remnants of Jim Crow from its legal and political systems.

The social crisis facing African Americans is certainly no secret; so long as a class of people remains economically and politically dispossessed, no real assimilative progress is possible. W. E. B. Du Bois noted that the color line was the emphatic fact of American society. That color line, however camouflaged, remains today, infecting every facet of American life.

For a southern state, the African-American population of Arkansas is relatively small (about 16 percent) and concentrated in the state's southern and eastern regions. The racial dynamic is different than in other southern states, largely because the legacy of slavery has had only a relatively minor effect on Arkansas. Since only 3 percent of Arkansas landowners kept slaves at the onset of the Civil War, and only a small minority of these held more than a few slaves, recent tensions between the races stem more from economic competition between blacks and whites than from a continuation of the plantation system. While white attitudes toward blacks in places like Mississippi, Georgia, and Alabama are informed by a certain *noblesse oblige*, Arkansas stands apart. The racism practiced in Arkansas rarely manifests itself in the "gentle" patronizing of black folkways associated with the stereotypical southern aristocrat. In Arkansas, racism is more fearful than condescending, more like the variety practiced in northern cities like Chicago and Boston than in, say, Oxford, Mississippi.

Take the example of Nolan Richardson, the flamboyant basketball coach at the University of Arkansas in Fayetteville. In 1987, Richardson was going through a tragic time. His daughter had died of cancer. More distressing to some was the fact that his teams were losing almost as often as they won. After a move to fire Richardson in the wake of his daughter's funeral failed, a heavyweight alumni association called the Razorback Club instructed the university's then-president Ray Thornton and athletic director Frank Broyles *never* to hire another black head coach.

Similarly, in 1989, a white teacher in the small town of England, Arkansas, defended the segregationist policies of the town's *public* swimming pool by explaining that she personally felt "uncomfortable around blacks." Bill Powell, a Little Rock radio talk show host, took to the air to defend the teacher, not on a First Amendment basis, but because it was "natural" to feel uncomfortable around people of a different color. In 1990, Ralph Forbes, a white supremacist and former associate of hate-monger Tom Metzger, ran a credible campaign for lieutenant governor.

Of course, racism of the most virulent sort is invariably a form of self-loathing, a fear fed by weakness. It is unfortunate that there are still many in Arkansas who loathe Bill Clinton largely because, as governor, black people loved and supported him in extraordinary numbers. Although Clinton's record on civil rights issues is not infallible and certainly not as good as advertised, he did at least appoint unprecedented numbers of African Americans to state boards and commissions, as well as to high-profile policymaking positions, providing role models while at the same time encouraging black political fealty. Dr. Joycelyn Elders, who served as director of the state Health Department, and who has also gone on to become surgeon general of the United States, is but one example of Clinton's able black appointees.

Stephen Buel, who is now the acting editor of *L.A. Weekly*, and who for several years published *Spectrum*, calls Clinton's record on civil rights "fearless."

"Race is the one subject on which Bill Clinton is unreproachable," Buel said in an interview conducted shortly after the Los Angeles riots. "It is the one issue on which he's consistently enlightened and where he's followed his own heart."

But political appointments—jobs delivered by a beneficient authority figure—may not carry much political currency. Selecting leaders, as opposed to electing them, is problematic. Black people who attain the necessary level of success to attract the attention of those who would select them to sit on boards or commissions have probably physically divorced themselves from the neighborhoods where most black people live. As they move into areas that are more affluent, they move away from the problems endemic to the black community—the fractured families, the crime, the psychological upheaval of ghettoization. Pulling oneself up by one's own bootstraps is fine, but it is a scenario that provides only individual escape, not the general uplifting of an ethnic group.

Gordon Morgan, a professor of sociology at the University of Arkansas who was that school's first black faculty member, said that although Clinton's appointees have, for the most part, been highly qualified and effective, people generally remain "suspicious of appointed leadership."

Paul Greenberg, the Pulitzer Prize-winning editorial page editor of the *Arkansas Democrat-Gazette* is perhaps Bill Clinton's fiercest critic. Greenberg, who was likely the first to use the phrase "Slick Willie" to describe Clinton, contends that Clinton's black appointments were not made at the risk of the governor's popularity.

"He has substituted patronage for progress," Greenberg said during the 1992 presidential campaign. "We do not have a state civil rights law . . . we don't have a fair-housing law in this state— that would also have cost him some popularity. He dodges and weaves whenever it might cost him something to support civil rights. I don't think appointing black folks to boards and commissions has hurt him. I don't think there's any great groundswell of opposition to black members on these boards and commissions. A state civil rights bill, a fair-housing law, that would mean that he'd be risking something politically."

Sadly, Bill Clinton, stung a dozen years ago, does not seem capable of making a habit of taking political risks. He abandoned his promise to make the U.S. military treat gay soldiers the same as straight soldiers, and he allowed Lani Gunier, his most creative appointment, to slide indecorously into the muck of history.

Soon these trees will give up their leaves, and the Capitol dome will be strung with Christmas lights. This year, the local chapter of the American Civil Liberties Union intends to challenge the state-sponsored nativity scene that routinely graces the Capitol grounds; the ever-excitable Bill McCuen has vowed to fight back.

Things are always entertaining here in Arkansas.

Just a few weeks ago, I stopped in Hope to buy gas in the middle of the night. There are, of course, many landmarks in the town now. One gentleman has taken to giving tours of these streets, pointing out both of the houses little Billy Blythe lived in as a child. Even this fluorescent-lit service station had a rack of souvenirs and T-shirts strung along its walls. Right by the register there was a four-inch stack of crude bumper stickers. For a dollar, you could signify that you "didn't vote for the dope from Hope."

Though Bill Clinton is in Washington, he still haunts the streets of my town. Every day, I drive past that too-famous McDonalds. Sometimes I lunch at Doe's Eat Place or at Your Mama's Good Food, where James Carville used to hang out. I used to work out in the same YMCA as Bill Clinton, and we were literally neighbors. When I saw him in the neighborhood, I waved and the governor waved back. It is difficult to describe how it is here, difficult to make people in Phoenix or Chicago or San Francisco understand. There is a kind of intimacy available in Little Rock that is at once comforting and stifling. We know our big goofy governor and we feel comfortable with him. It is odd to see him paid such deference, to see him so examined.

I am no friend of Bill Clinton, at least not in the way I understand friendship. He is—was—a person one saw, one ran into, one thought and wrote about. Most of the people interviewed in this book know him much better than I do; some of them say they were his friends and intimates.

But I wonder if any of us ever knew Bill Clinton, if we ever got past his bluff innocence and flashy intellect. Almost by accident I discovered there were gaps in his knowledge of pop culture, that despite his prodigious reading there were things Bill Clinton did not know. I have seen him look positively gooberish, like he wants to mouth "Hi, Mom!" and wave into the camera. He often seems out of place, with his triathlete's watch and his blooming ripe body. He should not wear those running shorts. His ties are atrocious. He still seems like the big redneck kid with the wild eyes and the talent no one seems to be able to account for. A happy freak of nature, Bill Clinton was born to run.

Though Bill Clinton disappoints me, I'm still fond of him. After all, it is not for lack of effort that he is not Thomas Jefferson or Jack Kennedy. And while it is difficult to take seriously an adult who says, in all apparent seriousness, "I feel your pain," there is something of the healer in this president.

As these interviews will reveal, Bill Clinton is a human being, not so innocent as he would have us believe but no demon either. He is a capable man, diminished more by the inoculating effects of constant exposure and scrutiny. He is, as someone once said of Voltaire, a "chaos of clear ideas." He is the most powerful man on the face of the earth and he is still that boy in the kitchen of his strong-willed mother's hospital-clean ranch house, listening to her denounce the world's idiocy and injustice. He is the slightly sheepish character who seems amazed at how far he's come, who delights in room service, and is too shy to approach Joe Cocker's musicians.

In the end, Bill Clinton is a Snopes, because he is from Arkansas and here we are all Snopeses, no matter how much we want to be Kennedys or Compsons. There is nothing wrong with that, but there is no getting around it either.

Philip Martin
Little Rock, Arkansas
Thanksgiving, 1993

1

The Kid From Hope

C ould any politician ask for a more politically convenient birthplace than Hope, Arkansas? Its very name seems to make the case for predestined greatness. Before Bill Clinton, Hope was best known for its watermelon crop. Now its chief industry seems to be the preservation of Clintoniana. Not so podunk as Plains, Georgia, Hope nevertheless represents origins humble enough to preserve the central American myth: Every little boy (and now girl) could grow up to be president. In retrospect, it seems that everyone who ran across the young Bill Clinton thought the child was bound for glory.

The same can be said for many who knew Clinton during his Hot Springs boyhood. Invariably, his high school buddies acknowledge his charisma and his almost too-easy charm. The young Bill Clinton reads like a Jimmy Stewart part; from the advantage of hindsight, even his foibles seem endearing. So what if he dressed like a geek, wasn't terribly athletic, and reminded some of his friends of *Leave It to Beaver*'s smarmy Eddie Haskell? It is clear Clinton bore his adolescent troubles well. Many did not realize the extent of the problems he was forced to deal with at home—Clinton's friends rarely mention his stepfather's drinking or black moods.

Bill Clinton was a serious child, uncommonly focused on his

schoolwork. But at the same time, he seems preternaturally concerned with building and maintaining friendships, some of which endure to this day. Early on, it was apparent Clinton was an overachiever with an uncanny political touch.

Dale Drake has known Bill Clinton since childhood. "I met Bill Clinton the second he was born. I was waiting outside the operating room when he was delivered. He was just a wonderful baby, a good baby, and very, very intelligent. You could tell he was observing everything that was going on around him. My house faced south and his grandmother's house faced west, so our backyards were right together. He was out in the playpen in the backyard every day that the weather permitted for him to have his sunshine and his warm, fresh air. He was one child who was almost raised completely by the book. By the time he was three years old he could read a little, and by the time he was four he could read the headlines off the paper."

President Clinton corroborates this. "I lived with my grandparents until I was four and they had a lot to do with my early commitment to learning. They taught me to count and read—I was reading little books when I was three. They didn't have much formal education but they helped imbed in me a real sense of educational achievement that was reinforced at home. So I would have to say they had a lot to do with it." President Clinton's mother, Virginia Kelley, agrees. "I think my mother, especially, had a great influence on Bill. She was a strong disciplinarian, and of course, she adored him. I guess like most parents and grandparents, we thought at an early age that we saw some special things in Bill. He was always so kind and caring and easy to discipline. He seemed to always want to do the right thing. Of course he got into stuff like all kids do, but we saw real sympathy at an early age."

"He went with his grandfather to his grandfather's store a lot and played and he learned to love all people—all races, colors, just whoever came in the store," says Dale Drake. "He was taught to be very nice to them, and to never, never act ugly toward anyone, regardless of who they were."

David Leopoulos, President Clinton's friend since second grade recalls, "We were pretty poor and had a very small house so I went to Bill's house mostly. One neat thing was what we called our kitchen debates. His mom would come home from work at the hospital and she would usually have something on her mind, something she was upset about, or interested in and she'd start talking about it. Here we were, nine, ten, eleven years old, and Virginia would be upset about health care because this guy didn't have insurance and he couldn't get health care soon enough. We would sit there and she would treat us like adults, and Bill understood the issues she was discussing. The older he got the more they would debate about the issues, but at first it was just this constant, 'This is wrong, this is right, that's the way it should be,' from Virginia. Even at eight years old, he would listen and have a lot of questions and was in tune with those kinds of things at that early age.

"I'll never forget Thanksgiving Day the year that we were eight years old. Virginia had sent Bill to the little local grocery store to get some extra food for Thanksgiving dinner. Instead of coming back with food he came back with another child. His mom said, 'Bill, who's your new friend?' And Bill said, 'Johnny. He was at the bus stop and I found out that he wasn't gonna' have a real Thanksgiving dinner so I brought him home to have Thanksgiving dinner with us.' The kid had a bag of chips in his hand and Bill said to his mom, 'You don't want him to have a bag of chips for his Thanksgiving dinner, do you?' Virginia said it just washed all over her; his empathy and caring and the fact that he acted on it at that early an age was a very special thing."

Virginia Kelley also remembers that Thanksgiving. "Bill came in—I'll never forget it. He came through the back door just as chipper as he could be and he said, 'Whoever heard of anybody having a bag of Frito's on Thanksgiving Day?' He said, 'Mother, we're not going to hold still for that.' And I said, 'You're right, we're not.' He was forever bringing people home to eat."

Bill Clinton's own memory of his childhood is haunted by a more poignant image, which he shared with *Newsweek* journalist Mark Miller. "He was staying with his grandparents and he came on the train to visit his mother. It was the first time that he had seen a building over two stories or three stories. But the burning image that he still spoke of years later was of his mother kneeling at the tracks weeping as he left to go back to stay with his grandparents."

President Clinton says, "My mother had a big influence on me because she was a good role model in three ways. She always worked. She did a good job as a parent and we had a lot of adversity in our life when I was growing up. She handled it real well and gave me a high pain threshold which, I think, is a very important thing to have in public life. You have to be able to take a lot of criticism—suffer defeats and get up tomorrow and fight again. And I think that my childhood had a lot to do with that. So I would give my family the lion's share of credit in terms of people who were influences on my life.

"The most profound event was something that occurred before I was born, which is the death of my father. It's a very difficult thing to be raised with a myth in a lot of ways. All of my relatives attempted to make it a positive rather than a negative thing, but I think I always felt in some sense that I needed to hurry because my father's death gave me a real sense of mortality. I mean, most kids never think about when they're going to run out of time, when they might die. I thought about it all the time because my father died at twenty-nine. By the same token now, I feel as if I've had a very full life. I mean whatever happens to me, I've already outlived him by fifteen years. So I've always had a different view than most people have. Being in such a hurry to accomplish things is both good and bad. Having my own child was probably one of the things that enabled me to get off that kind of career track. It was one of the reasons in 1987 that I decided not to run for president. Just being able to have a family life mattered to me and having that whole set of experiences that I didn't even imagine when I was a child growing up had a big impact on me.

"But before Hillary and Chelsea, I thought I had to live for myself and for my father too. I sort of had to meet a very high standard of conduct and accomplishment, in part because of his absence. It's a funny thing, but the older I get, the more I realize how much that shaped my childhood."

Joe Purvis has been a friend of President Clinton's since the two were four years old. He says: "The good guys were the guys that you liked being around, that were good to play with, were fun to be with, that you could have a lot of fun with. Bill was definitely a good guy.

"I remember playing cowboys and Indians and jump rope and stuff like that with Bill and the rest of the kids there. I remember when Bill broke his leg in kindergarten, which has now become legend. At that time, if you were really with it fashion-wise, guys wore blue jeans rolled up or denim overalls with a little short-sleeved shirt or whatever underneath and cowboy boots. I mean you had to wear cowboy boots if you were a guy because of Roy Rogers, Gene Autry, and all those people; cowboy boots were the mode of the day. One of the things we'd do was high-jump over a rope. A kid at each end held the rope at a certain level and then you'd jump over that. When everybody'd cleared that they would raise it up. Anyway, to make a long story short, somebody pulled the rope on Bill and he caught his boot heel and began screaming. People said, 'Get up. Get up. Stop crying.' He kept screaming and kids were chanting things to him like, 'Billy's a sissy, Billy's a sissy.' Anyway, his grandmother had to come pick him up and bring him home. At that point, his mom was in New Orleans going to nursing school and he was living with his grandparents. It ended up that his leg was broken in several places and I remember my mom made me take flowers out to him which years later Virginia (Bill's mother) used to embarrass the living fool out of me.

"I was working for Bill as his assistant attorney general and one day I saw his mom in the office and she smiled and said, 'How are you?' Well, the next thing I know, people are coming out of the coffee room giggling. Virginia had tacked up a photograph on the bulletin board of Bill with his leg up at almost a 90 degree angle—a 45-degree angle at least. But the worst thing is there's this kid wearing a jughead beanie, a three little pigs T-shirt, and a pair of blue jeans holding a little bouquet of posies, and it's me. Boy, did Bill and Virginia ever get revenge on me but Bill was just a good guy. He was a good guy."

Pat Harris, who wrote a series of articles on Clinton for the *Hope Star* newspaper, notes, "I called Little Rock and I started investigating his record in office, and talked to quite a few people up there to see if a lot of the things that he was saying in his campaign were true. I found out that everything he said was true. The jobs *had* increased in Arkansas. People *were* making more today than they were say, four, eight, ten years ago. Most of the people that I met said the same thing. Now it's my opinion that if the guy's a jerk somebody out there's gonna' say it, I don't care how well they know him. What really struck me was that everyone was saying the same thing, that he was a caring person, a good person—even though he was ambitious he was also very caring."

Dale Drake also was impressed by President Clinton's caring, even after he reached the White House. "A number of years ago I had this antique couch and I had asked my daughters if they would like to have it. They said, 'Oh, no, Mother, it doesn't go in our houses and we don't really want it.' Bill said, 'I want it,' so I gave it to him, and he took it to Little Rock and had it in the Governor's Mansion up there. And the first thing that he said to me when I saw him in Washington was 'I brought the couch with me.' This was when were having lunch at the White House, the day after his inauguration.''

Virginia Kelley remembers when her second husband, Roger Clinton, was dying and ''how wonderful Bill was to him before he died—he was a student at Georgetown when his father died of cancer. Bill said, 'I'd like to be here and like to have him know that I'm here.' I'll never forget how sweet he was. Roger was vain and as much as he drank he was one of the cleanest individuals you ever saw—he was always well groomed. And when he got so that he was not able to go to the bathroom, for example, Bill would bodily pick him up and take him to the bathroom so that he could maintain his dignity. It's just these sorts of things that people don't know. I could write volumes of the wonderful things that he's done for people—significant things.''

In Hot Springs, Clinton was known as much for his quick mind and wit as he was for his caring, concern, and sympathy. David Leopoulos recalls, ''I always used to think he was just inherently smart. That he didn't have to study. Carolyn Staley (Clinton's neighbor) told me there'd always be lights on in his room well into the morning. So he did all of his schoolwork when no one was around and usually after hours. But in school he never settled for just the basics, he always went beyond. Teachers loved him because he challenged them. But he wasn't cocky or arrogant, he just really was excited about knowledge. In fact my phrase is that knowledge is recreational for him because he never stops.

''I was the opposite of him. He was a great student and I made C's and D's. I was failing an algebra course, and I needed to pass the last test with at least a B to get a D in this class. He found out about that and he said to me, 'You're coming to my house tonight and we're gonna' study.' It was the only time we ever did that. So I went over there and he's trying to get me to work and I'm Mr. Funny Boy, you know, joking and all that stuff, and I just wouldn't concentrate. Finally he got real mad and his face turned red and his nose turned bright red just like Rudolph's and he said, 'If you're not gonna' help yourself, how can I help you?' And he was really mad at me because I would not take myself seriously. I still flunked the test, but he tried as hard as he could to get me to study. And one other time, just before graduation, I needed a typing course to graduate. I had to pass a physical typing test to pass the course by typing sixty words a minute with less than three mistakes. I could type seventy words a minute but I never could keep my mistakes down. They let me take the test day in and day out for the last two weeks of school until the final day of school, graduation day, which was the last day I could take the test. Well, we were all pretty nervous about whether I'd graduate. Bill was really nervous about it. The night before the last day of school I was lying in bed scared to death when the doorbell rang. My mom answered it and it was Western Union with a telegram for me. Now people in our neighborhood didn't get telegrams—they were for rich people. The telegram was from Bill, and it said, 'Good luck on your test tomorrow. I know you'll pass it. Your friend, Bill.' Well you cannot imagine what that meant to me. I was stunned. He obviously walked down or his mom or somebody took him to the telegraph office to send the telegram. And I passed the test the next day. You know, a high school kid doing something like that doesn't happen very often. He was always so humble and so helpful and so generous. I mean I know he sounds like a saint, but that's just the way he was.''

Virginia Kelley talks about President Clinton's inclinations to help others even as a child. ''Our housekeeper prayed that he'd be a minister because she could see his leadership qualities and she'd say, 'Have you ever thought about how he could lead people to Christ?' Bill went to St. John's Catholic School in the second grade. A few years ago, one of our campaign workers in El Dorado came to me and said she had been campaigning door to door. At one house a nun answered. The campaign worker asked for her support and the nun said, 'My goodness, you've had my support since he was in the second grade.' The nun told the campaign worker, 'You ask his mother. She'll tell you that I once told her that he can be anything he wants to be, and if he wants to be president, then he's going to be president.'

''He always got perfect report cards, but once he came home with straight A's except a D in conduct. 'I thought, oh, my dear, that teacher needs my help.' I scooted up there to see what the problem was and she said, 'There's no real problem. It's just that he is so sharp and he's so alert he knows the answer immediately and will not give the others a chance. I have to get his attention one way or another and this is the only way I know to do it because he is so competitive he will not be able to stand this D.' It worked.

''And I'll never forget Bill sitting on the couch one morning, before he went to school—he was in junior high school at that point. He saw in the paper the same old thing that we read all the time, that Arkansas's on the bottom. He turned around and he said, 'Let's say Maine was on top. Mother, aren't the kids in Arkansas born with the same brain that people are born with in Maine?' And I said 'Sure.' He asked me the same question about black and white people. He is the one who taught me about civil rights. He is the one who taught me about integration. And I said to him 'You're right, but you're going to have to be very patient with me Bill, because this was not the way I was brought up.' We talked about this when he was just a youngster because he was seeing black people mistreated in school. He felt that it was just because of their color and he could hardly stand it. Could hardly stand it.''

But Bill Clinton also was a normal teenager with the same interests as other people his age. David Leopoulos says, "He didn't have a basketball court in his yard but there was plenty of room to play football. So we played touch football. We would hike a lot, go up into the mountains. There was a mountain behind my house that we could hike and go all the way to downtown Hot Springs. And then we played Monopoly, listened to Elvis Presley records—we were fanatics, we listened to him all the time."

"I remember driving down this route and Bill singing Elvis Presley songs at the top of his voice," says high-school friend, Patty Criner. "He loved to sing. He just loved music and he's always played music. I think that's one of the reasons he went to church so much by himself as a kid. He loved the music. I've seen him walk down Park Avenue carrying his Bible going to Park Place Baptist Church, which I thought was real telling. I thought it was unusual but kind of neat because my mother had to drag us out of bed on Sunday mornings and force us to go to church and make us behave. Bill just walked from his home, and went alone. He dressed up in his suit. He was just a kid but he took his religion very seriously but he also was very private and never discussed it. Didn't realize you had to until he ran for the presidency I think."

According to David Leopoulos, "Our high school was large for Arkansas but small in that everybody knew everybody else. Bill was in the band and very, very much the leader of the band. Typically on the weekends or after football games or after basketball games or whatever, we'd get together and go over to his house or to Carolyn Staley's house. Carolyn played the piano and sand and Bill, of course, played the sax. We just sat around and either sang or talked or played hearts or watched a movie or whatever. It was a very simple, *American Graffiti*-ish kind of life.''

Kathy McClanahan first met Bill Clinton when she was twelve and he was thirteen. ''Everybody called him Billy. I don't know why. It was mostly when little girls were screaming, 'Billy, Billy. Throw me the football.' And the girls had crushes on him. He was always the center of attention. Bill was so giddy with these girls that it really was obnoxious. Even though I was only twelve I remember thinking . . . 'Oh, what a jerk.' The very first time I saw Bill, my mother and I drove up to the dormitory where I was going to stay and Bill was trying desperately to throw a football and he'd never been the most athletic human in the world. He threw the football to some girl who threw it back to him and he would drop it every time. I got out of the car and I've always been kind of a tomboy so when the ball almost hit me in the head, I just reached up and I caught it. He said, 'Good catch.' All the girls were giggling and I just threw it at him and, of course, he dropped it.

''Once I got to know him, I realized that he just likes the challenge and he wasn't interested in those girls who were giddy and giggling. We got to be friends and we would sit out on the front porch and talk. I guess we had a lot in common; we would sit and talk and play music. He talked of politics even at fourteen or fifteen: we talked about the world order, the economy, John F. Kennedy, and what did I think of what was going on in Russia. I said to him, 'I don't care. Bill. We're going to a dance.' This went on all the way through high school.''

According to Little Rock journalist Mara Leveritt, who is now associate editor of the *Arkansas Times*, his interest began even earlier. ''He explained to me that he had as a young child watched the Democratic National Convention and he loved it. He and I are the same age and I remember that convention. I remember it because we had just gotten a television in our house and I thought that the convention was the biggest adult intrusion on the good programming that should have been on. To think that someone at the age of about seven years old would have found that interesting was pretty weird to me.''

Kathy McClanahan adds, ''We didn't go skating or do whatever kids do at that age because all he wanted to do was talk about politics. He wore his hair the wrong way. When guys' hair was supposed to be long and not greased back, his was curly and it was pulled back—everything about his fashion sense was wrong.

Bill was such a dork. He dressed like a geek but I really liked him. I mean, we had fun. We laughed. He enjoyed being with my parents. He would come with us out to the lake house where all my family wanted to do was ski. We were good water skiers. All of us skied and all Bill wanted to do was to sit on the porch and talk politics. Well, I finally found out the reason he didn't want to ski is because he's not athletic. He's just not made that way. We used to tease him about being uncoordinated.

"We had a sign that we would give each other if he wanted to go out in the car or get away from the house or go be alone. Once I embarrassed him to death. He still talks about it. He was giving me the sign and I think we were playing hearts and I didn't want to go anywhere. It was dark and I was having a good time where we were and he was nudging me and finally I looked at him and I said, 'Quit nudging me under the table. I don't want to go parking right now.' And he said, 'One of these days, I'll get even with you for that. I don't know what I'm going to do, but I'll get even for that.'"

Kay McClanahan, Kathy's sister, remembers Clinton's visits to the family lake house. "He made people feel comfortable and would direct questions to everyone in the room. I can remember my parents saying that they knew that he would do something . . . I don't remember the exact words, but they knew that he would achieve something very important because he had such energy, an inner drive. It was hard for him to relax, really and just take it easy. No matter what he did, he did it with enthusiasm."

Kathy McClanahan says, "I used to tease him when we were in high school about being a politician in the womb and I surely believe that. Do you remember Eddie Haskell from *Leave It to Beaver*? He was obnoxious but he was always so overly pleasant to Mrs. Cleaver. Bill was like that. Parents loved him and he was so complimentary. If your mother had shorts on that she'd worn for forty years, he'd say, 'Oh, I love your outfit.' He didn't not mean it, but you just wanted to slap him and say, 'Give it a rest.'"

Joe Purvis recalls attending Boys State with Clinton during high school. "Boys State is a week-long seminar that was put on every year at Camp Robinson by the American Legion. Each high school would select several male students who had just finished their junior year and send them to Boys State to teach them American government and local government. It was set up along the lines of a mock government, and boys would elect city officials and county officials and then state officials and listen to speeches and that sort of stuff. I remember running into Bill who said, 'Hey, look, I'm running for Boys Nation.' And I said, 'What's Boys Nation?' And he said, 'Well, we elect two delegates to go to Boys Nation. It's in Washington and it's like a National Boys State.' Bill ran to be one of the delegates to Boys Nation and won hands down. That's how he got to meet President Kennedy.''

Edith Irons, President Clinton's high school guidance counselor remembers ''when he was in eleventh grade, he was elected to go to Boys State and then he was elected to go to Boys Nation. And he loved Jack Kennedy. He adored Jack Kennedy. He came into my office one day and he was holding this manila folder with his arms crossed over it, just holding it with both his arms. He said, 'Mrs. Irons, I bet you can't guess what I've got.' And I said, 'No, Bill. I don't have any idea. Show me.' It was a picture of him shaking hands with Jack Kennedy and, of course, that was the beginning of his senior year and Jack was killed that year.

''I remember him coming in the second week of school when he was a sophomore and saying, 'Mrs. Irons, where would you go to school if you wanted to be a foreign diplomat?' and I said, 'Off the top of my head, Georgetown University.' He asked, 'Why Georgetown?' And I said, 'Well, in the first place, it offers the courses. In, the second place, it has the proximity to Washington.' 'Why is the proximity to Washington important?' And I knew that he was real interested in political things and I said, 'Well, it's your love of politics. You'd probably learn as much in Washington watching the goings-on, as you would at Georgetown.' And he never did apply to another school. I told him that it was most difficult for a southern kid to get into an Ivy League-type school and that he needed to apply to at least two more. I sent college catalog after college catalog for him to look over but he never applied to another school. I was just a nervous wreck. By the time school was out we still hadn't heard from Georgetown. Finally he called me one day and said, 'Mrs. Irons, I got in.'

''He just had the confidence that he was going to get in. When Bill and his mother went up for their orientation, a Jesuit showed them all through the school. They got back to his office and the Jesuit said, 'Son, how many foreign languages do you speak?' 'Oh, not any sir, but I've had three years of Latin and three years of French and three years of Spanish.' 'And what religion are you?' 'Southern Baptist, sir,' Clinton said. The Jesuit threw his hands up in the air and he said, 'What in the name of the Holy Father is a Southern Baptist who can't speak a foreign language doing in the mother of all Jesuit schools?' So they laughed and went outside but Bill could tell that Virginia was really worried. He walked over and put his arm around her and said, 'Mother, don't worry. They'll know what I'm doing here after I've been here a while.' ''

Virginia Kelley laughs at the memory: ''And they did. They have given him a gorgeous chair—one of his first honors when he left Georgetown, as far as the school was concerned. He sat on their board as liaison between the students and the faculty right after he graduated.''

Edith Irons continues: ''He graduated third in his high-school class but he was involved in everything. The principal called me in one day and said, 'Edith, Bill has got to quit missing so much school.' I said, 'What are you talking about?' 'He's missing too much school. He's missing too many classes.' You see while he was in high school he was in demand to speak at the civic clubs, both the women's and the men's civic clubs. I said, 'Miss Mackey, let him alone. We're not teaching him what he's learning speaking to these organizations.' She let him go. He has a charm and a charisma that just draws people to him, I think. Now, maybe I'm biased. When these clubs would ask him to talk, he'd ask, 'What do you want me to speak on?' And they'd say, 'Oh, you just talk on anything.' He'd say, 'No, I want to know what your theme of the day is and I'll speak on whatever you're discussing.'

''Bill Clinton had a rough time in school which I don't know how many people know. When I was at Little Rock at a state Democratic Convention, the chairperson came up to me. 'There is a friend of Bill's from Georgetown here and he'd like to have an interview with you.' I said, 'Oh, that'd be fine.' And he told me that Bill held down three jobs while he was in school.

''Virginia's a big fan of horse racing. Bill called her one day and said, 'Mother, this boy in the class wants to bet me that I'm not third in my class at Georgetown.' She said, 'Well, are you?' He said, 'Yes, Mother.' She said, 'Are you sure?' and he said, 'Yes Mother.' She said, 'Bet him.' So he made the bet and Virginia told me that he sent her the twenty dollars he won. She told me that she needed it the most of any twenty dollars she had ever had.

''There were family problems that nobody knew about. I didn't know about them. Carolyn didn't know and she lived next door. I think it was a great mark of character that they didn't go crying in their bibs. A lot of people would have wallowed in it to use an old southern expression but I knew nothing about it. I respected them and think it was a mark of character to not discuss it and I haven't known many people that did that.''

Virgil Spurlin was President Clinton's high school band director. ''He was good. In fact, he was first chair for the entire state of Arkansas on tenor sax. He was good not only on sax, but in everything. His leadership abilities and his common sense and his maturity—everything about him. He was so sincere and mature in his actions that everything memorable that he did was something outstanding rather than something that teenagers do or act silly about or get in trouble over. I never had to correct him once. He was a leader; he already knew what to do. He was a tremendous leader. The thing I liked about that, he never crossed paths. He never had cross words with any of his peers or teachers. They all admired him and thought he was great. No envy or jealousy that I know of. He just had a knack of getting along with people.

''He was interested in just about everything. He joined everything that was available to him and he was either a president or a leader of some sort in all the clubs and organizations that he was a member of. He was certainly a top officer in my band and I've already told you he was first chair in tenor sax in the state. He liked the same music as most teenagers only he was a little more serious about his music than most. He was in a little combo during high school with Joe Newman who was my drum major that year and also Randy Goodrum, a piano player who composes music and arranges it for Anne Murray, and a bunch of other great people. The three of them would get together during their lunch break in a little group called the Three Kings. They wore shades and a lot of the kids jokingly called them the Three Blind Mice but they were good and they played for the kids during their lunch break instead of going to lunch themselves. That's just how unselfish and sharing of their talents they were. He was a tremendous influence on our stage band. We went to state competitions and he played as a lead soloist in our band and he won trophies that way and helped us to be the number-one stage band in the state that year. He might have gone the route of music but since he met and talked with JFK personally, that had a great influence on what he turned out to be.''

By the time he reached Georgetown already, his friends testify, Clinton's ambitions for a political career were set. He wanted to be like William Fulbright, Arkansas's great statesman in the Senate.

Already, he was considering the possibility that Arkansas might be too small a state from which to launch a national career. He was dreaming of the Supreme Court at the same time he was working three jobs to pay his tuition and watching his gas money.

Tom Campbell was President Clinton's college roommate at Georgetown. "The first day we came as freshman at Georgetown, we were assigned roommates alphabetically. We got on very well. That's why we were roommates for four years. He was there with his mother and they had come in the room and he just said, 'Hi, I'm Bill Clinton. How are you doing?' And that was it. It was very comfortable. We got along great. We just did a lot of hanging around. There were some great people. That's where we met Tom Caplan and Bob Billingsley and a whole lot of people. Bill became involved in politics right away. He was class president of the freshman class.

"He's very much the same man now that he was then. He was very focused on where he was and what he wanted to do and he's really changed very little.

"My impression at the time was that his hero was Fulbright and that he probably wanted to be like Fulbright. It was sort of a running joke that he was the politician who was going to run for president all this time and that he thought that Arkansas was too small a state but that he would probably go back to Arkansas and get into politics. He certainly had ambition. There was no denying that.

"I remember we were in the ROTC during freshman year, the Air Force ROTC, and he was not a very good marcher. Didn't know how to put on a uniform very well and I knew a lot about that because I had been in military school in high school. I remember a lot of good times working on his campaign and making all the flyers and working on the football floats and things like that.

"Doing well in school seemed like it came very easily to him. During freshman year, he developed that habit he has of sleeping only four hours a night and then taking a couple of twenty-minute naps during the day. It drove me crazy. He'd come in and he could look at his clock and say he had twenty minutes or a half hour before the next class and he would just lie down and boom, he would sleep. I think being able to get by on four or five hours of sleep was a conscious decision. He taught himself to do that because of that famous remark that Quigley made about Napoleon and all the great leaders having the ability to put themselves to sleep instantly and get by on very little sleep so he almost jokingly tried it and found he could do it. He could lie down and go to sleep instantly. He still does it in a car ride or an airplane.

"He was endlessly putting two dollars worth of gas in this big Buick. I don't know why but I remember we would drive for hours and then we would put two dollars worth of gas in the car. We would drive a little longer and then put two more dollars in and we would take these little trips. And he's always talking. He's an awful driver for that reason. He just gets on a subject and starts going.

"He knew all the professors. He knew everybody in the class. He was always talking to people. He was involved in a couple of the organizations and he ran for student body president again in his senior year and lost, which was probably a good thing because he concentrated on his grades and was able to get the Rhodes scholarship."

Lee Williams gave the young, ambitious Georgetown student his first job in Washington. "I had been in Arkansas for a campaign of some kind. A friend and law school classmate of mine, Jack Holt, who is now the chief justice of the Arkansas Supreme Court, talked to me about Bill Clinton who had worked for his uncle, Frank Holt, a candidate running for governor. He said Clinton was an outstanding young man, interested in politics, and that he was a student at Georgetown who had to have some income to complete his education. His description of Clinton intrigued me because Senator Fulbright was the type of man who sought out bright young people who were interested in education. He had been an educator most of his life and believed that education was the solution to most of the world's problems. I was his administrative assistant at the time, so were always on the lookout for bright, politically oriented, intelligent young people who had demonstrated some kind of a desire to complete their education, or to get an education. When I got back to Washington, I called Bill Clinton. I told him that Jack Holt had recommended him for a job in Senator Fulbright's office. After we had talked for a bit I said, 'Well, I'll tell you what we'll do. We have two jobs here, and you can have either one of them. They're both on the Foreign Relations Committee staff. One of them is a part-time job that pays thirty-five hundred a year and one of them is a full-time job that pays five thousand a year.' Immediately, he just popped back, 'Well, how about two part-time jobs?' I said, 'You're just the kind of fellow we're looking for. If you want the job, come on up as soon as you can get here.' I think that was on a Friday and he was there bright and early Monday morning.

"My first impression was by telephone conversation and that impressed me enough to offer him the job sight unseen. When I met him, it confirmed my telephone analysis of his sincerity, his dedication, and his desire to complete his education, but it did more than that. I mean, he was an unusual young man. As I said, we had a lot of students. He came walking into my office and he was a big, good-looking kid with a smile on his face and he just ... there was an aura about him. He was self-assured. He was articulate. He was relaxed, but serious if you know what I mean and it just made an impression on me that continues to this day, obviously. A deep interest in wanting to do something for people is to me, the essence of Bill Clinton. Politics is a very, very tough business and it requires keen interest in order for one to be able to put up with what one has to put up with and I never saw in Bill Clinton that lack of concern or lack of interest in people. He's got another trait that would demonstrate that too. I don't think Bill Clinton has ever forgotten a person that he ever met and had more than a few words with. I don't mean to sound like I'm an expert on memory but ... you can have it in two ways, I think. You can have a trained and disciplined memory, or you can have a deep abiding concern for people and an interest in people deep enough to make you remember them as individuals, and I think the latter is what Bill Clinton's memory is based on.

"I've been a touter of Bill's since I first met him. With contemporaries, my colleagues, I've always extolled his qualities and virtues. So, I'm one of the old-timers in that respect. It was because I thought I got to know him well enough to understand what he was as a young man. And, what you see in him as a president, are basically the qualities that he already had as a young man."

Hoyt Purvis, now director of the Fulbright Institute of International Relations, first met Bill Clinton when both of them were working for Senator Fulbright. "I started working full time for the senator early in 1968 and so I heard a lot about Bill Clinton, a promising, very friendly young man from Arkansas. I met him a few times but really didn't get to know him very well until the spring and summer of 1968. I had heard that he was an outstanding young man with great promise and he was very well regarded around Senator Fulbright's office and around the Foreign Relations Committee. I immediately took a liking to him. What was particularly noticeable about Bill Clinton was that he not only had the qualities of friendliness and being very pleasant and someone who enjoyed talking to everybody but he truly was interested in the substance of what was going on. I don't want to overstate the relationship between Clinton and Fulbright. I mean there was a great difference in their ages and it wasn't that Clinton was at the right hand of Fulbright or anything like that but when Clinton very recently presented the Presidential Medal of Freedom to Senator Fulbright, he recalled how important Fulbright was for many of us from Arkansas who were interested in politics and government and international relations. This came at a time when Arkansas had suffered a considerable strain on its national and international reputation as a result of the Central High School desegregating crisis so many of us from Arkansas were very proud of Fulbright and what he represented, and I know that Bill Clinton felt that way. He and all of us looked upon the Rhodes scholarship as an extraordinary opportunity for him, but in some ways he hated to leave.

"I'd be surprised if Bill Clinton changes. I saw him last month in Washington and he seemed in many ways the same as the first time I met him more than twenty-five years ago but obviously he has a much heavier load to carry. He's a more serious, more mature person but he still has that basic quality of friendliness and he always remembers his old acquaintances. He is very open and he's great about remembering things. I mean, he really has all the qualities one associates with Bill Clinton's successful political traits. I think he radiates ambition but not in an offensive way and I think that in itself is an important distinction. There are a lot of ambitious people who don't hide that ambition very well but some people can be ambitious in a much more acceptable way and I think part of it was the fact that Bill Clinton was always so open about it. I mean, he wasn't coy. Being coy is not something that one associates with Bill Clinton. He is what he is and he's very open about it. Years ago when I first knew Bill Clinton, he talked about the fact that he wanted to be in politics. At that point, if you had asked me in 1968 where I thought Bill Clinton would be twenty-five years later, I would have said there was a real good chance of him being in the Senate or being in the state department, or even secretary of state because he was interested in foreign affairs at that time and studied at Georgetown and was going off to Oxford. I think any of us who knew him then in Senator Fulbright's office in the Foreign Relations Committee would not have been at all surprised by that. I think Bill Clinton became convinced early on that politics was a noble career, that it was a way to have impact and influence on very important issues. The kinds of issues that we were dealing with in those days, particularly civil rights and Vietnam were issues of such significance that many of us were drawn in and felt compelled to try to do all that we could to have an influence on those areas. I know that Bill Clinton felt that way. We talked about those kinds of things. It was evident from what his interests were. As I mentioned earlier, he kept up with what was going on in the Senate. I mean, here was a guy who was going to school full time who was involved in all kinds of other things but he knew what was happening in the Senate and was keeping up with the development of the Vietnam policy and other policy issues. He considered politics to be a positive instrument, that government could serve the interests of the people and I think that's been reflected in his entire approach to his political career.''

Chris Ashby became friends with President Clinton during their freshman year at Georgetown. ''I met him the first day of our freshman year. There was a corridor meeting. I remember when I walked in noticing that he had an accent and since I'm from Dallas I had an accent and nobody else did. Well, actually, I thought we were the only ones who didn't have an accent. I was attracted to that because I had never been in the East before and I was surrounded by all these Yankees so he was somebody I felt akin to.

''In 1964, in Washington you talked about what was going on in the world and certainly at that particular time, the civil rights movement was the major event. It very much influenced student life and it influenced us. We talked about courses and social life—I suppose the things that kids of that age normally do talk about.

''He was interested in student politics. A lot of people who were interested in politics became involved in the young Democrats or Republicans and that was a presidential election year so there was a lot of goings-on in downtown Washington around the election. Bill ran for student freshman class president and won and became very involved in that.

''There was a required course in the school foreign service called the Development of Civilization. It was taught by a fellow by the name of Carroll Quigley who had been an institution at the school of foreign services and there had been a number of articles written about his influence on everybody. Even to this day, people can recite verbatim some of the lines of some of Carroll Quigley's lectures. He was a very dramatic individual and an excellent teacher. In addition, in those days, the Catholics had to take theology so non-Catholics had to take a number of other excellent courses. That freshman year, we took something called Comparative Cultures, which was actually comparative religions taught by Father Sebes who was a Hungarian Jesuit. He also was an excellent, dynamic teacher and we still talk about those classes. Clinton was moved by Quigley and enjoyed the class a great deal. Father Leo O'Donovan (who's now president of Georgetown) gave as his gift to Bill some tapes of a Quigley interview that had occurred a couple of years after we attended Georgetown.

"Our senior year a good part of my education took place around the dinner table. I used to work for Senator Scoop Jackson and Clinton worked for Senator Fulbright and we would come home and talk about whatever was going on that day, like when Martin Luther King was assassinated and when parts of Washington were burned down. It was just one thing after another in 1968. In January, the Pueblo was taken and February brought the Tet Offensive; in March, Lyndon Johnson said he wasn't going to run and in April, Martin Luther King was assassinated. In June, Bobby Kennedy was assassinated. In July, Czechoslovakia was invaded and in August, late July and August, was the Chicago convention. It was one thing after another. And always the war. Clinton was very influenced by Fulbright. Fulbright was among the few people who were against the war on geopolitical rather than humanitarian grounds. I mean everybody else was against it because we were doing bad things to the people of that country. That was not Fulbright's position at all. His stance was that, from a power point of view, it made no sense to be there.

"I kept in touch with Bill a lot during his campaign. The first time we saw him was in New Hampshire and after it was all over, looking back, he said that was the low point of the whole thing. He dropped points in New Hampshire that weekend. New York was very tough. He was not ready for it. He was too depressed at how New York politics were conducted. He had and has tremendous endurance but even so he often was quite drained. Once in June, I went to an event in Greenwich and then drove back into New York with him and he was third in the polls and very down. I remember at the end of the trip, I said, 'Bill, I've been trying to get you to smile for about forty-five minutes and I haven't been able to.' He smiled then but it was a tough time."

Virginia Kelley recalls, "Bill was in New Orleans for his final hearings for his Rhodes scholarship and I did not leave my phone all day long. I never refused to come in for an emergency before in my life. But this was on a Saturday, and they had an emergency, and the doctor called and I said, 'I'm sorry, you'll just have to call somebody else.' I gave Bill a London Fog raincoat to take to New Orleans for good luck. And it was around five o'clock in the afternoon and he called and said, 'Well, Mother, how do you think I'll look in English tweed?' I'm telling you, it's just one of the thrills that he's given me in this life.

"He called me when they first suggested to him that he qualified for a Rhodes scholarship. He said, 'Mother, I think I'm going to go for it. But I want you to understand now, my chances of getting this are literally one in one million. Because, you know, everybody wants it.' I said I understood that. It is a tremendous process that they go through. They have to have four different hearings—they keep narrowing it down, and narrowing it down. The luckiest thing in this world, I believe, was that he picked up in an airport a *Time* magazine that had an article on the first heart transplant. And the questions they asked him were about this heart transplant. A man of destiny if there ever was one, I promise you. Yet, he doesn't believe in luck. He really believes you make your own luck. But you don't make that kind of luck.

"I was at an anaesthesia convention in Chicago one year after Bill came back to the states from his Rhodes scholarship. And the president of Rhodes House called me at the hotel where I was staying. He was in America and he had traced me some way or other, I guess, maybe somebody at my home told him where I was. I'll never forget what he said about Bill. He said, "Do you know the only thing that keeps your son from being one of the greatest intellectuals of all time?' and I said, 'No, what?' And he said, 'His love and understanding of people.' I'll never forget that man saying that. And I thought, he doesn't need to be an intellectual. They paid him to come to Yale. And he still has a year of his Rhodes scholarship and it's good for the rest of his life because the president of Rhodes House said this is an offer you cannot refuse."

President Clinton himself remembers his years at Georgetown "as an incredible experience for me. I mean it was like a feast. I'd never been out of Arkansas much and there I was with people from all over the country and all over the world, going to school. Teachers from all over the world. Then I had the opportunity to work for Senator Fulbright on the Foreign Relations Committee staff, something I'll always be grateful for, because they gave me that job when I was nobody from nowhere and my family had no money, no political influence—nothing.''

If Georgetown was heady, then Oxford must have been sublime. ''Slowly, the spell of Oxford grew, until one was suffused with it, its majesty and largesse,'' Willie Morris, the writer and a Rhodes scholar some dozen years before Clinton has observed. Morris, in his memoir *New York Days*, remembers the twenty-one-year-old Clinton who turned up at his *Harpers* magazine office the day before he was to set sail for England. ''He was intelligent and inquisitive and funny and warm and wanted to go into politics someday, he said, and his hero was John F. Kennedy, whom he had once shaken hands with during a Boy's Nation ceremony in the White House,'' Morris wrote. ''As we later cruised around midtown in a taxi . . . the conversation was of the great adventure before him, and of Oxford University, what it was really like and what to look for in it as a young American, inevitably turning to the South and including the specific topics of watermelons and boll weevils, and growing up in American places like his birth-place, Hope, and my Yazoo; against the glittering Manhattan back-drop we talked of how poor Arkansas and Mississippi were, and how much he loved and felt for his native ground. We spoke of history books and family, and dogs and cats, and the feel of be-longing in this country. I think we talked about women and love. The youngster had grit.''

Hoyt Purvis spoke with Clinton as the Rhodes scholarship win-ner was preparing to leave for Oxford. ''In particular I can recall a discussion we had in the Old Marion Hotel. I had spent some time at Oxford, not as a student but I'd just visited there so I was able to offer my insights about Oxford. Also we had both read a book written by Willie Morris (who is now a mutual friend of ours) called *North Towards Home*. This book was widely read among young people, particularly southerners, because Willie was from Mississippi and he wrote about his experiences. Willie was a friend of mine because he had preceded me by some years as editor at the *Daily Texan* at the University of Texas and so when Bill Clinton found that I knew Willie he wanted to meet him. Bill was going to New York to leave for Oxford to sail with other Rhodes scholars and he wanted to try to meet Willie Morris when he was in New York. I arranged an introduction and they did indeed get together, had a big time in Manhattan, and became

friends. Not long ago I came across a very nice letter that Bill
wrote me shortly after he arrive in Oxford in the fall of 1968. He
described his trip and his first impressions of Oxford and thanked
me for getting him together with Willie Morris and of course
wished all of us well in Fulbright's campaign.

"We were all very proud of Clinton and particularly because
Senator Fulbright had been a Rhodes scholar and many of us felt
that Bill Clinton was carrying on the Fulbright heritage. Also Bill
was a Rhodes scholar from Arkansas, which hadn't produced very
many Rhodes scholars."

Investment banker David Edwards first met Bill Clinton in England in 1968. "A friend invited me one evening to a party a
friend of hers was giving. Her friend was Bill. We went into what
they called his rooms, which was basically a tiny little bedroom
and a tiny little sitting room with a wash basin in it and a shower
down the hall. Bill was having a sherry party. I don't even know
if he could afford sherry; I think a lot of people were drinking tea.

"I have one memory from that first time that I laugh about to
myself all the time. Twenty-four years ago, we were sitting in a
Chinese restaurant in Oxford for Sunday lunch. He was about
twenty-two and I was about twenty-three or twenty-four. We were
both in a sense discovering and dating women about the same
time. This gal walked in and I said, 'Wow, look at that gal,' and
he said, 'Listen, don't bother with her. I have had one date with
her and when you scratch the surface, you'll hit rock bottom,' and
I still laugh at that joke or that off-hand remark. I found he was
right when I did take her out. I think that illustrates his wit and
sense of insight and that kind of clever lightness he has about
himself."

Kathy McClanahan reads from some of the letters that Bill Clinton sent her from Oxford: " 'October 23, 1968. Dear Kathy, For-
give me for taking so long to write. It's only in the past week
that I've been settled enough to write a letter. Left Arkansas about
three days ago after I was with you and was on the run constantly
after that. . . . I flew to Washington from Little Rock and while
there was fortunate enough to see Senator Fulbright a few minutes
and to run into David Pryor in one of my old Georgetown hang-
outs. . . . I think [Fulbright's] positions on issues are too fuzzy,
too practical. I think he and Mack [McLarty] are very much alike
in that way and therefore will probably please more people and
be far more successful in politics than I'll ever be. After Washington, I spent three days in and out of New York. The ship sailed

October 4th. A great voyage despite a bad day and sea sickness. The air was so clear. . . . We landed at Southampton that night and took a bus to Oxford. Characteristically, it was raining. The sun seldom shines till March, or so I'm told; however, there have been a few beautiful days, great for taking long walks through the centuries-old buildings. Most of my college buildings are mid-seventeenth century. I walk down wooded paths which then follow quiet rivers across the most lush green meadows you ever saw. It's a beautiful and serene place. I read a lot, explore a lot, talk a lot to people from all over the world, try my hand at familiar and unfamiliar sports, take French lessons and an economic tutorial on the side and attend a few lectures a week. The place is much slower than I'm used to. I have decided to pursue the B. Litt. degree which is like an American M.A. except that the only requirement is one long paper, no tests. At the end of the year, if I'm still here, I'll have the option of applying for the B. Phil. Ph.D. program. Please write. . . . Love, Bill.

" 'December 1, 1968. Dear Kathy, . . . Oxford and England are more to me everyday. I'm continuously on the move, save the unavoidable work in the library. Trying to get to know town and country people. . . . I have not yet been to Blenheim Palace. I have seen Kensington Palace in London but most of my sight-seeing has been typically traveling around the country getting to know the everyday things. Have been twice to Stratford-on-Avon and all over the place. . . . The Royal Shakespeare Theatre isn't very impressive on the outside though the swans on the Avon are, but the company and actors are perhaps the finest I've ever seen. . . . Love, Bill.' "

Kathy McClanahan says, "He's a real caring person. I was in a singing group that went to England while he was at Oxford. I took a side trip and stayed with him for a couple of days and all we did was walk around and look at things and see the trees and just be old friends.

"Years later, I took my parents to the National Cathedral and I had the strangest feeling. I said, 'The last time I was in Washington in this church, I was with Bill because we sang in Washington at the Pentagon and he was at Georgetown and he took me on the grand tour. It's so ironic that the next time I'm here in Washington, he's the president.' Now that was a weird feeling. A weird feeling. After I read those letters last night, I sat down and wrote him a long letter. I don't think that he would mind that I share some of these letters because they're good ones and they make me feel good inside and I care about that side of him. I'm not saying that I agree with every one of his ideas on politics but there is no way in the world that I could be objective because he's too good a friend so I don't think there's anything he could do that I would really disagree with.''

Little Rock attorney Cliff Jackson first met Bill Clinton in the fall of 1969. ''I met him either in Oxford or on the *SS United States* going across to Europe. He was very friendly and talkative; he liked to surround himself with people. We were the only two Arkansans at Oxford and as such we visited each other often. Also, both of us played on the Oxford University B-basketball team and traveled throughout England to different universities playing basketball. For people who had not played in college we were quite good. We won our league.

''Bill was at University College, Oxford, and I was at Saint John's College, Oxford. Oxford University is divided into different colleges so we were at different locations throughout the city. He was interested in politics. I was interested in politics. We had that in common. I had no doubt that he would go into politics. He was from Arkansas and so was I. We knew of people back here. I was at Oxford only a year as a Fulbright fellow and came back to Arkansas at the end of May of 1969.

''I was the person who essentially arranged for him to avoid the draft. Right toward the end of the year Bill got a draft notice at Oxford. He was very concerned about it because he didn't want to go to Vietnam and fight and die in a war that he opposed. He came to my room and asked for my help because before I'd gone to Oxford, I had worked for the summer as the statewide campaign coordinator for a Republican candidate for statewide office and was going back in the summer of 1969 to become research director for the Arkansas Republican Party, which was under Winthrop Rockefeller. Winthrop Rockefeller was the first Republican governor since Reconstruction. He had appointed as the head of selective service Colonel Lefty Hawkins who was also a Republican. I knew Colonel Hawkins but more importantly, I knew people who knew Colonel Hawkins including the top aides of Governor Rockefeller. That was crucial because after a draft notice is issued, only two people in the United States can kill or recall the draft notice. One is the head of selective service in Washington, D.C., and the other is the head of selective service in the respective state.

''Bill wanted my help in killing the draft notice, telling me that he wanted to look for an alternate means of serving his country in the ROTC or army reserve to the ROTC. He told me that he wanted to serve his country honorably in some other capacity if I would only help him get the draft notice killed. Because he was my friend, and because I also opposed the war, and because he told me he would honorably serve his country if this draft notice was killed, I agreed to help him. I arranged a meeting although he may have had other people help him arrange the meeting too because that's the way Bill is. He would have covered his bets and very well may have had other entrées to Colonel Hawkins but I know I arranged a meeting with Colonel Hawkins and Bill went over there with his mother. Quite frankly, I believe Strobe Talbott was there although he's claimed he had no recollection of that. Basically, Colonel Hawkins agreed to kill the draft notice and to let Bill serve in the ROTC.

"I myself did not serve. I had a 1Y, which is a deferment for medical reasons. I could have been called for duty, but only after the 1A's were called, so I was second tier and was never called.

"Bill and I had conversations throughout that summer. I was invited to his birthday party in August, but declined to go because by that time he had begun—to use a word I used in a letter written contemporaneously at the time—he had begun to 'wiggle' on the commitment he had just made to the ROTC and by that time I was sensing that I'd been used simply to kill the draft notice and that he had no intention of serving his country. The *Los Angeles Times* articles on the subject discuss what happened. Some involve me, and others mention other people who tell about Bill's earlier efforts to get preferential treatment, even before he went to Oxford. In the first place, he wasn't even drafted until about eleven months after he was reclassified as 1A, which was about ten times longer than the average person coming out of Garland County. That's because the draft board was essentially handled by Judge Britt in Hot Springs, who was Bill's uncle. Around the first of September, Bill went back to England by way of Washington. He went to Washington to work in the national headquarters of the Vietnam moratorium after leaving Arkansas. But by that time, he had already decided to breach his commitment to the ROTC, not to enroll in the law school that fall and enroll in the ROTC program there, which was part of the package, and I did not have any correspondence with him. I was here in Little Rock and he was at Oxford."

*   *   *

Nancy Bekavac was a classmate of Clinton's during their first year at Yale Law School, but she didn't know it the first time she spoke with him. "A fellow came up to me who had a beard and ginger hair and he asked if he could borrow my notes. I said, 'Who are you?' and he said, 'I'm Bill Clinton.' And I said, 'That's nice. Who are you?' And he said, 'Well, I'm in your class.'" And I said, 'No, you aren't.' And he said, 'Well, I've been real busy running Joe Duffy's campaign for Senate but I'm here now.' And I said, 'Well, we started in September.' And he said, 'That's why I need your notes.' I was sort of taken aback and I said something like, 'Why don't you borrow Bob Reich's?' [Reich is now Secretary of Labor.] And he said, 'He writes too much.' And I said, 'Do you know him?' And he said, 'Oh yeah.' So, I was pretty charmed by this discussion so I said, 'Okay, you can have these two notebooks but I need the other two and I've got to take some stuff out.' He says, 'Are those love letters?' And I said, 'No, poems.' And he said, 'Well, I'll read them.' And I said, 'No, you won't.' So that's how I got to know him. I think we probably went and had lunch. He had sort of asked around and figured I was the one to ask for notes because I didn't write everything down. I mean, I thought that was pretty neat.

"I would have asked Bob Reich for notes. If you're with Bob for ten minutes, you figure out that this guy's got it locked. He's smart. He's talkative and he also writes extremely neatly. He had this beautiful kind of printing handwriting.

"The next semester, I persuaded Bill and two of his roommates to take a class in natural law in the graduate school and we sat around and read Aquinas and argued. There was a graduate student in philosophy in the course who was probably just beside himself that we clearly didn't know a philosophical discussion from a shoe and were in there wasting his time but we had a great time. I think there were four of us and a professor. It was wonderful.

"Someone who knew Bill Clinton once asked me, 'When did you figure out he'd be a politician?' I said, 'Well, that was clear in the first five minutes.' And I probably figured in the first day he could be president. It's like meeting Wilt Chamberlain. You meet Wilt Chamberlain, you think, 'Gee, this guy could be a great basketball player.' You meet Bill Clinton, you think, 'This guy could be president of the United States.' I mean, I never met anyone else like that and I've met a lot of people.

"One of the things I always think about was how kind he was. I guess all of us had an abiding interest in politics and Vietnam and all those issues and I remember he had worked for Senator Fulbright in Washington. He was an undergraduate and Senator Fulbright came to Yale at some point in our first year to give a talk and get an award and it was one of these very fancy affairs which I realize now were fund-raisers but I think I was very innocent and didn't understand why it cost so much money. There was a reception and then there was the fancy dinner and Bill was very anxious. He had talked about what an influence Bill Fulbright was on his life and he said to me, 'I want you to meet him. It will only be for a few minutes.' He stationed me on the stairway and when Senator Fulbright came out of the upstairs reception to go down the stairs to the commons for dinner, Bill brought him up and introduced me and I'm sure Bill Fulbright had no idea who I was and I was just ga-ga but it was something Bill enjoyed doing.

"I remember eating at a place called the Elm City Diner a couple of times with him and then there was this joint like a diner out toward Milford. It had cheap breakfasts that they served till three. That was great. Unlimited coffee. This was important. It was sort of like a truck stop diner and it was on the way to where the big movie house was; it was off Highway 95 so you also could get matinee tickets. It was real cheap on Wednesday afternoon. I remember a couple of those.

"Bill was the kind of guy who always knew everybody's name. I mean, people in the serving line. All the secretaries' names. It was clear to me by the second semester that he was the one person who could get a paper typed for him any time day or night because he knew everybody. There were all these sort of sharp guys who looked like they were going to wreck the world but I knew damn well they probably couldn't get someone to open a door for them. It was just an observation I made.

"He liked country music. He loved Joe Cocker. He liked real rock and roll. He liked jazz. He loved gospel music. I got really sick and he brought me Janis Joplin's *Pearl* which is I think her best album. He adored *Nashville* by Robert Altman. He loved that film. I was going down to New York for something and there was a wonderful show of Van Gogh, maybe fifteen Van Gogh oils at the Brooklyn Museum. He had a car and since it was way out in Brooklyn, it was kind of hard to get to by subway. We went there together and we saw "Cornfield with Crows" which is a pretty shattering picture. Just an incredibly moving picture.

"He had this huge long blue winter coat he bought in England.

It probably was a navy wool . . . it might have been like a surplus navy coat. It didn't have a braid or anything on it but it was almost like a maxi coat. Now that I think of it, it wasn't that it was a maxi coat, it was just too big. It was huge. I mean, my impression of him is this tall guy with his mop of ginger hair sticking out over six feet of navy blue wool. I have a very clear memory of that.

"Their house was a beach house with junk everywhere and rat-hand furniture. And decorated? Guys don't decorate. I mean, Bill decorate? No. I remember the house. I remember the cat. I remember the beach. I remember the TV. It was a big deal.

"There was a kind of culture at that time to maintain an indifference toward studying. It was not cool to be anxious about it but he genuinely wasn't anxious about it. You knew from a very early point like the first conversation, the first lunch, by the end of the first day, that he was going back to Arkansas. Everybody knew that. A lot of people said, 'Well, I'm going back to my home state to be a senator.' And you sat there thinking, 'Right. They won't get elected dog catcher.' But it's not what you thought about Bill Clinton.

"Bill didn't inspire jealousy because he was too easygoing. Apparently easygoing. There were some people who probably bristled at the fact that he literally knew everybody in the Democratic party and there was, I'm sure, jockeying about the McGovern campaign but because he was gone for those two large chunks of time, not everybody knew him. I thought he might practice for a couple of years but no. He was born to be a politician. It would make as much sense for him to be a practicing lawyer as for a greyhound to carry in the snow. He wasn't bred for it. He wasn't made for it.

"I thought Hillary could do almost anything. The difference between northern and southern culture is she is more concise. She is more articulate in a certain way. She might have gone on to medical school. She might have been much more like someone who would run a social welfare agency. She could run a hospital. She didn't have to go into politics. I mean, she could be effective as an administrator but that wasn't Bill's thing."

Donald Pogue also met Bill Clinton the first year of law school. "A friend of mine from the Dartmouth debate team had roomed with Bill Clinton at Oxford. He said that Bill was looking for a housemate and that we ought to hook up. There were four of us. One of the other Oxford roommates, a guy named Doug Eakley, found a house before the rest of us got there—one of those houses that's literally right on the beach—Fort Trumbull Beach in Milford, Connecticut. We only lived there one year but it was a great year. It was a lot of fun. Bill was a tremendously lively person. Doug Eakley, the guy who found the house, was an exceptionally bright guy and we found a fourth in William Thadeus Coleman III who was a very interesting fellow. I didn't know it then but his father turned out to be William Thadeus Coleman, Jr., who was one of the lawyers on Brown v. the Board of Education. It was a very interesting group.

"Bill read a lot and he did other things besides law. He would do political campaigns. I just have this recollection of him walking around with a book in his back pocket all the time and if he couldn't find somebody to chat with, he'd read the book. He always said he wanted to do two things with his life, one was run for president and the other was write a great novel. He's done one of the two, and he's young enough to do the other.

"We cooked but Clinton cooked only briefly. Bill was a fryer. Cooking was not his strength. He fried eggs and he fried cheese sandwiches and he fried just about everything and I think we all would have taken a few years off our lives if we let him cook often. But he was an excellent dish washer. I hated dishwashing so I worked out a deal with him early on that I would cook and he would wash dishes.

"The war was clearly still an important focus but we were really moving on to other issues about the direction of the government. It was the peak of the Nixon administration and that seemed to be still unraveling. On the other hand, we were studying with a tremendously interesting group of professors who had such a deep range of experience because they had spent their lives building a national body of law whether it was in procedure or it was in torts or first amendment or national relations act law or business units. During their lifetimes, law had gone from being local or state bound to a real national system and so it gave us a tremendous exposure to try to gain from that experience and get a piece of what they had learned and had to teach. Many of the professors, many, not just a few at Yale, were awesome intellects and it was a very humbling experience.

"I always thought Bill's favorite professor was J. Willie Moore who is a professor of procedure and really crusty. Bill is a process person and he's a learner. My favorite story about him is that everybody else I ever met during that period would go off and they would work in campaigns and come back at some point and say, 'It's hopeless.' They met somebody who was so difficult that they just had to give up. Bill's reaction was always different. He was always learning from mistakes. He learned from the experience and it was like that in law school. I think procedure gave him an orderly way to learn. I think that's what he found so compelling about it and also that Moore was such a giant, a little guy giant.

"We had to write a paper together once and I slaved at this thing. I thought I did a tremendous job and he decided it wasn't good enough and went off and wrote by himself. I was always pissed off when he got an A and I got a B but it was fun. He had such a tremendous fluidity with words. He had very high standards and still does. He was very outgoing and very charming as he still is. I think a lot of people were disarmed because they thought, 'Well, he's a good ol' boy' and then they were surprised to discover that there was a fierce mind behind that charm and that was one of the most interesting things about the relationship with him.

"I think he and Hillary did a moot court. I mean, he was very serious about his legal education and I thought he was an excellent writer and a very good speaker as he is now and so I saw him as an advocate. He met Hillary around January, I think. All the lights went on. It was just immediate. It was a powerful, immediate attraction and very, very strong. She was a lot of fun. They were a great couple to be around."

President Clinton remembers when those lights went on. "The biggest thing that happened to me at law school was meeting Hillary. It was sort of a fluky deal how it happened. I'd just broken up with another girl and the last thing I wanted was to get involved with anybody. We were in a class together where—I'm embarrassed to say this, I don't want to set a bad example—neither one of us attended this particular class very often because the guy who taught the class had written the textbook and it was one of those deals where the book was better than the movie. He was a great writer—not a particularly great lecturer, you know.

"But, anyway, I saw her there one day and I followed her out and I didn't have enough courage to talk to her. The truth is I followed her out of the class. So a couple of days later she saw me in the library, and this guy was trying to talk me into joining the Yale Law Review and telling me I could clerk for the U.S. Supreme Court if I were a member of the *Yale Law Review* and then I could go to New York and make a ton of money and all that kind of stuff. I told him I didn't want to do all of that. I wanted to go home to Arkansas. It didn't matter to anybody down there whether I was on the *Yale Law Review* or not. And they were trying to get southerners. They wanted geographical balance on the *Law Review*. They didn't want everybody to be from Connecticut and Massachusetts so they were hitting on me to do it. I just didn't much want to do it. All this time I was talking to this guy about the *Law Review*, I was looking at Hillary at the other end of the library. And the Yale Law School Library is, oh, about eight or nine times longer than this room—but not much wider. It's a real long, narrow room and I just sat there staring at her while this guy was banging me about the law journal. She closed the book she was looking at and she walked all the way down the library—all the way across to where I was and she came up to me and she said, 'Look, if you're going to keep staring at me and I'm going to keep staring back, I think we should at least know each other. I'm Hillary Rodham. What's your name?' That's how we met. I couldn't remember my name at the time. I was so embarrassed. But that's a true story. That's exactly how we met. It turned out she knew who I was which I didn't know at the time. But I was real impressed that she did that. And we've been together, more or less, ever since.''

Under the circumstances, Bill Clinton's return to Arkansas after his academic career may have seemed unlikely. One of the state's most pressing problems had been what is colloquially referred to as the "brain drain"—the traditional reluctance of its best and brightest children to return after being educated elsewhere. But Clinton seemed to harbor a real desire to return to Arkansas and the University of Arkansas was delighted to welcome Clinton home. It wasn't long before his inchoate political ambitions began to bloom. He lost a race, married his law school sweetheart, and began to insinuate himself into the state's collective consciousness. Soon every Arkansan would know Bill Clinton's name and many of them would have shaken his hand.

Professor Al Witte met Bill Clinton after receiving a letter from Clinton indicating an interest in joining the faculty of the University of Arkansas Law School at Fayetteville. "We did have a vacancy at that time. A letter from one of his references spoke very highly of him. I think it was from Burton Marshall, who had formerly been number-two man in the Justice Department under Bobby Kennedy. So we arranged to meet for Sunday brunch at the Fayetteville country club with my two sons. I recall he was going around the room shaking hands and talking and he was about as charismatic a person as I had ever met. And he had sold me about fifteen minutes after we first met that he would be a welcome addition to our law school. When he first applied he hadn't yet received his degree and I thought that showed a certain amount of chutzpah. It was unprecedented. Also we didn't have many applications from people who'd been Rhodes scholars, and I'm impressed by that sort of experience and accomplishment. He'd also taught constitutional law at a night law school in New Haven. All those factors mitigated his lack of experience. And then once people met him I think they were captivated by his personality and his obvious intelligence.

"I was perhaps the last person to realize that a political career was his number-one goal, and it seems to me that I didn't really understand that until he had already been teaching for a couple of months. I do recall that after he'd been here a while we had a conversation in which he talked about running for Congress, which he ultimately did. And when I realized that he was serious I encouraged him.

"Senior members of our faculty visit the classes of the younger members of the faculty just to observe and evaluate how they're doing. And I was asked to visit his class in constitutional law. I recall the experience rather vividly. The class was starting the chapter on equal protection, and in most of the case books I'm familiar with, the first case is usually, as it was in this instance, Justice William Douglass's opinion in Railway Express v. New York. That's basically the case that's set forth, the principle of deferential review toward social and economic legislation, and I thought he did a brilliant job of analyzing the case and then conducting a conventional Socratic dialogue with the class. So I think his potential to be a great professor was always there. On the other hand, he was, how shall I say it, distracted by his political career, particularly since the university at that time did not have a policy of giving leaves of absence to members of the faculty who wanted to run for public office. They had no policy stopping that, of course, they couldn't, but he was faced with both teaching and running for office in two very heated campaigns—one for the primary, to get the nomination, and the other again in the general election. I don't know if he missed classes but I'm not sure that he was as prepared as he ought to have been always. My recollection is that he had the intricacies of the case locked away in his mind and was able to carry on a question-and-answer dialogue, a Socratic dialogue with the individuals he called on in class without what might be called outside aid, or the need for any outside aid. He was just a very intellectually well equipped classroom performer.

"I think those of us who had some age on him didn't know what to make of him. I know I didn't. He was simply different from our conventional academics, particularly since he was so well read, so well informed and so energetic, so ambitious, and still in his twenties. As far as I can tell, he was universally well liked and respected and supported.

"I think students saw all of his good qualities. I don't like to put words in their mouths, but I think some of them wished that he were here in residence more rather than out on the campaign trail, but that's natural. For that matter so did some of the faculty. But we understood that he wanted to take a leave of absence. It wasn't his idea to try both challenges simultaneously. He wanted to take a leave, and in fact later on the university, largely in response to his situation, did adopt a policy whereby members of the faculty who run for public office could take a leave of absence. State Senator David Malone from Fayetteville was our assistant dean for many years and did exactly that whenever he had to run a campaign.

"When Clinton was offered a position in the Watergate investigation, he asked me what I thought about that opportunity. I remember at the time urging him not to accept the job on the grounds that by then it was pretty clear that political life was his first choice and I felt that service on this committee would only slow down his political career—that kind of activity would not mean much to what I'll call the ordinary voter. How he felt about my advice I don't have any idea. I suspect he asked a lot of people what they thought about it. I don't think he relied on any one person's advice. By then it was clear that politics was where his heart was. By that I mean holding elected office, not being appointed to something. I remember seeing him more often after he was attorney general, and having dinner with him and Hillary one night during the first two years of the Carter administration. He was close to Carter at that time and we would talk about his future in terms of whether he should shoot for state office such as governor or federal office, either Congress or the Senate or even try to be appointed to some top job in the Democratic administration. But he was just considering options, he wasn't focused on any one choice. I'm not sure I understand the desire for a political life because I share none of it myself, so it's like a lot of other human desires that, unless you share them they remain a puzzle. I think that given his personality, the emotional charge that he gets out of campaigning and his relationships with the people with whom he comes in contact, whether it's longtime associates, intimate associates, or just people out on the campaign trail, give him a very rich emotional life that I suspect most people never experience.

"I think he could be a great teacher if he chose to do that after his presidency. Hillary also would be a great teacher. I have the utmost respect for their abilities in whatever they turn to. I would be delighted if either one expressed the desire to teach here again. I think the only problem would be holding him to this smaller stage. I mention Hillary because I think that most of us know both of them well and know them as a husband and wife team know that they have a partnership; it's difficult not to think of one without thinking of the other.

"My clearest memory of Clinton came more recently, during the campaign last fall when he came to Fayetteville just about ten days before the general election. By then it looked like he really was going to be elected president. And instead of being part of the crowd on the campus to listen to him I went out to the airport. When he came along there wasn't a very large crowd. We saw each other and he gave me a hug. I began to realize that it had been almost twenty years since a twenty-seven-year-old fellow with a blue suit that looked like he wore it in his high school graduation because the cuffs were about ankle length—he looked like Li'l Abner in his Sunday best—had come to Fayetteville and now was going to be president. It was just more than I could handle. I started to tear up and so did he and so the words weren't very easy to utter. I guess that's the one moment that I remember best."

Mark Grobmyer met Bill Clinton for the first time at the University of Arkansas in Fayetteville. "A third-year student who lived on my street had a party, and somebody brought Bill Clinton along. Right away I was impressed by his friendliness and his fun-loving demeanor. You could tell he was obviously very smart. And then I became managing editor of the *Arkansas Law Review.* Because of that I had a small office within the law school and that's where I used to go every night. Bill Clinton did not have an office because they didn't have space for him; he was the youngest faculty member and the lowest man on the totem pole. I was a little bit lower than he was, so they booted me out to a desk outside the door of his office, and so basically it was almost as though we shared an office. We'd both be there late at night talking. One note of interest was that my wife is from Tennessee and grew up knowing the Gores very well. The Gores had given Libby's parents a book written by Senator Gore, Sr., called *The Eye of the Storm.* It was about his stand during the Vietnam War and the fact that he didn't get reelected was in large part because of that. So I thought Bill might be interested in the book and brought it back to Fayetteville and delivered it to him one night. And he went on and on about Senator Gore, and how much he admired him and what a wonderful man he was. He had known something of him because he was on the Senate Foreign Relations Committee when Bill worked for Fulbright.

"I took his antitrust course that last semester in law school and he was a very good teacher; he particularly was good in that subject because the summer before he had written a brief for the lawyers who were handling the case for a local bank involving MasterCard and Visa. At the time MasterCard and Visa had a rule that if a bank sold one it couldn't sell the other. This bank wanted to sell both, and Bill figured out it was an antitrust violation because it limited competition. So, the case made its way to the U.S. Supreme Court and Bill wrote the brief for it. Unlike many of the teachers he was not just teaching something he was interested in, but he actually had firsthand experience, which was rare for somebody just out of law school. At Fayetteville one of the things that they pride themselves on is good, close relationships between faculty and the students. For example, the *Law Review* would have a party and invite the faculty and we'd have a keg of beer and there was a lot of camaraderie between the faculty and the students. Unfortunately, it didn't carry over to the grading.... He was young, he was fun, enthusiastic, he obviously knew his subject matter quite well so he was well liked by students. The antitrust course was interesting because it dealt with a lot of constitutional law issues. He didn't really use the standard text. He had three or four books that he urged us to read so we didn't just stick to the casebook. He didn't use the traditional case study method. The class examined a lot of issues about the philosophy behind monopolization and why we passed laws to prohibit it.

"He was always interested in politics and I think when he moved back up there he probably knew he was gonna' run for Congress, which he did. And I remember that nobody expected him to win, but quite frankly nobody expected him to do as well as he did."

Woody Bassett also knew the Clintons from the University of Arkansas Law School. "I took a course that Hillary taught in the fall of 1974 in criminal law. Bill taught the course in constitutional law in the fall of 1975 so I had both of them as teachers. Bill's class was very conversational, informal, and very relaxed just like you see him when he's out giving a campaign speech. He taught that way too. Hillary was more organized. She was probably more vigorous and rigorous in the way she asked questions. It was much more formal in her classroom. Bill very rarely used notes. Hillary was an excellent teacher and so was Bill. They just had different styles.

"One thing that I remember about Bill's constitutional law class was that we spent about three weeks of class time talking about Roe v. Wade. He was fascinated by the case and told us it would be a controversial case for many years to come. It's ironic that now he's president of the United States and he's fixing to appoint somebody to the Supreme Court to succeed Justice Blackman who wrote the majority opinion in Roe v. Wade.

"Hillary had just moved here. She'd only been in Fayetteville for three days when she walked into that classroom that first day. It took a lot of students a while to get used to her. It didn't take very long for people to know that Hillary and Bill were a couple. When Hillary wasn't in the classroom she was helping Bill with his campaign.

"Bill was the kind of guy who, when he wasn't in class, would be shooting the breeze with the students in the lounge. You know, he'll talk forever as long as somebody will stick around."

David Matthews, who later would volunteer in Clinton's campaign, thought that Clinton's classes were very good. "He has so much knowledge on so many things. It's really important to him that his listeners learn everything that he knows so he's a fountain of information. His habits then were typical of now too. He would frequently be late but just as frequently he would stay late. If there wasn't another class coming in, he would stay another hour to answer questions or visit with the students. He's willing to talk about everything. Politics. Sports. Any subject imaginable. I mean that's the way he was then and that's the way he is now. He'll talk about a whole lot of different subjects. He was just a good ole' boy who spent a lot of time talking. Everybody knew without any question that this was just a temporary stopping point. We knew he wasn't going to be a law professor for the rest of his life. We knew his interest was in politics but he was a good teacher. They both were. I think Hillary was probably a little tougher in the way she ran her classroom. Quite frankly, both of them flew by the seat of their pants from time to time, particularly Bill. With Bill there was no telling what preparation he had done just before he came into the classroom, but as the class went on, he got more energized and more excited and more into it.''

Kathleen Barnham first met Bill Clinton just after Hammerschmidt beat him in the 1974 third congressional district runoff. ''In the course of Bill Clinton's campaigning, he had gone to Harrison, which is my hometown, and had met my mother who worked in Harrison's only bookstore. I remember her saying that she thought he was the most wonderful person in the world. She loved his politics. She thought he was just so true blue and so eager to really help the everyday man and the real folks of Arkansas.

''Well, I lived on a hundred and fifty dollars a month and I had a dog who had worms. He was an Irish Setter and I loved him dearly. I was stupid to have him but I knew I couldn't afford to take him to the vet so I proceeded to go down and rip off this dog food supplement and IGA proceeded to arrest me. I peed in my pants, I was so scared. I wasn't a real thief. I would never have stolen anything for myself. I wasn't out there ripping off cars. I would have died before I ripped off something for me but I couldn't afford to take my stupid dog to the vet. They arrested me and they threw me in jail. My bond was ten dollars and my boyfriend had to go to three different people to borrow the ten dollars. I was hysterical and I went home and thought, 'Oh, my God. I'm going to jail. I'm going to prison. I don't know what I can do.' Anyway, I had to have legal representation and this was Sunday afternoon. The only thing I could think of was my mama saying, 'Bill Clinton was the sweetest politician. . . .' I knew he taught at the University of Arkansas at Fayetteville because after he had gotten defeated, he went to work as a professor at the university and his number was listed. I called him on a Sunday afternoon just screaming, blithering.

''At first, I was really incoherent and so he said, 'Why don't you come to my house and we'll talk about it.' For whatever reason, I have no idea why, he gave me directions to his house. He lived by himself on a dirt road off Highway 16. I was a shoplifter. There's no reason in the world why anybody should have ever gone out of their way for me. So I went to his house and he was very calm and quieted me down a bit and just asked me to repeat my story. I whined to him about my dog and I whined to him about being a waitress's daughter and told him that I was on grants and work study and lived on a hundred and fifty dollars a month and I didn't have enough money to go to the vet and whine whine whine. He said, 'Okay. I'll take you to Judge Webb and I'll represent you.' Judge Webb was the hanging judge for shoplifters at that time. In fact, when I was in the jail cell, somebody wrote on the wall, 'Don't rip off Moon Pie because Judge Webb'll get you.' They had had such a flurry of shoplifting that the stores really got up in arms. They were gonna' prosecute any time they could.

"We went to court and I wore my high school job-hunting dress and a bra. Good Heavens. When I was at his house he had said, 'Please don't cry at court.' It was all real straightforward. He got up and appeared before the judge and just explained that I had never had a record and that I'd taken the medicine for my dog and that maybe some leniency of the courts should be realized. The judge just said, 'You've got to be kidding.' Clinton came up and shook my hand and apologized that I wasn't found not guilty. They charged me $25.00 plus court costs. My boyfriend had to go borrow more money to pay the fifty bucks, whatever it was. But the cool part was that Bill asked for an expungement after a year. You know, that was a big thing. If I didn't shoplift or do anything wrong then after a year, I could say, 'Yes, I've never been a shoplifter.' And I could never have done that without Bill's help.

"He asked me to remind him in twelve months so that he could take the steps necessary to expunge my record and sure enough, a year later I did that. I remember there were some flowers growing by the law school building and I thought he needed some flowers so I picked some. I showed up at his door and said, 'Hello. It's me again. I'm sure you don't remember me but. . . .' He did say, 'I have to charge you something because if my counterparts ever find out that I don't charge, they'll get mad,' so he charged me ten dollars. So my boyfriend went off to three more people and got ten dollars. In fact, I mailed it to him later. I didn't have the ten dollars then.

"When I mailed the ten dollars, I wrote him a note that said, 'If you ever need any help at all, please call me because I will help you. I'll even wash the bathroom at your headquarters if you ever need it.' He got my record expunged and then a few months after that, I got a postcard inviting me to the inaugural ball for his first term as governor. When he was vacating his office, he called and asked if I could be a volunteer and I said, 'Sure.' By the time I got down there, pretty much everything was done. I felt real sheepish. I was in flip-flops and cutoffs and a halter top and I just said, 'Okay, I'm here.' They handed me the only piece of furniture left in the place, which was the lamp and I took it downstairs. I just carried that lamp down and it was all that I had an opportunity to do. I would have done more if I could."

The Clinton guy's charm did not win everyone in Fayetteville. Ernest Oakleaf, a political consultant who now lives in Little Rock, says, "I remember a conversation with Peggy who's a waitress in Fayetteville. This was a friend of ours from our Fayetteville days and she said Clinton would come in and he was just rude and full of himself. She couldn't stand him and at this point we didn't know much about him and so we were saying, 'What is it about this Clinton guy?' She said, 'Oh, he's just an arrogant son of a bitch.' "

Ellen Brantley, now a probate judge in Little Rock, taught at the University of Arkansas at Fayetteville at the same time as the Clintons. "I remember that I had a car that I bought right before I started working at Fayetteville. It was a 1974 BMW 2002 and I had a Clinton bumper sticker that I had gotten that spring that just said, 'Clinton.' It didn't say Clinton for anything because when they had it printed, they didn't know what he was going to run for. He was trying to develop his political contacts in general but not specifically running a given race. He was an unknown. He was really young. He was not well financed and he ran a great race against Hammerschmidt and so even though he lost, I think his political star was seen as very bright after that loss."

Carl Whillock first met Bill Clinton in Fayetteville in 1973. "I was a vice president of the University of Arkansas at that time and some of my friends in the law school called me one morning and said they were going to take this faculty member, Bill Clinton, to lunch and wanted to know if I'd go with them. I said, 'Yeah, I'd be glad to.' We were talking about President Nixon and the Watergate inquiry because Nixon was still president at that time. He had not resigned and each one was telling what he thought about the president. I told them that I thought that President Nixon would be extremely unkind to his mother if he thought it would help him politically, and Clinton, ever since then, I think, has had a soft spot in his heart for me because of what I said at the time. He'd come by and we'd sit in front of the fireplace and talk. If he was hungry, our daughter Melissa would make him up a peanut butter and banana sandwich, which he seems to have a weakness for. We'd just sit around and talk about a lot of things and I became convinced that he was a very bright young man, a very caring person, and I just had a great affection for him.

"It was not until December of 1973 that he mentioned running for Congress. I encouraged him to run. I told him that if he wanted to run and that was in his heart and the election was something he wanted to do, I thought he should do it, but I said, 'You'll have a hard time being elected because the man that's in there is very popular.' I think there were about 175,000 votes and Bill lost by only 6,000 votes. If there had been a switch of something like 3,100 votes he'd have won the election, but he ran a very good race. He tells people that I was the first person after his mother to encourage him to run for Congress. It was his idea. I didn't suggest it to him but I think I was one of the first ones he talked to about running.

"To the best of my knowledge, he had not been outside of Washington County where Fayetteville is located to do any campaigning and there are about twenty-five counties in that congressional district. I told him that he needed to get out and meet some people who could help him in other counties and that if he wanted to, I would go with him and introduce him to people I knew. We left Fayetteville about 6:30 or 7:00 in the morning I guess. We went first to Berryville where I introduced him to Victor Nixon and his wife Freddie. Victor was the pastor of the Methodist Church and the clerk of Carroll County. I introduced Bill to the chairman of the Democratic party in Boone County, Virgil (Bo) Forney, and to the postmaster, Beryl King, over at Yellerville and to the owner of the newspaper in Harrison. I introduced him to some people in Mountain Home. One of them was the county treasurer at the time. Her name was Vada Sheid and since then she has served many years in the state legislature. She noticed that a button was loose on Bill's coat sleeve so she asked him to take his coat off and she sewed the button back on for him. In the conversation, they found out that they both have the same birthday, August 19th. Last January, Vada Sheid told me that she has received a handwritten birthday wish from Bill Clinton every year since then.

"I also introduced him to a fellow name Hugh Hackler who was a good friend of mine. We served in the legislature together back in the 1950s. I told Hugh that I was with Bill Clinton, this young law school faculty member from Fayetteville who was running for Congress and I wanted him to be for Bill also. He said, 'Well, I've already committed to a state senator, Gene Rainwater from Fort Smith.' And I said, 'Well, I'm sorry you've done that because you really ought to be for Bill Clinton. I think he's a really bright guy. He's a caring fellow and committed and a hard worker and he's got a bright future in front of him.' And I think I said that someday Bill would be governor or a United States senator so you need to get acquainted with him now. So Hugh agreed to meet Bill. We met in a drugstore on the east side of the square at Mountain Home and sat there and talked a little bit. I told Bill that Hugh was already committed to Gene Rainwater. Hugh asked, 'Bill, where you from? Where did you grow up?' Bill said, 'Well, I grew up in Hot Springs.' Hugh said, 'Do you know Gabe Crawford? He and his family and my family are just best friends. We're over at their house a lot. They're over at our house a lot and just really good friends.' And Bill and Hugh sat there and talked about twenty minutes and then Hugh looked over at me and he said, 'Carl, I'm going to call my friends down in Fort Smith and tell them I'm not for Gene Rainwater. I want to support Bill Clinton.' It's my opinion that if Bill Clinton could sit down and talk to every voter in the country, he would convince two-thirds of them to be for him. He has such an ability and a presence about him that people believe in him when they get to know him."

Skip Rutherford met Bill Clinton when Clinton was campaigning for Congress in Arkansas. "Steve Smith, Clinton's campaign manager, and I were fraternity brothers at the University of Arkansas. Steve had run for the state legislature when he was twenty years old and we ran that campaign out of our fraternity house.

"Steve wanted me to meet his friend who was running for Congress. Nobody thought this guy had a shot against John Paul Hammerschmidt at that point. Smith kept telling me, 'You watch, he's going places.' Well, by going places, I thought he meant Congress, governor. I think Steve had a much bigger radar screen. I think he saw him at a much higher level. We were sitting in the bleachers on the Capitol steps overlooking the inauguration and watching the swearing in and I remember saying to him, 'I think you knew this day was going to happen.' He just smiled.

"The first time I met Clinton I thought he was impressive. He was very outgoing. He remembered names quickly. He had a very good grasp of the issues, the type of campaign he was going to run against Hammerschmidt. I didn't even know all the counties of the third congressional district so listening to him talk about different strategies for different counties was fairly impressive to me. I remember thinking, 'This guy's pretty sharp.' He wasn't going to come close to beating Hammerschmidt and I thought it was a suicide run, but it wasn't the first time I thought he was going to make a suicide run."

David Matthews volunteered to chauffeur Bill Clinton during his congressional campaign. "I went to his office and reintroduced myself. He always remembers everyone's name and what you had talked about so he remembered me. I offered to help him. Told him that I knew people up in the Benton County area and that I would like to become a volunteer, a chauffeur, if you will, during his campaign. The qualifications for being a chauffeur were you had to own a car and have a tank of gas. Periodically I would meet both of those criteria. He sat in the front seat. I was driving a 1971 Subaru, unairconditioned, standard transmission, knocked down in three corners. He'd get in and push the seat as far back as it'd go, and take a nap or he would take along a large stack of correspondence and he'd write letters in the car. We'd talk about the race and the issues and volleyball and school and everything else imaginable. If you're traveling with him, you don't stop for a meal. He keeps eating high-energy food in order to keep going. He doesn't have time for a sit-down meal. I do remember we were traveling over in Hiwasse, a little bitty town in Benton County, I mean like eighty-six or eighty-seven people. He had heard that the Dunnaways were important in that county and he wanted to meet them so we went and knocked on their door. He introduced himself. 'Mrs. Dunnaway, I'm Bill Clinton. I'm running for Congress. This is my friend, David Matthews.' 'Oh, won't you come in?' And we had a nice visit and sat down and had some of Mrs. Dunnaway's peach pie, which was terrific. Bill told me as we were leaving, 'You know, the first rule in politics, you always eat if somebody offers you food. You hurt their feelings if you don't.' Of course it was a great peach pie so that wasn't a problem but listen to how he remembered Fleta Dunnaway twenty-three years later because this tells you a lot about Bill Clinton. She and her husband were not people of means but they'd always been his supporters. Bill'd just been elected president of the United States. I was in Little Rock about three weeks after and went by the Governor's Mansion to visit. My law partner, George Rhoads, said, 'How's Fleta Dunnaway? I heard she's been sick.' I said, 'She has been sick. She broke her hip and she's in Gravette Hospital.' Two days later she got a card in the hospital from Bill wishing her well—this from the president-elect of the United States while he is trying to pick a cabinet. That's the kind of fellow he is. He is capable of thinking about the weight of the world but he is human enough to remember the small kindnesses that people have shown him and to return them. That to me is a man of character. We're not talking about the Jack Stephenses of the world or the Sam Waltons of the world or the people that had funded the campaign. Willie and Fleta May Dunnaway gave fifty dollars and some peach pie.''

Ernie Dumas, now a columnist for the *Arkansas Times,* first met Bill Clinton in 1974 when he was running for Congress. ''I guess everybody in Arkansas has an anecdote about the first time they saw Bill Clinton, about his charm and charisma and how he could affect a crowd. Mine took place at the Hope County Democratic rally in Russellville. David Pryor was running for governor. He remembered looking back and seeing this young man—Clinton— whom he hadn't met before. Clinton was writing something on an envelope and Pryor said that he had this impulse to turn around and say, 'Look young man, just relax. Don't try to write anything out and read it. You'll do much better if you're just off the cuff. Just tell who you are and why you're running and just make it very short and light.' But he didn't do it. Something told him not to.

''So the crowd up there is noisy; everybody's eating their chili and talking and nobody's paying any attention to the speakers. You had to strain to hear what the candidates were saying so Pryor finished his speech and then Bill Clinton came on. As he began to speak, within seconds, the noise kind of dissolved. It became quiet and everybody was listening to what this guy had to say. Something about his voice and manner up there just caused people to be quiet and listen to his little two-minute speech in which he said nothing. I mean it was just an empty thing but it sounded at the time really inspirational and kind of tugged at your throat but he actually said nothing of substance. In fact, you looked

at your notes later and said, 'I don't have a story here.' But he
got a thundering ovation. He was the only candidate that night to
really get that kind of response and Pryor was amazed. 'Boy, was
I glad I didn't say anything. I would have made a fool out of
myself telling that guy how to make a speech. Who is this guy?'
Which was what we were both asking. 'Who is this guy?' ''

George Jernigan, now president of the Democratic National
Party in Arkansas, also recalls the Russellville rally. ''My first
recollection of Bill Clinton was when he was running for Congress
in 1974. He was a young man, a college kid, even though he was
a law professor. Very dynamic, in fact when he spoke that night
at the rally, it was the first time any of us had ever heard him
speak, and he was just outstanding. He gave his three- or four-
minute spiel about why he should be elected to Congress. He just
mesmerized the whole crowd. He won that election that night. The
whole crowd was just stunned that this guy got up there and gave
the kind of speech we'd never heard before in Arkansas. All of a
sudden this kid gets up there and gives this spellbinding three-to-
five minute speech. And when we left, everybody in our car coming home said, 'Hey, he's the next one.' As I recall he had a
runoff with David Stewart. And then he went on to run against
Hammerschmidt. I don't know that we gave him any money or
supported him at all at the primaries but at the general election
we did help raise some money for him and contributed to his
campaign for Congress.''

Judge Richard Arnold first met Bill Clinton in 1974. ''I remember listening to him speak. I wasn't doing anything then, just
carrying a brief case for the governor. I wasn't anybody you would
ask for political advice because I had run for Congress twice and
got beaten so I knew all about running for Congress except how
to end up the campaign trail on the right side of the ballot. I
remember a particular occasion when we heard Bill speak at a
little town called Greenwood. On this occasion he spoke against
inflation. I mean it was a very eloquent, well spoken, well articu-
lated talk about how terrible inflation was and how something
ought to be done about it. I guess I had gotten to know him well
enough so that I felt that I could joke with him and I said, 'I've
heard that line of bull so often that I'm beginning to believe it,'
and all he did was laugh. I was referring to the fact that he didn't
say much of anything except that he was against inflation. Nobody
was for it. It wasn't that the incumbent congressman was advocat-
ing inflation or that either of them had any particular recipe of

what to do about it but what struck me was that he was able to make this speech and that people liked the speech and liked him. Well, there's nothing surprising about the fact that they liked him but it surprised me that they liked the speech because I didn't think that there was any substance to it. Well, that proved how little I know about politics.''

Now a professor of journalism at the University of Arkansas, Roy Reed covered Bill Clinton's congressional race for the *New York Times*. ''In the 1970s I was covering the South, rather a large region of it, and an old source in Little Rock said that I should come up to Fayetteville and look into a congressional race against John Paul Hammerschmidt. I came up and wrote a story about this brash young man and was taken with him. I remember I followed him around a day or two. He was just a kid who had all these political ideas that you never would expect to hear in the Ozark Mountains. Back then, multinational corporations were in the news and they were regarded as villainous. Clinton took out after the multinationals in a very effective and articulate way. He knew a lot. Obviously he'd read deeply on this subject and had some progressive ideas—as it turned out a little too progressive for the third congressional district of Arkansas, although Clinton came so close in that election in what is truly a Republican district. Hammerschmidt was not an anomaly. He fairly represented the people of this district.''

David Matthews recalls just how close the race between Clinton and Hammerschmidt ran at the end. ''Late in the campaign, with about a week to go, Clinton was out of money. I mean he had no money at all while Congressman Hammerschmidt had saved a substantial part of his money and was just flooding the market. We were ahead. We had the sense that we were ahead and grew very frustrated. We knew we could win and hoped we could hold on. Then a large corporate concern approached Clinton about a campaign contribution. It would have meant the difference in the election but it had strings attached—nobody ever said that but we just knew it did. Clinton turned down the money. He said, 'We'll go with what we got, win or lose.' And of course we ended up losing.''

Bob Steele covered Bill Clinton's first political campaign. ''I met him while I was a rookie reporter at KARK-TV, when Clinton ran against John Paul Hammerschmidt. The rest of the reporters were out in the field but I was very new and they felt it would be better for me to pick up any folks who came in to be interviewed. They already had live shots from all the big candidates. They didn't have a live shot from Hammerschmidt or Clinton because they were out of the viewing area and out of the district. Clinton had lost the election but that night he drove for four hours from Fayetteville to Little Rock to be on television. He had run a pretty good race for the first time out of the box but he'd got beat; so we talked about it on the air and I thought, 'God, this guy's good.' He was lucid and outspoken and brilliant, really, and he enjoyed the process. I think he was really eating it up, the fact that he was on live television. When we got off the air he said, 'How did I do?' and I said, 'You were great.' He said, 'Well, I was a little bit nervous but thanks.' I said, 'I'm real curious about why the hell you're on. Why did you drive four hours to be on television?' He said, 'Name recognition.' I said 'So, you're gonna' run again, right?' And he said, 'Maybe,' and at that moment I thought, this guy understands the power of this medium. He knows more about television than I do. I'm twenty-eight years old. He's twenty-eight years old and yet he's figured it out and that's really what I think the presidential campaign was. I think it was a name recognition race. I mean, you're looking at a president with a 70 percent approval rating and this guy ... nobody's ever heard of him and he wins. I just think he was running to get his name out there. George Bush took this guy for granted. Clinton ran a brilliant campaign. There's no way Bush should have lost but everybody who knew Bill Clinton knew the day he announced that he had a shot.''

Bill Harrison and his wife, Merlee, friends of the Clintons during their Fayetteville years, recalled less frenzied times when they socialized with Hillary and Bill. ''He had a lot of hair, but we liked him. He easily made a bridge to people older than himself as well as to people now younger than himself, of course. But we're ten, twenty years older than Bill.'' ''Ten,'' Merlee Harrison said.

''And we were quickly friends as were other people in the law school and in the community. Hillary was a great movie buff, of course, so we started going to the movies.''

''They both are,'' says Mrs. Harrison. ''But I remember Hillary wore those big thick glasses and we liked to sit down up front, the two of us, and we were never quite close enough. Bill would always say, 'No, come on, we've gotta' go down further. Hillary can't see.' ''

"We sat around on the living room floor of our house frequently."

"We were great wine drinkers in those years," says Bill Harrison. "We had a glass of wine once in a while and snacks and sat in front of the fireplace talking about everything."

"And it was mainly good humor but it geared down into serious things. But what I remember is that we laughed. I remember Hillary's laughter at not just our joke telling but her people stories, knee-slapping howlers about mutual friends, especially about stuffy people. They still don't like stuffy people, nobody does, but they have bull's-eye visions of these people."

The Reverend Vic Nixon was present at a more significant occasion for the Clintons. "I think it was in August that Bill called me one day and said, 'Hillary and I are going to get married. Would you be willing to marry us?' and I said, 'Well, of course. I'd be glad to do that.' And he said that it was going to be a rather small, private sort of wedding and he wanted to know what he needed to do. And I said, 'Well, we need to visit.' And he asked what the visit would be about. He said, 'Well, are you going to ask us questions?' And I said, 'Well, I don't know. I may ask some.' I think Hillary wanted to know what the questions were so she could study for the visit. The wedding was a very intimate affair in the house that they had bought and the ceremony was very, very simple—just family basically."

Anne Henry, a friend of Bill and Hillary's, says, "They all went to Mexico on the honeymoon together. Bill said, 'How many people do you know who take their mother-in-law and father-in-law and two brothers on their honeymoon with them?' I think that shows you how easy Bill and Hillary are; they thought it would be fun. They went to Acapulco for their honeymoon and Hillary's family went with them. The whole family went. Bill did the eulogy at Mr. Rodham's service. I preached the ceremony but he did the eulogy and Bill told this story about how they went to Acapulco on their honeymoon and the whole family went."

Morriss and Anne Henry had a reception for the newly married Clintons at their home. "It was a party. We had a great party," says Anne Henry.

"Two or three hundred people. A lot of campaign people who worked in his campaign," adds Morriss Henry.

"The wedding was just their families," says Anne Henry. "Her best friend from high school was the maid of honor but other than that just their immediate family members were at the wedding itself. Hillary's mom came on Labor Day weekend. She came for lunch and we sat and talked about the fact that they were going to get married and we offered the house for the reception, which was perfect for them.''

Reverend Nixon says, ''There were hundreds of people at the reception. It was a wonderful event and I had a grand time and I think all the campaign staff was there—students, advisers, friends—people from all over came to the reception. That was quite a nice event.'' Anne Henry noted that ''everything had been a compromise from day one because Bill's such a gregarious sort and Hillary's much more private. Some said the wedding day itself was a compromise because Hillary and her mother wanted the private small ceremony and, of course, Bill wanted to see everybody in the state.''

2

Governing Arkansas

In Arkansas, the attorney general's office has traditionally been seen as a stepping stone to the statehouse. So, in retrospect, the most interesting thing about Clinton's run for the office was that his competition seemed so thin. Everyone remembers Clinton, who had lost his only previous race, as nearly a preemptive favorite. His constant campaigning from the time he arrived back in the state had paid off. He did what one must do to win elections in Arkansas—he met people.

The trajectory of Clinton's career is by now well known; the stint in the attorney general's office was simply a requisite for his run at the governor's office two years later. When he became the youngest governor since Harold Stassen forty years earlier, his national aspirations seemed suddenly attainable.

But like any classic hero, Clinton had his hour of disgrace. Hubris crept in and Frank White took away the office the boy governor had come to see as his birthright.

George Jernigan, now president of the Democratic party in Arkansas, ran against Clinton in the 1976 race for attorney general. He was surprised, "that Clinton did as well as he did (in his 1974 bid for Congress against Hammerschmidt). Everyone commented that had they known he was that close they all would have done

73

a few more things and he might have won. So things definitely
would have unfolded differently had he won that election—no
question about it. Had he gone off to Washington he probably
would have tried to be a senator or house member. He probably
would have run for the Senate four years later when there was an
opening. We had a classic battle at that time but I think he could
have gone for the presidency by the other route. I ran against him
two years later in 1976.

"In 1974, in the fall, Kelly Bryant, our secretary of state for
many years, died. David Pryor was governor and Pryor and I had
been to law school together. He appointed me secretary of state.
I had a great time being secretary of state. The next year was the
bicentennial year and I met Clinton at two or three Democratic
party functions around the state. He was teaching law and there
were comments that he was gonna' run for attorney general the
next year and I knew that Beryl Anthony was also going to be
running for attorney general. Beryl was a fraternity brother of
mine and he and I had supported the same candidates all along
and so I was gonna' be for Beryl and for Pryor for reelection as
governor. And all of a sudden Beryl dropped out of the race.
Clinton had spent the two years since he had been defeated just
traveling the state. He had the county sheriffs working for him.
He had the county officials. He had gone into every single county
and had stayed in somebody's home; that was his great technique
of campaigning. He would call somebody to meet him, stay at
their house that night, eat supper with them, and visit, and then
he had that somebody locked. He had their vote. Clinton did the
best job I've ever seen of an individual sitting on a statewide
organization. He had that knack of going and staying in people's
homes, which I just have a problem doing. I always stay at the
Holiday Inn and watch TV, have some room service. He loves to
come into their homes, meet with their families, be part of it. It
was a very personal campaign. He never stops asking and visiting.
He makes you feel like whatever is your problem, he is going to
attend to it and take care of it, he's listening to everything you
say. The other candidates would go sit on the stage. He wouldn't
be on that stage, he'd be out there working the crowd row by
row, table by table. Anyway, Beryl got out of the race the weekend
before the filing deadline, and folks convinced me that I ought to
run for one reason or another and I wound up Monday morning
filing to run for attorney general against Clinton. This liberal, left-
wing kid, we couldn't let him be our attorney general.

"Well, he just beat the hell out of me but I had only forty-two days till the election. He had raised money, he had a statewide organization, he had commitments. He tried to keep me out of the race by calling Pryor and asking Pryor to talk me out of running. Of course, Pryor said to me, 'What you run for, that's your business.' Obviously Pryor and I were good friends. He probably could have talked me out of it but he just said 'That's your business. Are you sure you want to get into politics?' And I'd had a good time being secretary of state and I was having a good time. But it's one of my great regrets that I ran that year. I spent a great deal of my own personal money because I didn't have time to raise any. I had ten thousand shares of stock in a corporation called Demographics, which is now Axion. They've gone public and with all the splits they've had they could be worth up to 3.8 million. 'Course I'd have eventually sold them anyway, but I sold it back for a dollar a share back then. People that said they were gonna' support me weren't there when I got in. When I went to my longtime friends in many counties, Clinton had already been there to see 'em. He had covered this state in a year and a half. And two or three backed off him and supported me. I couldn't believe he made the state, really couldn't believe that he had worked this state for a nationwide race. He had just gone out there and done it.

"I think Clinton has been campaigning for the presidency since day one. He's the best campaigner I've ever seen. I'd go to rallies and go sit up on the stage where they introduce the candidates to speak; come Clinton's turn he'd still be out in the crowd shaking every hand of every person there. I'd get up in the morning and he'd have already been places shaking hands and visiting factories and what have you. Plus he had this phenomenal ability to remember names. I am the worst with names but he knows everybody's name. And we'd be working a crowd, I'd be working, campaigning, giving 'em my card and he'd be calling all the people by their first names. He has this ability to go up to somebody and focus entirely on them for about fifteen seconds, and they think, 'I'm the most important thing in the world. He's interested in every word I say' and then he moves on to the next person and has the same intense focus. I saw it a hundred times in the summer of 1976. Hell, I'm just giving 'em a card and passing along and don't even care what their name is. He wants to know all about their families. I've seen his aides trying to drag him along and he's saying, 'Well, how is Aunt so-and-so? Last time I heard she had an operation for such and such.' And I'd look around and say, 'Who is this guy, where'd he meet all these people?' He's just a natural, he is a natural at this kind of thing.

"He already perceived the attorney general's job as a two-year stepping stone even while he was running for it. He wasn't worried about the campaign for his second term, didn't gear up, didn't raise the money that he should have. So he was defeated. We all speculated about what would he do, could he come back. Politics in Arkansas are like that. I guess everybody loses a race, but not that quick. I think he sincerely did want to help Arkansas and had been places to see what a better place it could be. All of us would agree we needed to go places. But at the same time I think he loved politics for the sake of politics."

Former Clinton supporter and his opponent in the 1990 Arkansas gubernatorial race, Sheffield Nelson, recalls, "I met Bill Clinton when he was running for attorney general. In fact, he was a law professor at the University of Arkansas and called me at home one night to tell me he was gonna' run. I told him that if a good friend of mine, a guy by the name of George Jernigan, did not run that I'd back him. George played with it for a long, long time and almost didn't get in the race. He got in at the last minute, which caused me to have a break with Clinton because Bill felt that he almost had me aboard. But I'd told him. When I backed Jernigan, Bill called me all hurt and he just said, 'I'm hurt over this.' And I said, 'Well, Bill, go back to our initial conversation. I told you at the time that the only problem I would have with backing you is if George Jernigan entered the fray.' And I had promised George long ago, before Clinton ever talked to me, that I'd back him for attorney general. And I just stuck to my word.

"I think as attorney general he was probably more aggressively against utilities than most attorney generals ever had been and I think he used this as his vehicle to ride to the governorship. I think it was a very well thought out plan. I think it was intentional. He later laid over and played dead with the utilities. I know that Southwestern Bell and a couple of other utilities did extremely well under Bill Clinton's years here in Arkansas. If you'll look at the financial records of the other two companies you'll see they did. So he played to the hilt to get where he wanted to be and then he backed off and went to sleep and let the utilities do basically what they wanted to do. The utilities were among his major contributors in his last gubernatorial race as well, of course, as in the presidential race, not only in terms of dollars but in soft dollars and in terms of personnel who could fly to New Hampshire and elsewhere to campaign for him.

"It was a ploy. Again, it's like Clinton's entire career. People say, 'Well, nobody's smart enough to think that through.' First of all, he didn't do all that thinking by himself. At every juncture he's had somebody aboard who was either university oriented or poll oriented or politically oriented and usually some from each of those categories who could help him fashion a plan. Anybody who knows Bill Clinton will tell you he's planned to be president since he was in high school. Since he met John F. Kennedy this has been a driving desire of his. It's been his sole ambition, and, of course, he achieved it."

Joe Purvis describes working for the attorney general. "I graduated and went to work at the attorney general's office. I've never worked as hard in my life as I did at the attorney general's office. There are a lot of people who laugh and make fun of government employees but I was probably working about seventy hours a week and knocking myself out. The office was so bad then, I had transcripts and briefs stacked up that not only filled my desk, but filled the floor; there was a narrow path from the front door to my desk. On Friday afternoon after 5:30 when most of the people had gone home, I was working on something that had to be filed with the court by Monday. I was working like crazy, sleeves rolled up, tie pulled down. That was back in the days when I smoked and I probably had a pipe and two cigarettes going at the same time. I was as exasperated as I'll ever get and here Bill comes. He walks in and grins. He sits down in the chair in front of me and reaches in and pulls out a pack of gum and unwraps it, puts his feet up on my desk, and offers me a piece of gum. And I looked up just exasperated and he said, 'Son, are you having fun?' And I think I said something like 'What in the hell are you talking about?' He said, 'Are you having fun?' He leaned over the desk and he looked at me. I said, 'Bill, are you out of your damn mind?' He said, 'Listen, if you're not having fun and you're not enjoying it, you better move on to something else.' And I said, 'Yeah, you know as much as I hate it, you have sucked me into a love-hate relationship with this thing. I have precious little family life and social life, but, yeah, I'm having fun because I'm enjoying what the heck I'm doing.' But that has really stuck with me. I apply it to so many things and I think how true it is. You know, if you don't enjoy what it is you do, if you don't have a passion for it, if it's not fun, then you better move on to something else."

Breaking Eggs

Dick Herget, Clinton's campaign manager for his second run for governor of Arkansas, believes Clinton tried to accomplish too much during his controversial first term. "There was so much to do in Arkansas. We're just so far behind. We're forty-ninth and fiftieth in any statistical area. Bill and Hillary were both very, very ambitious. They were committed to the well-being of Arkansas. It was almost as if he had some sort of personal mission to fix all of the state's ills. He was concerned about the plight of minorities in the state. He was concerned about the Delta areas of eastern Arkansas where we have a Third-World country economy. He was very concerned about the environment back when the environment wasn't even a real issue or something that politicians hung their hat on. He got into a major battle his first term with the timber industry over clear-cutting and he totally alienated the timber industry in Arkansas, which is a major economic force in the state. He had a group of young advisers and operatives who didn't understand the old political ways of Arkansas. They did not have the courthouse touch and, even to this day, you've got to have the courthouse touch in our state. I mean, the Democratic party lives and dies by the local committees and what we called the courthouse crowd. He did not make those attachments, and that was fatal.

"Initially, there was an awful lot of excitement about his election. He was thirty-two years old and the youngest governor in the United States. He's a bright young man and we were proud of him. He brought a shine to Arkansas that we hadn't had in a long time. David Pryor and Dale Bumpers had been wonderful governors. They were both young men, very bright and ambitious, and they moved on to their proper places in history but Bill Clinton seemed to have a different level of activity and brought a different level of intensity to the job and he attracted a lot of out-of-state people. He brought in advisers and talent from all over the United States and it was almost like we were having a reunion of the peace corps as far as his advisers were concerned. The first indication that he had lost touch was in the Democratic primary when a seventy-year-old turkey farmer from Kingsland, Arkansas, by the name of Monroe Schwarzlose got 36 or 38 percent of the vote. That was the wake-up call to Bill Clinton. Clinton's campaign could have been salvaged at that point. We had an early primary so we could have put together a successful campaign to beat a local businessman who really had no political connections. Frank White's a very amiable personality and meets people well and is a hard worker but that shouldn't have been enough to beat Bill. Bill got caught in a set of circumstances. He got caught in Jimmy Carter's decline while White got lifted up by Ronald Reagan's wave of popularity. Then Fidel Castro decided to put every lunatic and criminal in Cuba on a boat to the United States, and Walter Mondale, who had been appointed the caretaker of all these people by Jimmy Carter, decreed that they would end up in Fort Chaffee in Arkansas. That was very unpopular. People felt that if Bill Clinton had this great chum relationship with Jimmy Carter, that he could have forestalled that and we should not have had the Cuban refugees dumped on us so there was a backlash there.

"Then Clinton had done something stupid in his legislative program. He had listened to the wrong group of people and had raised license tag fees in Arkansas by some astronomical amount and there was a terrible backlash from that. His losing was the result of a series of circumstances, the drought, the Cuban fiasco, the Jimmy Carter decline, along with Clinton's lackluster first-year performance, which was to be expected. As a young man, he was stepping in and trying to deal with the old establishment party system with stars in his eyes—he was focused on all the great things he wanted to do. All these sets of circumstances caved in on him. I remember being asked on June 8th by Mack McLarty and Wally Deroeck, who was finance chairman of the campaign, if I would become the campaign manager. They said they really needed new blood, that Bill wanted to give a new look to the campaign and diminish the role of his advisory group while adding a more professional style to the campaign, so I became campaign manager. Mack was treasurer. Maurice Smith, former director of the Arkansas State Highway Commission, was campaign chairman. Woodson Walker, a very bright young African-American lawyer here in Little Rock was vice chairman of the campaign. The campaign really didn't become a strong organization until about July. I likened the campaign to a house that was on fire and the new campaign team was the fire department. By the time we got there, the house was consumed. It was just very, very difficult to control the blaze.

"I felt very, very strongly that Hillary should change her name. I could not get her to do it. I spoke before a Democratic women's group and at the conclusion, before I let them ask me any questions, I said, 'Let me ask you a question. How important do you think it is that Hillary be Hillary Clinton rather than Hillary Rodham?' And oh my Lord, I wish I had never asked that question. There was a mass eruption. The average age of the group was about sixty-five so these were older voters but I left there with the firm opinion that the issue was strong enough to cause us to lose on the average a thousand votes per county. There was such a strong feeling in Arkansas because it's a Bible-Belt traditional type of state. I talked to Hillary about it but it's a personal thing. I could only press it to a point. We made the point as well as we could and very shortly after the election, she changed her name. Hillary's a crackerjack lawyer and a very good businessperson. She is very capable of being president of the United States someday. She was very capable at that point of being governor of Arkansas. I think that Hillary just felt very strongly that she wanted to maintain a professional identity of her own and I can understand that. She's worked hard to accomplish what she has.''

Arkansas Times columnist John Brummett, however, rates Clinton's first term as governor his best. ''Most viewed his first term as governor as disastrous. I'm one of the few people who thinks he was a better governor in the first term than in any after that. He was bold and he did some things that needed to be done. I have a curious political philosophy. I don't think someone should be measured only when he succeeds. I think you measure someone based on what he tried to do. Clinton tried to set up a system of rural health clinics in impoverished rural Arkansas where people can't get doctors. He tried to increase the authority of nurse practitioners so that more medical care could be delivered. This pissed off the medical society and cost him politically, but I don't think that means he's a bad governor. He appointed a timber management task force to go to war with the timber companies over some clear-cutting and, of course, that cost him politically. He did battle with the utilities. This was in the early 1980s and so called liberal-minded people thought that utilities shouldn't invest in power plants, that they should invest in conservation rather than building a plant, go right in and put in storm windows and things. Clinton believed that and he set up an energy department and that got him in trouble with utilities so he's alienated that special interest; he didn't get anything done there but I was really proud of what he tried to do. He really didn't get beat because of all those things. He got beat because of his silly car tags and the Cubans.''

Meredith Oakley, a columnist for the *Arkansas Democrat-*

Gazette, agrees. "Raising motor vehicle fees was not only a political fiasco, it did more harm to his administration and to his political standing than anything. It hit those on fixed incomes so hard. Now you might think increasing a certain fee from a dollar to eleven dollars to be a drop in the bucket. But it's not. The impact of seeing a tax increased 1100 percent was very strong. He showed incredibly bad judgment. He talked about the need for it in terms of improving rural roads, but it's gasoline taxes that fix rural roads, not license fees. So he was really trying to expand the income of the wealthiest agencies in the state, in effect, splitting off those revenues to a different division, but it all went into the same pile.

"And he started an energy department that was totally unprecedented. We were essentially a very clean, unpolluted state, but suddenly energy and pollution controls and all these things that had to do with a clean environment became the in things to do. His staff people were the precursors of yuppies but they were the offshoots of flower children. You probably didn't have a flower child among them, but it was that philosophy."

Herbie Byrd is a retired broadcast journalist who first met Clinton during the 1974 congressional race. "My first impression of him from that campaign was that he was an extremely brilliant quick study, highly capable young man who appeared to me to be politically sophisticated beyond his years. Clinton came from virtually out of nowhere and became the rising star of the state Democratic party obviously destined for higher things. Back in those years, who would have thought those things would lead him to the White House? All things considered, he made a good attorney general, although his political views back in those years were a lot more liberal than my own personal political views. He stayed in public office and ran for and became governor. When he lost his second term and had to sit out for a couple of years before he got back in the governor's office, it taught Bill Clinton a lesson that he will never forget. It taught him not to ever isolate himself from the voters, and you see that very creed in play today. He's given the Secret Service hell I'm told. They can't rein him in and they're not going to rein him in. He is going to press the flesh and meet with the people because not doing that almost ruined his life and resulted in getting defeated for what has been traditionally an automatic second term as governor of Arkansas."

Mike Trimble, *Arkansas Democrat-Gazette* reporter, observed in a 1986 article that "Arkansas voters seemed ready to get mad at the man they had endorsed only two years before and it's hard to figure out exactly why. His youth probably had something to do with it. Clinton was so obviously smart and capable and charming that we felt compelled to vote for him but way down inside where we keep our prejudices chained to the wall, some of us felt a little guilty about handing over the reins of state government to someone who, in the context of political precedent, was little more than a kid. 'I can't get used to having a governor who has zits,' one voter confessed to me over a drink during Clinton's first administration.''

Former reporter Bill Sadler first met Clinton in 1978. "He was young, energetic. I met him on a Sunday afternoon and he was in the office working. That impressed me. However, his loss to Frank White didn't surprise me. There was a sense going into the election that Clinton was in trouble. He was in trouble with the common person. He had lost touch with the common Arkansan and it wasn't any one single event in the term that had caused the problem. It was a series of things from staff members who were making contact with the constituents. It wasn't Clinton himself or the Cubans or the license tag fees. The man was out of touch with his people.''

Long-time state legislator Lloyd George first met Bill Clinton when Clinton was running for attorney general. "Bill Clinton impresses you. He impressed me even way back when he was just a kid running for office and running for governor, he was still just a long-haired kid. We old-timers kind of take all of them with a grain of salt but he'll impress you very quickly if you just give him a few moments. He's smart. Nobody has ever questioned the intelligence of Bill Clinton.

"But he wouldn't listen. He didn't listen to anybody. You couldn't tell him anything. You couldn't talk to him. We old-timers just from experience could have told him some things. The worst thing about Bill's first term and what really got him beat was his staff. His people wouldn't even let his constituents see the governor. You couldn't get in to see Bill Clinton. He didn't even know who was trying to see him. Even the legislators who were trying to help couldn't get in to see him. You had to talk to his staff.

"Bill was kind of arrogant the first term and either he really didn't care or else he didn't know it. Bill Clinton wouldn't be president today if he hadn't gotten beat for a second term as governor of the state of Arkansas. He was too arrogant and he thought he knew all the answers. He is smart but then there's

some practical, political sense that he just did not have. The legislature did not like him the first term. Nobody did. I mean, how
can you like a guy that you can't even work with? Those of us
who have been here twenty-five or thirty years have learned that
the art of an intelligent legislator is the art of compromise. You
don't get everything you want done and the governor doesn't
either but you don't have to give up everything. If you can't get
the whole pie, at least get a slice. That's the way we work and
during Bill's first term he didn't want to negotiate anything, which
ultimately led to his defeat for a second. You know, what amazes
me about Bill getting beat by Frank White was that a lot of people
said afterward, 'Well, I didn't have any idea he'd get beat. I just
wanted to teach him a lesson.' "

As Arkansas legislator Ernest Cunningham recalls it, "Bill
really started out popular with the legislature his first term as
governor but by the end of the session, things had changed. Partly
because legislators felt he was too young and also I think he was
perceived as being a liberal in a very conservative state—probably
more conservative than it is now. The legislature was mostly very
conservative Democrats who didn't like it when Clinton tried to
come in and do some innovative things. He wanted to set up an
office of energy to be placed in an advocacy position against the
increase in utilities and the utility companies saw it as a power
move, so that was one of the things that I distinctly remember as
controversial. Some members of the legislature disliked him because they didn't feel that the legislature was included in the decision-making process. The decisions were made by Bill Clinton
and maybe some of his staff and they were kind of passed down
to the legislature. You know, anybody who has run for legislature
usually has a pretty good size ego and would want to be involved
and feel part of the process. Part of the problem was that legislators just didn't feel that they were involved in solving the problems. I think his first term was a learning term with the legislature
as well as the general public.

"When Clinton lost the election to Frank White I was shocked.
I stayed up very late that night but when I went to bed, Clinton
still had a small lead. I believe they even gave him the election
at one point. He had a 7 or 8 percent margin when the returns
from the rural areas began coming in and then he started slipping.
I was not only shocked, I was deeply disappointed. I remember
going out to the Governor's Mansion the next day and Bill and
Hillary came out on the porch with Chelsea who was just a baby

at that time. Bill gave a very, very stirring speech and there were tears in a lot of people's eyes. A lot of us had felt that Bill was in trouble, but didn't believe he was going to get beat. I think that at that time, a lot of us felt like, 'Well, if we had thought this was going to happen, we certainly would have worked a lot harder on his behalf.' "

Steve Barnes, anchor at KARK-TV in Little Rock, claims that Clinton's first term as governor was a failure because of Clinton's "abundant hubris. I went with him about once a year into the Mississippi Delta. They've got very small communities there, and in these kinds of communities chamber of commerce events tend to be the pivotal political happenings of the year. Your local bankers, auto dealers, the local Coca-Cola bottler in addition to the beauty queens and the John Deere tractor dealers, they all show for these things. And Clinton went through the crowd as he will always do in a crowd, shaking hands, touching shoulders, seemingly oblivious to the fact that most of the political establishment kept their distance from him. I was struck by that. This was not a warm and hail-well-met crowd. The whole tone of the political establishment in that little town was decidedly cool to him and he seemed not to notice. His abundant hubris blinded him. This guy had never done anything wrong in his life. Even his losing the congressional campaign was a victory of sorts, and I honestly don't think he could see what was sneaking up on him.''

State Senator Nick Wilson says, "I wasn't surprised when he lost to Frank White. You'll hear all these crazy theories about what happened. I'll tell you what happened. The mayors and the county judges and the local businesspeople throughout Arkansas had had Bill Clinton shake their hands and say to them, 'I really want to see you in Little Rock. When you're down there, come on by the office.' He says it very sincerely and I'm certain that he means it but he had told a couple of hundred thousand people and when they came to Little Rock and walked in that office and some overly protective staff person said he's there but they couldn't see him, they left unhappy. The car tags and the Cubans and this kind of stuff weren't really the issues."

Meredith Oakley speaks about Clinton's sincerity. "I think that he was sincere about wanting to help people. The problem was his concept of what would help people. Although he was a product of Arkansas, he was also a product of our generation and the politics and societal concerns and movements that were taking place then. His way of helping was to bring in an awful lot of intellectual people to take care of us because we were not bright enough to know what we needed. Obviously he could not hire his cabinet in Arkansas. He went out of state for his key people. And they were going to come here and take care of us because we were not capable of taking care of ourselves. That is not true.

"No one thing did him in. Cubans, car taxes, his arrogance, Hillary Rodham, a lack of accessibility, an administration that was far removed from his constituency. All these things contributed. It was this notion that to make us self-sufficient we had to be kicked in the tail and kicked in the teeth by people who had no concept or respect for where we were coming from. I felt as though a bunch of snotty-nosed little pompous asses were trying to save us from ourselves because we were so backward and so unenlightened that we couldn't make a contribution to this state."

For political activist Brownie Ledbetter the governor's inaccessibility contributed significantly to the failure of Clinton's first term. "I think it was a flaw in his staffing as much as anything else. Actually Governor Faubus had the best and most effective criticism of him that I remember. I ran into him at the old Coachman's Inn one morning and he said, 'You know, that boy had everybody from every constituency,' and I think that's the best way to put it. His staff people were pretty full of themselves. I remember calling the woman who kept his schedule and saying I really wanted to talk to Bill and being told I couldn't. I told her, 'Look, I'll go wherever he is, I'll drive to town, I just need twenty minutes,' and she assumed I wanted something. She never would let us get near him. The last time I called she said to me, 'Well, what do you want? Just because you've given money, what position are you after?' I wasn't after anything."

David Matthews sums up Clinton's failures as follows: "I think Bill Clinton got beat by the five C's. He got beat by the Cubans, car tags, coattails, Carter, and Clinton. Ronald Reagan's coattails in the 1980 election. The antipathy toward Jimmy Carter because of the Cubans and because of the hostages. Finally there was that fifth factor of Bill Clinton and his perceived arrogance. 'I'm not voting for that little whippersnapper. He got elected and it's gone to his head.' Nobody ever said that about him but they did say it about the people that were around him. He didn't realize he was being protected, that there were two levels of hierarchy that folks had to get through to even talk to him. Bill Clinton is at his absolute best when he has direct contact with the people; when roadblocks get put up between him and the people is when he begins to have trouble. That's why he's stopped allowing barriers. He's got to do that for his presidency to succeed because the fact is, Bill Clinton has better instincts about what's on people's minds and what's in their hearts than anybody I know. He was upset when he lost but determined to come back. He later hung a quote in his office that I think summed up his feelings after he lost. It was a quote by Abraham Lincoln. The story was that Lincoln had been up late at night waiting for the returns in the race between him and Stephen Douglass and he learned that he had lost. As he was making his way back to his home along a muddy trail, he slipped and almost fell. Lincoln said, 'I thought as I went down, it's a slip and not a fall.' And Bill had that printed in calligraphy and put up on his wall. That's the attitude that he had after the loss: 'It's a slip and not a fall.' ''

George Frazier, longtime Clinton supporter, says, "I see some real similarities to his first term as governor and his first term as president. He manages to keep bright young people around him. That doesn't always sit well with the old legislators whether it's at the state level or whether it's at the national level. They resent being talked almost down to by young brain trusts and I think that's what happened. Also Bill got a couple of bills passed in his first term as governor that were unpopular and which defeated him when he ran for the second term. One had to do with increasing the cost of car licenses; that hit everybody and it just did not sit well with the state and so they kicked him out of office, but he learned from that.

"I think he knew from the moment he lost the election that he would be back at the end of the next two years and we talked about how he would do it. He threw himself on the breast of the people and said, 'I made some mistakes and I'm sorry. I have learned from them.' And he did learn from them.

"If he has a flaw, and we all do, I think Bill's flaw is that he sees so much that needs to be done. Whether he is governor or whether he's president, he's eager to get it done and thinks he can do more than he actually can instead of biting off a little piece at a time.

"He had a staff at that time who were very loyal to him, and I think they sort of closed the door to his office. Old legislators, especially in a small rural state like this one, are used to having an open door governor whom they could go in and discuss things with. I think he was shielded a bit too much from the public and from the legislators who wanted to talk to him.

"They were trying to protect him. Maybe they saw their responsibility as guiding his day. I think you see the results of his losing that election in the open door policy that he adopted for the White House. We visited him and were in the White House almost all day watching people come and go, being ushered in and out of the president's office. It was all very methodical but also very warm and friendly. People didn't get the feeling that they were being rushed through for a photo op so I think he's learned that he's got to be more open to people. That's why he's back on the road taking his message to the people. He sort of got steered away from that in his first one hundred days. He was so busy trying to do other things but from now on you're going to see him do more and more of the town hall type stuff because he knows that's where his strengths lie."

Bob Steele was a field reporter when Clinton became attorney general. "I saw him mostly at press conferences. He was obviously running for governor at the time so he was prosecuting cases and making filings against the public service commission and he formed the consumer product division in the attorney general's office to protect Arkansas. He was in the news a lot so when I saw him it was always on a professional basis. We weren't pals or anything but I saw him often. I did a live shot once from the Governor's Mansion the day that it was announced that the Cubans were coming to Arkansas. The photographer snapped a picture of the two of us right before we were getting ready to go on the air so I've got this picture at home of myself with now the president of the United States and it seems like we're both about twelve. While the cameras were rolling, Clinton talked about whether we would be able to handle this and about a facility at Fort Chaffee that could house the Cubans and it will not be a big problem and blah blah blah. It was all very official. As soon as the cameras were off and we were carrying down the live shot trail he said, 'I cannot believe Carter did this to me after all I've done for him.' I said, 'Do you feel double-crossed?' He said, 'Yeah, he knows we've only got six electoral votes and this will hurt him the least but it's gonna' cost me the election. I could get beat over this.' And it was a very honest aside. I said, 'Are you angry?' and he said, 'Well, there's not a whole hell of a lot I can do about it. Yeah, I'm angry but there's nothing I can do about it.'

"Sure enough, Frank White jumped on that; Cubans and car tags became the theme of his campaign trail. Car tags meant that Clinton raised the licensing fees for boats, trailers, and motor vehicles. Guys who were bass fisherman, who were Joe Six-pack, had to pay a whole lot more for their licenses, and it was a big deal. Then the Cubans rioted and some of them were even shot and killed. It was a massive deal and the folks in northwestern Arkansas, which is a Republican stronghold anyway, didn't like the fact that all of these folks had been placed up there. Those two issues were what White harped on.

"In 1980, I was the assignment editor at the ABC affiliate and I was asked to cover Frank White. I didn't want to cover White because I knew he was going to lose. He's a Republican and this is a Democratic state. I didn't think covering White would be as much fun as covering some other candidate. I knew Clinton was going to go to Barnes or some other top-dog reporter but I just didn't want to cover White. They said, 'Cover him.' So, I started following Frank White on the campaign trail and the guy was getting a response. He was good with people and he was really hitting chords. I had a sneaking suspicion that maybe he could do something but I had no idea he'd win. Monroe Schwarzlose getting more than 30 percent of the vote showed there was some discontent out there. Frank White kept coming up with new charges, and Clinton didn't respond to them. He didn't counter or anything. He just kept his campaign going. We'd get faxed responses to charges we hadn't even heard yet. It taught him a huge lesson. Now, any time he's attacked, he will counter instantly."

When the Cubans were brought to Fort Chaffee, Freddie Nixon was one of the people responsible for handling problems that arose. "The governor's office was sort of caught in the middle because there were a lot of phone calls and letters and even people coming by on both sides of that issue. There were people who were irate that the Cubans had been brought here and didn't want them at Fort Chaffee and were concerned about it, angry about it, and afraid. On the other hand lots of people were glad that the Cubans were there and wanted to help or were family members trying to locate loved ones. So we were trying to work with the different agencies from that perspective. We were caught between two groups of people, and trying to respond to both sides."

Meredith Oakley believes Clinton didn't think he could lose. "He was totally taken by surprise. I said at the time that if a viable candidate comes along, he'd be history. Like everyone else (except, of course, for Bill Clinton who even failed to pay his property taxes on his vehicle) I had to go stand in a line at the revenue office to get my car tags renewed for my motor vehicle license, not the operator's license. I stood in line at the revenue office on the Capitol grounds for about an hour or so. And the whole time I'm standing there and inching along to the front, I was looking at a color portrait of Bill Clinton smiling. And I thought of all the people who would have to stand in this line looking at that man smiling at them, the man who raised those fees. That's when I had my first inkling because people in line with me were saying, 'That son of a bitch, look at that grin of his.' And they're personalizing it, they're internalizing it. I knew he was in trouble before any expert told me he was in trouble. When Frank White came along with the brilliant one-horse campaign he ran, I knew there was a very good chance that Bill Clinton was going to be beaten.''

State legislator John Miller views that portrait differently: "Historically, the governor's photo hangs in the revenue office and most of the time, when the governor has his photo taken, he is smiling. It'd be foolish to send out one of him frowning."

Clinton's aides were more a source of contention than his portrait. About Clinton's aides, Mike Trimble says, "Clinton delegated authority to three men who basically were very smart but they also just had a real good time running the state. John Danner, Rudy Moore, and Steve Smith were sort of the gang of three. They were pretty arrogant, pretty cocky, and they were young. My impression of that first administration is that it was very progressive, very assertive, and it just seemed to piss people off. There were a lot of alligators in the legislature who didn't like to be condescended to by these guys with peach fuzz on their cheeks. These guys had beards and the old guard didn't like beards.

"They also didn't like the fact that Hillary Clinton went around using her own last name. She was not known as Hillary Rodham Clinton even. It was just Hillary Rodham and that pissed them off."

Senate Chief of Staff Bill Lancaster says, "I think, to be quite honest, that there were three or four people who thought they could do anything because they were in the governor's office and their attitudes reflected that. Despite what you think about this legislature, there are many people with vast knowledge here who have been here many years and who knew the governor was committing political suicide but they couldn't get through that layer to tell him. He later came to realize that there are some people here worth listening to."

Bank president Bill Bowen offers his impressions of Clinton's first term. "I was involved with two aspects of controversy. I was a member of the Arkansas Good Roads Committee that persuaded him to use car tags as a source of revenue for state highways. The other controversy involved Steve Smith who was campaigning that year as a tree hugger against almost any cutting in the national forests. He was trying to ban clear-cutting even on private land. John Ed Anthony called me one day and said, 'Bill, he is offending the entire timber industry.' So I went to see Clinton as his older friend, and I said, 'Bill, these things are hurting you. Believe me, they're hurting you. I don't know what your polls are.' He said, 'You've got to understand that Steve and his associate, Rudy Moore, are like brothers to me and I'm not going to tell them what to say or do.' I said, 'All I can say is it's going to hurt you.' "

Bobby Roberts, formerly a Clinton staff member, recalls, "His administration was one of the first in history to try to really move the state forward. That impressed me. I was unimpressed with his inability to surmount his image problems. This is a conservative state. He had three guys working for him all in their thirties, all with beards, and some people didn't like it. It was killing him politically and I couldn't see why he allowed that to continue. He seemed to still be trying to be a private person instead of a public figure, and you just can't do that.

"Bill is far more sophisticated than most of us. He's far more articulate than most of us. He's far better read than most of us. That would be true in any state but I think in Arkansas there is a populist mentality that is put off by that kind of thing.

"I think Bill needs constant reassurance. He constantly needs to hear from people what he's doing right, what he's doing wrong. You would get that almost ad nauseam, almost to the point where you'd think, 'Let's talk about the football game. Let's talk about something else.' But he would say over and over, 'What do you think happened?' I would say, 'Look, you can blame it on Frank White's ads. You can blame it on the Cubans and the car tags. You can blame it on trying to do too much too fast, but I think the main thing was image. You were going too far too fast. You've got long hair. You've got a wife who doesn't use your name. People perceive you as different from them.' And then he would argue about it. 'No, no. That's not what happened. Here's what happened.' And he'd go through all the statistics and so forth. So we would have some fairly heated arguments about that."

Orval Faubus, former governor of Arkansas, discusses his view of Rudy Moore, John Danner, and Steve Smith. "Their positions were considered by the people to be important, prestigious positions. These young fellows conducted the affairs of the office in cutoff shorts with ragged edges and sandals. No one complained to their faces because you usually go there wanting something so you're not gonna' displease the person you're talking to, but this had an effect statewide. And then Clinton himself ignored the duties of the office a great deal. He scheduled too many public engagements, too many trips out of the state, and paid more attention to the politics than to the duties of the office. He gained almost instant notoriety by being the youngest governor in the nation. So he got a lot of invitations and he accepted a lot of 'em. And then back at home were these 'hippie-types,' some people called them, conducting the affairs of the office. It had an adverse effect on his political fortunes. A turkey farmer down in a little town in a very small county, an old man named Schwarzlose, had no political standing whatsoever, but he filed in the primary against Clinton and carried several counties where I don't suppose a half a dozen people knew him. It was a protest vote against Clinton's activities and his policies.''

Former Clinton staff member Sam Bratton, who is now chairperson of the Arkansas Public Service Commission, answers the charges that Clinton's staff wore cutoffs. ''For the most part, it was a professional atmosphere although periodically on Fridays, folks who didn't have appointments would wear jeans to the office. A bunch of us would go to the White Water Tavern, which was right down on Seventh Street and Capitol and eat cheeseburgers and play pinball. It was a real good group of people to work with. It was a very colloquial group and Clinton really set the tone for that. People enjoyed staying till 7:30 or 8:00 on an odd Thursday night to argue about some opinion that we were in the process of preparing. Clinton might be out on the road doing things, come back in late in the afternoon and say, 'Well, let's talk about such and such opinion.' There were intellectual discussions that were challenging and fun.''

Longtime political consultant, mostly for Clinton's opposition, Jerry Russell says, ''His staff members were kids with beards and long hair. His wife didn't even call herself by his name. I mean, he got in his limo and sped down the highway, got arrested for speeding one time, and was a jackass about that. Well, by God he's the governor. He treated legislators with a great contempt that they probably deserved but were unaccustomed to getting. Those kids just went in there and acted like a bunch of obstreperous children, and the power structure of the state said, 'By God, we've got to get rid of this guy.' And so they did.''

Russell believes the media was enamored with Clinton. ''He stayed above it all. He tap-danced and temporized and lied and kind of floated along and the media let him. They let him get by with stuff during his campaign that they never would have let Bush get by with and they're now suddenly realizing, 'He slickered us.'

''Clinton beat a token Republican and he waltzed into his office on the euphoria of liberal youth. His staff decided they owned everything and knew more than anybody else and proceeded to operate the governor's office that way. He got a lot of criticism and he always waffled around and apologized and said, 'Gosh, I'm sorry.' And then he went out and did it again. I mean he's kind of like a kid. You say, 'Don't track mud in on the floor.' And the kid says, 'Oh, okay. I'm sorry.' And the next day he tracks mud in on the floor and you say, 'Goddamn it, I told you not to track mud in.' It's not a question of whether he means it or not; I don't think having to mean it is part of his agenda. I don't think he says things and thinks, 'I'm going to lie.' I don't think a concern for the truth inhibits his conduct in any way. I think he says whatever he wants to and then somebody else can go back and clean it up later.

''White, on the other hand, was in the right place at the right time. He was a known quantity. He was a symbol of propriety rather than impropriety. He could be counted on to do things the way they were supposed to be done. I don't mean Clinton's people were corrupt but these kids, boy, they were just shaking the social and cultural mores of state government wherein Frank was steady and dependable and he and Gaye were good Christians. The Clintons, during their first term were taking instruction at St. Marks Episcopal Church. After his defeat, Clinton began attending the largest Baptist congregation in the state. He sang in the choir where everyone could see him on Sunday morning TV.''

State Treasurer of Arkansas Jimmie Lou Fisher disagrees. ''Bill Clinton, to my knowledge has always been a religious person and always gone to church. In December, after that defeat, when he started singing in the choir at Emmanuel Baptist Church, a lot of people who love to cast stones said, 'Oh, he's just doing it because he wants to run again.' I don't believe that. He thoroughly enjoyed it. He was very faithful, he was a very dedicated member. Rex Horne was the minister at that time, and I think Rex Horne was a very good source of strength for him when he needed it.''

Now a University of Arkansas professor, Steve Smith offers another perspective. "I think if you look at what was accomplished in terms of legislation passed and things like that it was a very active and fairly successful administration. But any time you start breaking eggs it doesn't matter what the omelette's like, the eggs don't like it. There were a lot of stylistic things that I think were not handled well, not so much on Clinton's part but by his staff, and I include myself in that. Because in politics generally and in Arkansas in particular I think that the style makes a difference, that personal relationships make a difference, and change is never easy. You can do things in terms of communication strategies with interpersonal behavior to make them less harsh or less jolting and I didn't always pay enough attention to that. It's a failing on my part because I understand now that's the way it works; and those years certainly reinforced that lesson.

"People tended to view Rudy Moore, John Danner, and me as a triumvirate. That's an easy handle but I don't think it's accurate. Clinton was always the governor and Rudy was in the traditional chief of staff role in charge of taking care of the staff and handling most of the legislative relations. He and Clinton worked together in coordinating those and the general political side of the office; I don't mean he was doing all the work—there would be liaisons to the agencies, the various staff people working with Danner and he coordinated that effort. And I was in two areas, community and economic development and natural resources policy. It was just a division of responsibilities that became unnecessarily visible. I think there was resentment toward Clinton's staff though. Rudy Moore and I had both been in the legislature so we still had a lot of friends in the legislature. It wasn't like we were aliens.

" 'Bearded hippies' became the icon for what people didn't like about us and Clinton's staff in general. Those things probably shouldn't have made a difference but it did. And they could have been avoided.

"I think he made some significant advances in education, certainly, and energy conservation and the energy policy and things like that. And he reorganized his economic development efforts.

"People have said he wasn't accessible but I think he was one of the most accessible governors ever as far as meeting with people and traveling around the state to meet with groups and things. If having access means being able to talk to him either on the phone or in person, I don't think he was any less accessible than any other governor in the past. Popular perception saw it as a problem, but I don't think it's an accurate perception.

"The Cuban relocation was something he had absolutely no control over, that was a federal government decision. The car tags became sort of a symbol for a tax increase or an uncaring approach to that. He raised the tax from seventeen dollars to twenty-five dollars and still Arkansas has one of the lowest car allotment taxes in the country.

"He got the negative consequences for raising revenues but didn't get credit for what that money brought Arkansas. He used those taxes to fund construction programs that he didn't get the political benefit from because construction contracts take a long time and all the road building began after his first term had ended. But part of it was just sort of the general mood of the country. Ronald Reagan was being reelected and I think that people didn't intend for Frank White to win but didn't want Clinton to have a landslide and some of the totals that he might have had. People in Clinton's campaign thought that Frank White's attacks and charges and negativism were at the very least a violation of decorum with the political discourse and his staff ignored the charges because they didn't think the public would believe them. Since that time Clinton has always answered every charge made against him and confronted it and let nothing go unanswered. Learning that lesson certainly served him well in the presidential campaign."

Sam Bratton thinks "there was probably some truth to the criticism that he tried to do too many things at once, to fix too many problems all at the same time, and got spread too thin. He took on some fairly controversial issues and perhaps didn't handle them as well as they should have been handled.

"Clear-cutting is an example. It is a forest harvesting practice. The governor appointed a task force to look at this issue and in the process, managed to alienate the timber industry, and that's a fairly significant industry in Arkansas. In retrospect, he clearly could have handled the issue with more finesse and diplomacy.

"We would have been better off if we had one or two more people who had somewhat more experience or broader experience. A very significant number of staff people were lawyers. Perhaps we would have been better off with a somewhat different mix of staff members. There are a lot of folks that want the government to just leave 'em alone. They don't necessarily want educational improvements if by improvement you mean getting rid of the local school that has a hundred kids in it and which hasn't had to change its curriculum since 1952. They don't want to be threatened by the idea of perhaps having to consolidate with folks down the road whom they never have liked. So even with education, which was a very popular issue with a lot of people, there were some negatives because some of the things that were done to improve the system and to better educational opportunities made some folks unhappy.''

Mark Grobmyer says, ''We had three good governors before Clinton—Rockefeller, Bumpers, and Pryor—so it wasn't as though things were terrible and had to be changed. All three had been clean governors, no scandals, no problems like that, and I think people thought he would kind of do the same things. I don't think they voted for him for a big change. I think there's a big difference between his presidential election and that governor's race. The people in Arkansas wanted more of the same, while Bill was headed on his road of progress. The legislature back then was made up of a lot of older guys who had a hard time relating to staff members under thirty. It was a culture clash. When Bill decided to run again he basically ran some ads apologizing, saying, 'I think I tried to do too much,' etc. He got the people's message to just settle down.

''The guy he was running against was well liked. He was a Democrat running as a Republican. Frank White was a savings and loan executive before savings and loans had a bad name, and people thought, 'Well, he's a businessman; if you call somebody in Little Rock and ask about Frank White, generally they'd say he's a nice guy.' I think people subconsciously thought, 'I'll vote against Clinton, send him a message, and if Frank White happens to win, it's not the worst thing in the world.' So Clinton lost.''

Tom McRae, Clinton's opponent in the 1990 Democratic primary for governor, notes, ''He had a four-year term when they were trying to put together a rural health care initiative. And Bill's agenda was to do the initiative and have the first clinic open when he kicked off his campaign for reelection. Well that was less than a year off with a two-year term. Administration and process are things that I happen to be familiar with so I was looking at all the bases that had to be covered and it was clear to me that achieving his goals in that timespan was impossible without making a lot of enemies. I said this to Hillary, and she said, 'Well, Bill needs to hear this.' She called him over and as soon as I got about a sentence and a half out of my mouth and he realized where I was going, he just turned and walked off. Well, a lot of other things happened, but the net result was that they got no rural health clinics because they had to cut out of the process the people necessary for this project to happen.

"The physicians got angry because they thought he had some sort of a plan to implement socialized medicine or some such idea. Many doctors, who often aren't active politically, ended up supporting Frank White. The groups that gave the most money to Frank White's campaign were physicians who were mad about this and timber industry people who were mad about a series of hearings done on land use over the state.

"I remember that because there was a governor's staffer who kept calling me and saying, 'We're gonna' really fix them, we're gonna' stack this hearing with people who are opposed to clear-cutting.' Now we're talking about private land. I kept saying, 'Well, fine, it's fun to have those kinds of things as issues. What are you getting for it?' And they kept saying, 'What do you mean?' Bill had a crew of people who were just absolutely convinced they were going to save the universe. I always worked based on the theory that if you're going to make people mad, if you're going to make waves, at least make sure you get something for it. Clinton's staff seemed to be making gratuitous waves for the fun of it."

Steve Smith responds to these charges. "People working on policy issues get involved in the minutiae and fail to take an overall view of what's going on and how the different constituencies might be alienated if the staff fails to see the overall picture. In health care we were doing rural health clinics that a lot of the doctors were opposed to, so we alienated one constituency there."

Tom McRae says, "I think Bill came back thoroughly chastened. I remember one night after he'd lost the election, we happened to be at the same dinner party. And he said, 'It was the Cubans, it was the car tax that beat me, I tried to do the right thing.' I tried to point out some of these other things and he didn't like it. I felt he was fairly resistant to it. We happened to leave at about the same time and I remember he looked at me and he said, 'If I thought that what you were saying was right, I'd go home and stick my head in an oven.'

"I think to say his staff was a bunch of young, bearded hippies is a little too much of a cliché and a little too strong. It would be a little fairer and more accurate to say they were a bunch of young people riding in on their white horses convinced they were going to save the universe, whether it wanted saving or not.

"Many of his friends would say that he never met all their expectations. And he created enormous expectations—whether they were realistic is another argument. You have someone who creates enormous expectations and achieves moderately good results. Now, do you criticize him because he was moderately good? What if he had been average or moderately bad? Is it bad because he inspires people and creates great expectations and then only achieves pretty good results?

"One of his gifts, which I suppose at one level threatens to become a curse, is that he has the ability to create vision and to inspire and to simply make people think he's going to move mountains. And it's not a bad quality, but if the expectation is that he's going to lift the mountain seven feet and he only lifts it four, people don't tend to say, 'We're up four feet.' Instead they want to know why we haven't made seven. And if you go back and look probably no one else has done better than four.

"He got some taxes through. Most of it was for teachers and at a time nationally when no one was getting taxes through and no one was even daring to try. He got a big highway plan through, again by increasing taxes. These were things we needed. No one could look at Arkansas and see where our teachers' salaries were, and see what the roads were like and not realize that both things desperately needed doing but it took a lot of political courage to belly up to the bar and get those taxes through. And you can't help but admire that."

Jeff Katz, then Little Rock correspondent for the Memphis *Commercial Appeal*, says, "I said Clinton was the greatest politician that I've ever seen. I didn't say he was necessarily the greatest governor. In 1980, I saw somebody who looked like he was on top of the world, the youngest governor in the country lose an election and he lost for several reasons. You've heard a lot about car tags and Cubans. Certainly those were two important issues. But Arkansas is a predominantly rural state with people who think that in addition to wrestling the weighty problems of the day, their governor should be down-home enough to visit all the local fish fries and leave folks with the impression that he gives a damn. Clinton didn't appear down-home. He had a convoy of young aides that people thought were arrogant and ruthless. I don't know if they were arrogant and ruthless but they were very much aggressive and go-getters. They wanted to accomplish a lot. Clinton has said that the fact that his father died before he was born gave him a sense of the shortness of time and wanting to do a lot. His administration tried to do so many things that they couldn't follow through on them and he got into problems in many different areas and pissed off a lot of people.

"Don't forget too that 1980 was a very difficult time for the state of Arkansas. There was a drought. A Titan missile had exploded. The recession was going on. Meanwhile, Clinton was seeing himself touted in the national media as a rising star. There was a very strong contrast between what was happening to Arkansas at the time and what was happening to Clinton."

Kathy McClanahan describes an uncharacteristic view of Bill Clinton. "This was probably in October right before he lost the election in 1980. He called and asked if I could come pick him up at the Old Post Office, a popular Fayetteville restaurant. I said, 'I'll be there in just a minute.' So I drove down there and he ran out to the car and just collapsed in the backseat. I said, 'What is the matter?' He said, 'I have been politicking till I'm just worn out. I can't go another day.' I don't know where Hillary was. I don't even think she was in town. He didn't have any other place to go, I guess. Anyway, on the way back, I was about to run out of gas so I had to stop. He said, 'Please don't stop.' And I said, 'Bill, we're going to run out of gas. Would you rather run out of gas with me on the freeway or . . . I'm stopping.' He'd crawled into the backseat. Got down on the floor. I said, 'I'll go to the self-service line.' He said, 'Just hurry.'

"He didn't want anybody to see him. He was so tired that he didn't want anybody to see him. That was the first time he had asked for my help. I've never seen him so stressed out. I had a bunch of people staying with me from Tulsa who had come over for the game and all these people were half drunk. Some of them were passed out. And here I walk in with the governor of Arkansas. He said, 'Can I talk to you in the other room?' And I said, 'Sure.' So we went to my office at the back of the house. As soon as I closed the door, he started bawling—really crying and I grabbed him and I gave him a hug. I said, 'What is wrong?' And he said, 'I'm going to lose this election.' "

Frank White, who beat Clinton for governor, says, "Bill was very immature. He was very young. He was the youngest governor in the country and he would put on these tirades of out-of-control anger and throw things in the governor's office. He surrounded himself with a bunch of what I call bearded wonders. He had these guys who came down from federal. They all had beards and were part of the hippie movement. When he'd have a picture taken with his staff, there'd be Bill Clinton with all these bearded guys. Most Arkansans didn't know that Hillary didn't have his name when they elected him. They knew her name was Hillary but they didn't know her name was Hillary Rodham. They thought she was Hillary Clinton. Well, she was very specific that she was Hillary Rodham after they were elected. I think it was a case of the people really not knowing what they were getting. Bill built this image that he couldn't be beat and none of the Democrats would run against him. I said, 'Well, I can't believe that's the best the state has to offer.' I had served in David Pryor's administration. I knew a lot of movers and shakers in Arkansas. And so I said, 'Well, heck, I'm going to run,' and I just came home one night and told my wife I was going to resign as president of a $100 million savings and loan to run for the governorship.

"She thought I was crazy. I called a hundred people to tell them and ninety-seven said, 'Don't do it.' I promised my wife that I wouldn't expose us to more than $50,000 and I put $50,000 in my account and then I got ten people in the state who were my friends and asked them each to raise me $10,000. It took them two months but they did and then I got through the Republican primary and began to get around. I began to build a little momentum and all of a sudden, I expanded my list of supporters to ten more and asked them to raise me some money—not big money—I only spent $200,000 to beat him in 1980. See, *now* these races cost a million, two million dollars.

"Even though nobody thought I could beat him I was just out there, knocking on doors and shaking hands day after day. He didn't take me seriously the first four months and they made a very tragic mistake. They decided not to haul the black vote. Now they can tell you anything they want to about politics in Arkansas but when you want to get the black vote in eastern Arkansas, you've got to pay the preachers and they take them to the polls. That's just the southern culture. That's just the way it is. I had the guy from the Associated Press in New Orleans tell me that it cost two million dollars to haul the black vote in New Orleans for Edwin Edwards. That's exactly the way you get it, and if you don't take them to the polls, they don't go and half of them don't know how to vote so the preachers tell them how to vote."

Dick Herget recalls, "I had breakfast with the Clintons the morning after the election. Bill was barefooted and had on blue jeans and a T-shirt and the phone was ringing off the wall. Walter Mondale called and Teddy Kennedy and people from all over the

United States called. That was the first time that it really came home to me that this guy had a national agenda. There are people out in the world who are interested in the welfare of Bill Clinton and wanted to know what had happened.''

Longtime Clinton supporter and U.S. District Court Judge Bill Wilson remembers: ''I had talked to him on the phone the morning after he lost. He could have played handball against a curb he was so low.''

Jeff Katz says, ''One of my most vivid images of that campaign was at the Governor's Mansion the day after the election. It was like a wake. I've never seen so many people in tears. I've never seen so many dark glasses. Thank goodness it was a sunny day so they could disguise it but people were just incredibly shook up. I remember him ending his speech saying something to the effect of 'With the grace of God, we'll have the chance to serve again.' And I was among those who thought that people needed some time to forget why they didn't want to reelect Bill Clinton.''

Sheffield Nelson avers, ''Bill Clinton has always been campaigning. Bill Clinton started campaigning the day after he lost, after he stopped crying and got his feet back on the ground. He realized that the Hillary Rodham thing had to change, it had to become Hillary Clinton. He realized he had to drop the arrogance and cut his hair, surround himself with new people and he had to go tell the people he was sorry, which he did very effectively. And again it comes back to if you tell them strongly enough and look them in the eye when you tell them, and if you're enough of a salesman, the majority will believe you. And that's what he's always capitalized on.''

Frank White says, ''When Clinton raised the title fees and the license fees and the title transfer fees, every old boy sitting down in Desha County who's got a pickup truck and a boat and a trailer now has to pay $125 to register when he used to pay just forty-two bucks. As I traveled around the state, these little girls would tell me, 'Listen, Mr. White, I want to tell you something. I've worked in the revenue office for fourteen years and I've been cussed at and yelled out and abused more in the last six months than all fourteen years put together and it's all due to one thing—the license fees.' It burned him so bad that he seriously contemplated calling a special session two months before the general election to repeal the license fees and title transfer fees. It cost more to transfer the title of an Arkansas car than anywhere else in the nation.

"The other thing was the Cuban issue; they played raw politics with the Cubans. Jimmy Carter told Dale Bumpers, David Pryor, and Bill Clinton that he wasn't going to send any more Cubans here. Now, we took the Vietnamese and there was never a question about it. It was a humanitarian thing to do and they came to Arkansas and many of them infiltrated the major parks of Arkansas and began small businesses with great success. There're some very wealthy families up in Fort Smith who came with the Southeast Asian influx of boat people. With the Cubans, it was different. I mean, we got the criminals. We got two barracks full of nothing but gays and misfits. Castro dumped the prisoners on us and it was a farce what he did to Carter.

"I did an ad on television in which I said, 'The governor of Nebraska stood up and said, "No more Cubans." The governor of Pennsylvania said, "No more Cubans." Where was the governor of Arkansas when we needed him?' I took twenty points off of him in two weeks in the polls and that's when he knew he was in trouble. It didn't matter where he went in Arkansas, people would get up from the audience and say, 'Why didn't you stand up to the federal government?' When I won, he never called me. (Dick Herget called for Clinton.)

"He did a lot of things that alienated people. He refused to set the death penalty. He commuted forty-five life sentences his first term as governor and wouldn't set the death penalty. I changed that policy and started setting the death penalty. When he came back in, he kept my policy and as far as I know, made *one* life sentence commutation the next twelve years in office."

James Merriweather, former political editor for the *Arkansas Gazette,* agrees. "Clinton's support for the death penalty always bothered me because I can remember a time back in the early 1980s when the prosecutors were on his butt all the time to set execution dates and he just wouldn't do it. It would be months before he would take any concrete action and get them set up to schedule the execution. I don't know exactly when the transformation occurred but at some point I guess he read the polls and decided that the public was in favor of the death penalty so he jumped on the bandwagon too. That was the big fault that I always had with him. I'm not sure that on a personal level, he favors the death penalty. I think it's more a political consideration to him.

"The case that really bothered me was Ricky Rector. He killed a policeman and another guy. In the heat of his campaign for president, Clinton flew home just to make sure that if anybody was going to stop the execution, it would be him. This death penalty issue is one area where I really question whether the governor made a personal decision that it was the right thing to do or if he'd read the polls and decided that it was the politically expedient thing to do. Three or four years ago there was a death penalty protest on the state Capitol grounds and I asked him about a study in Louisiana that showed that prosecutors were much less likely to seek the death penalty in cases in which the victim of the crime was black. Clinton's answer to me was that there was no doubt that that was true but then he followed up by saying that 'Still, two wrongs don't make a right.' That baffled me and it's stuck with me ever since then. After thinking about it for a couple of years, I still haven't sorted it out. I always said if I ever get a chance to talk to him again, I'd ask him about that comment.''

Katharine (Kit) Seelye, a political reporter for the *Philadelphia Inquirer,* remembers one execution. ''Clinton doesn't schedule public events on execution days because he doesn't want any action. He thinks it will be misconstrued as heartless. The day after the Gennifer Flowers story broke was conveniently an execution day so he didn't have any public events. He came down to Little Rock from New Hampshire that night and even though this execution was about to happen, everybody was talking about Gennifer Flowers. It was the only thing on the news and I was really concerned about this guy scheduled to die. There had been no claims that he was a threat to society. In fact, his lawyer told me that the man had spoken of voting for Clinton in November and making up a pecan pie that night. This on the day of his execution. He was really out of it. The lawyer also told me that he had tried to call Clinton during the day because one of the other reasons that Clinton doesn't schedule any public events on execution day is so that he can be available to lawyers to grant clemency; if there's some last-minute change, he would be able to respond to it. The lawyer told me he tried calling the Governor's Mansion and couldn't get through. Clinton was holed up with his political advisers brainstorming on what to do about Gennifer Flowers.

''I'm not convinced that Bill Clinton believes in the death penalty but I think as a southern governor, there's no way he could get elected without going along with it. I once asked him why he believed in it or why he supported it and he gave me this long convoluted answer. It was one of the most tortured sentences I had ever heard. It went on and on and twisted all around itself. I had to transcribe my tape so I could really understand what he said, which was that he believed that the death penalty was a deterrent but in the same breath, he acknowledged that there's no evidence that it's a deterrent.''

Clinton's friend Paul Berry argues that ''Clinton's critics from time to time will try to paint him as totally expedient. I wouldn't give two cents personally for anybody in political office that didn't have an understanding of the proper utilization of a modicum of expediency from time to time. But to say that he takes positions only because that's the way he thinks the winds are blowing on something as crucially a matter of principle as the death penalty, is untrue. I know firsthand that that's just not true. I personally oppose the death penalty. As young men, Bill and I talked about political candidacies. I once thought about trying to be a candidate for something and I said that among other liabilities was my opposition to the death penalty. A majority of people would not vote for me based solely on that. Bill Clinton had no problem with the death penalty as long as he felt there'd been a fair trial. He felt that man-made institutions can provide justice and that if he were ever governor and in a position to set an execution, that he would as an officer of the court. He's been very consistent..

''Strange thing. We didn't even talk about it for ten years or so. But the first time someone on death row was executed since Governor Faubus's administration occurred while Clinton was governor. The person under death sentence was named Swindler. Clinton kept his publicly stated position and set the execution date. The evening of the execution, Governor Clinton called me and I went out there. I spent the evening with him that first execution.

''I guess he called me because we're friends and although we hadn't talked about it I'm sure he recalled our conversation of many years prior. I said to him that night, 'Governor, if anybody ever says you're a hypocrite on this issue, I could put the lie to that.' His position never changed. He was very calm and serious about it. A final call comes to the governor just moments before the execution in case there's any last-minute reprieve. I was present when he took that call from the warden and he did not flinch. He told them to proceed and moments later, the call came back that it was over and that the execution had been done. I disagree with the death penalty but I must say that I was impressed . . . he took it very seriously and didn't flinch. He was as objective as I think a human being could be in that circumstance. He took no pleasure. He was not lighthearted. He did not indulge in any sort of speech like 'That guy deserved it.' He was executing the law. In those kinds of crucibles I don't worry about him. The Bill Clinton that I know will be the calmest person in the ring.''

The Comeback

Bill Lancaster remembers the effect that defeat had on Clinton. ''After Bill's defeat to Frank White, I invited him to a party, just a neighborhood party out in Maumelle where I live. He was so down, he just didn't come. It indicated to me how down he was. I got a note from him when he left office as governor. I still have it framed. It says, 'We'll have another day.' ''

Ernest Oakleaf also recalls Clinton's reaction to the 1980 loss. ''Bill Walker, who used to be the lobbyist for AEA, told a story of Clinton coming into that grocery store in the Heights, the Food Emporium, which used to be a Safeway. Anyhow, it's close to where Clinton lived. Clinton would just kind of wander through the aisles looking for a familiar face and then he'd sort of catch 'em at the meat counter while they were trying to figure out if they wanted hamburger or chicken. He'd say, 'Why'd I lose?' He'd follow as they carried their bags out to the truck, and say, 'What'd I do wrong?' He was sort of like a puppy. He'd come up and say, 'What do you think I ought to do?' ''

Lloyd George found Clinton bemused by the defeat. ''Six months or so after he got beat, I started seeing him around. He'd want to talk and he'd ask some of us senior citizens, 'What did I do wrong?' Everybody said, 'Frankly, you made the whole legislature mad. You made everybody mad. We appreciate you but you're going to have to listen a little every now and then.' And we told him just that. He listened and he came back a changed man.''

Brownie Ledbetter says, ''He did his *mea culpa* in every grocery store and filling station. And a lot of us thought he shouldn't run for governor, including Betsey Wright. We thought he'd lose, that he ought to go for the Senate. I've always felt that he was more of a legislative person than an administrative person. But Betsey really organized it. There's just no question. Betsey had known both Bill and Hillary during the McGovern campaign. She's from Texas where she was Ann Richard's assistant. She

said, 'You will pick three things and that's it. You're not going
to do a hundred and fifty things. And you've got to be focused.'
She saw to it that what needed doing was done. There were no
files of names of contributors, there was no traditional sort of
political-favor-your-friends kind of stuff, there was none of the
building of the political organization that he'd needed to have
won. She did all that for him.''

Jerry Russell asserts that ''Clinton campaigned for governor the
whole two years after he lost and they put the network back together. That's when they made the overtures to Betsey about coming back up here and helping him. He . . . groveled is the only
way you can say it. If you could get a copy of those television
spots that he ran shortly before the ticket closed in the 1980 election—he went on television and said, 'I'm just so sorry. I just
really made bad mistakes. I'm just so sorry and if you'll just let
me have another chance, I promise you I will do better and blah,
blah, blah.' From a professional standpoint, I was kind of embarrassed that he would go on TV and grovel like that. Just as Bill's
actions cost him the governorship in 1978, Frank's actions in 1980
cost him the governorship. Bill Clinton would not have won that
race if Frank had not campaigned so poorly. Bill Clinton has had
only two tough races in his whole career—only two races against
well established, well financed, credible candidates: the race
against John Paul Hammerschmidt, which he lost, and the first
race against Frank, which he lost. Every other race he's run has
been against weak or flawed candidates. He also decided to have
a child after he got defeated. Remember the timing on that. Chelsea came after he was defeated by Frank White. 'Oh, wait a minute, you take my name and we have a kid and we join the Baptist
Church, none of this Episcopal bullshit. We're going to be at the
Baptist Church.' You can hear them sitting there talking.''

Jimmie Lou Fisher recalls, ''I'd go up and see the house; they
were very proud of it. Chelsea would be in the high chair. They
got it all fixed up and renovated and had a lot of folks over. It
was all very down to earth. He stayed busy. After he got over the
initial shock, he seemed to be almost reinforcing himself, kind of
reevaluating, reassessing, maybe girding himself for battle. And
he did run, he'd pick up the phone, he'd get in contact with
everybody in the Democratic party. He was not one to go off and
hide. He did not do that.''

Steve Barnes thinks the sense of failure both on election night
and in the months afterward when Clinton had to move out of the

mansion was "a little like a sixteen-ounce glove in the solar plexus. All the air rushed out of his lungs. The blood drained from his head and I think he was profoundly affected by it. The guy had never really failed in life. And I got him to make what I think was his first public appearance after he lost. To say he went into a period of hiding is overstating it. He simply canceled all of his public engagements or didn't accept any. I was president of the Little Rock Chapter of Sigma Delta Chi and I called him to see if he could come and talk to the membership at a Saturday luncheon meeting. I called his press secretary at the time but I heard nothing back so I called again and heard nothing. Finally he called me and said, 'What is this thing?' And I said, 'Well, it's a bunch of reporters and you know most of them. We're going to get together and have lunch on Saturday and they want you to come and speak.' And there was hurt in his voice even then. I felt as though he was thinking, 'What would that accomplish?' And I remember coaxing him a little bit. I said, 'You know, I don't know what your plans are in the future but you're going to have to do this sooner or later.' After mulling it over for a while, he accepted.

"Fairly soon after he lost, it became obvious that he was planning a comeback. He was a sought-after interview and I'm aware of him turning down very few of them. So it was a serious effort and everybody knew what he was up to. He made it a point to dump the hubris, publicly at least. He ran a series of television advertisements that were basically self-flagellation. He lashed himself publicly. The prevailing wisdom is that he overcooked it. He went from hubris to never brushing his teeth without reading a poll. He became so sensitive to public opinion that many believed he sacrificed a measure of leadership he could have exerted and thus began a great era of compromise."

Ernest Cunningham recalls the changes in Clinton. "When he came back, he was very cautious. To give you an example, John Miller and Bill Foster passed into the House and sent into the Senate a four-cent increase in the gasoline tax. It takes seventy-five votes or three-fourths votes to pass a tax like that. I voted for it and we got it over to the Senate and they passed it through. Highway programs are popular with people. Taxes are never easy to pass but when people see that money being used on their roads it makes it easier. Bill Clinton vetoed it, which was a real surprise. It was one of the few times that his veto was overridden."

Ernest Oakleaf characterizes Clinton's second go-around as governor: "I always felt that from then on, his eye was on the bigger prize and that he was very cautious and would do whatever it took to stay in office. He did things that would be interpreted from beyond our border as progressive and positive but would never take any serious chances. The one exception was the teachers. By the time he came up with teacher testing, teachers had already endorsed Jim Guy Tucker in the 1982 Democratic primary. Tucker didn't make the runoff so the teachers were waning in political force by the time he took them on. By and large he became very cautious—some people would say poll-driven."

Charlie Cole Chaffin, for years the only woman in the Arkansas Senate when Clinton was governor, describes his second term. "I was not a member of the legislature during his first terms so I don't really know about that. During the time that I served, which was 1984 through the present, Bill Clinton was a very accessible, hands-on governor. Prior to a session, for example, he would call in ten or twelve legislators. We'd sit around the big dining room table and he would say, 'Okay, here's what I'm thinking about for my package,' and he would talk about an idea for a couple of minutes and then he would go around and let each one of us comment on that particular idea. We then knew what was going to be in his package before the sessions actually began and he had our thoughts. He got a lot of advice from the legislature when he felt that it was appropriate to do so. I don't think Bill Clinton could be faulted for the way he worked with the Arkansas legislature or the way he worked with the people of the state of Arkansas during all the time that I worked with him."

George Frazier compares Clinton's two terms as governor. "There was a maturing process that would have happened naturally anyway. He learned to work with the legislature. There are detractors who say that's a weakness but I don't see it as such. Running the government requires the art of compromise. Bill always seemed to feel that although he would go gung ho for what he believed, if it could not come to full fruition, he was willing to work out some kind of compromise with the legislators, bearing in mind that they had responsibilities to their constituents back home. Bill would work with all sides and come up with a compromise that was acceptable to everybody and that's a real art. I think that's what you're going to see the Clinton administration do. They'll give up the idea of keeping the whole package knowing full well that some of it will have to be eliminated. Some of it will be changed to some extent but he will always end up with some good part of his package.''

Betsey Wright says, ''He called me about a week after the election in which he was defeated and asked if I would come see if there was anything that could be salvaged of his political career in case he ever had an opportunity to run again for something so I went back and helped close down the governor's office.

''That was one reason why he wanted me to come and help. I initially stayed at the Governor's Mansion and I stayed a little while at their house on Midland Street before I got a place to live. When Wright, Lindsey, and Jennings took Bill into the law firm, they also provided space for me. I worked on computerizing his political records and then put together his comeback campaign in 1982.

''We weren't sure he was going to run two years later. We didn't really know whether it was possible or not until we did a benchmark poll in the fall of 1981 so for almost a year running in 1982 wasn't exactly what we were working on. He spent every single day going around the state, running up to people and asking them to tell him what he did wrong, but I mainly listened to him regurgitate all of that. He was just getting a sense of where he got so off kilter.

''First we did a benchmark poll to figure out what people's perception of him was. We also did a very thorough opposition research on Bill to determine which adversaries could do the most damage. Once we knew where his vulnerabilities were we tried to figure out what kinds of things we could do to protect them.

''One of his greatest vulnerabilities was all those clemencies he granted in the last few days he was in office. We knew that one of the people whom he had commuted had murdered again, so we knew that that was a tremendous vulnerability. That's why we began the campaign as we did with an ad instead of an announcement. The ads were not apologies. He talked about being out of touch and said it won't happen again. Dick Morris, Bill Clinton, Hillary, and I agreed that this was the way to begin this campaign.''

Jeff Katz says, ''It was very clear to me in 1982 that he was going to present himself in a different way. He was putting aside some of his loftier, more visionary speeches and dealing much more directly with voters. He talked about Frank White and the issues he had raised more directly. The 1982 campaign was the single most remarkable political campaign I have ever covered and I've covered a lot of campaigns. I've never seen somebody so driven.

"Here was a guy who was extremely proud, maybe even arrogant in some ways, and the first thing he did before he even announced he was running for governor was to air a TV commercial in which he basically apologized for having made mistakes. That, in and of itself, was an extraordinary, almost desperate statement but I think that really helped set the tone of his campaign.

"He kept an incredible schedule. In one story, I counted how many places he visited. In a thirty-six hour period, he visited ten small towns in Craighead County, opened a campaign headquarters, visited two small towns in Mississippi County, and attended meetings with supporters in Greene County and Clay County. I particularly remember one beautiful sunrise I saw on this trip. I was in the car with him and I remember being in the backseat trying to watch the sunrise and there was Bill Clinton already expounding at great length about some aspect of politics in Arkansas. He went after it with a certain verve and gusto, with a stamina that I had never seen before and have not seen to this day. I feel the reason that he was able to make this comeback is that even though people wanted to dismiss Clinton at the time and take him down a notch, they felt that he represented the possibility—the hope—of something better.

"I think one woman in Monette, Arkansas, spoke for many voters. Her name was Karlene B. Redman and she was a teacher with twenty-six years of experience. She came down to this little coffee shop that we went to in Monette. We were there at 7:30 in the morning. It was a bare dingy coffee shop and it was the kind of place that Clinton was practically living in during 1982. Afterward, she followed us out to the parking lot and she told him, 'The number-one thing I had against you was a lack of communication. We got everything secondhand.' As a teacher, she was particularly upset that he had given them a nice raise one year and then because of the recession had cut back. What she said was really telling. She said, 'Put me on your mailing list,' and then she said, 'I'm begging to be convinced.' I thought that's how a lot of people felt in 1982 in Arkansas. They were begging Clinton to convince them.

"Karlene Redman later told me, 'What really makes me mad about Bill Clinton is that he forced me to vote for Frank White. For a dyed-in-the-wool Democrat, it was very hard for me to vote for a Republican.' "

Bobby Roberts remembers, "The night he lost was one of the worst nights a lot of us spent. I knew he was in trouble in the polls but I just couldn't believe that he could lose to someone like Frank White. That campaign was one of the first really negative campaigns. White ran a very clever campaign on two or three issues and made everybody mad as negative campaigns do. I couldn't conceive that voters would respond to that so there was a great deal of shock when that happened, and a great deal of guilt. I talked to a number of faculty members at the University of Arkansas at Little Rock, a fairly progressive bunch of people whom you would think would support someone like Bill Clinton. I came across faculty member after faculty member who had voted against him. They gave lame excuses like, 'I just wanted to send him a message.' 'I didn't want him to win with too big a margin' and all of 'em said, 'If I'd known White was going to win, I wouldn't have done that.' So there was disbelief among people. I said, 'God, if you're going to cast a vote, cast it correctly. Don't do it just because you're mad at somebody.'

"I've always tried to tell him the truth. I told him when I thought he tried to go too far too fast. People perceived him as being uppity and out of touch with them, and people didn't like the fact that Hillary didn't use his last name. Stupid. That's really stupid I'll admit but people didn't like it. The perception was that Clinton was not one of them and that's really what defeated him. The excuses for voting against him included the taxes and car tags and Cubans and all that kind of stuff but that's not why they did it. That didn't have anything to do with it."

Bobby Roberts continues, "Traveling with him during the campaign was an experience I'll never forget. It was interesting to watch the campaign grow. When we started out, the two of us were in a rented 1971 Oldsmobile with a Kennedy sticker on the back of it and we would get in that thing and go for hours and hours. I didn't like to ride with him. I will not get in the car if he's driving and now, of course, he doesn't do much driving, thank God. It's good that he doesn't because he talks and doesn't watch what he's doing so I always drove until a state trooper took over. He actually gets car sick in the back so he always rode in the front seat. We would sometimes drive three or four days. We would normally stay at the homes of campaign coordinators. He likes to stay in people's houses. He rarely stayed in a hotel. I would say probably 80 percent of the time, we stayed in somebody's home. I think he preferred it. He liked being able to sit down, get away from the campaign, and talk to his friends. He just likes that kind of atmosphere. Normally we would stop in some small restaurant in some small town. That was his favorite thing to do. We would stop, go in. He would not eat that much. I mean, he would walk around the room with maybe a sandwich in his hand, talking to people. I would try to get something to eat but he would mostly be campaigning. He never failed to go into the kitchen and to make sure he met everybody who was working the back, the cooks, the people cleaning up, the people who did the work. He'd ask them a few questions and visit with them. I used to think he did that for political reasons but I'm not sure that's the case. I think he is curious about people and he just likes meeting people. He's not shy. He's real thick-skinned too. I mean, I've rarely seen him get off balanced, you know, where somebody would get him in a corner and he couldn't get out of it. I really think that Clinton learns a lot from those discussions. I think he has a lot of faith in the basic wisdom of everyday people."

Woody Bassett says, "I think the campaign in 1982 was the best campaign he ever ran and it was critical. Had he not won, he wouldn't be president of the United States now. In fact, you could make a compelling case that his opportunity for elected office might have ended at that point although I'll say this— anybody that counts out Bill Clinton is making a mistake. He's been counted dead more times than Elvis and he keeps coming back, but that year, 1982, was incredible because he went on statewide television and basically said, 'I screwed up my first term and I'm sorry. I learned a lot from it. I want another chance.'

"What I remember about 1982 is what the rest of the country would probably remember from 1992 when he ran for president. His incredible energy, the nonstop campaigning, the unbelievable perserverence. I mean, he just refused to quit. He was bound and determined to win that thing and he went out after it. It was just unbelievable how hard he worked. I remember one night, in 1982, getting up at 3:30 in the morning in the fall. It was cold, rainy, and dark obviously. We had been out the night before until midnight. We'd been to a bunch of political things and we retired to some local night spot. So just hours later I picked him up and we went to the Campbell's Soup plant for the four o'clock shift change. I remember standing there in the cold rain. The people going in for the shift change were amazed that somebody would be out there at that time of day. All of these people were going in and out of the plant and Bill was shaking all their hands and this one lady comes out to speak to him. She said, 'Mr. Clinton, I was going to vote for you but I don't think I can vote for you now. Anybody who would stand out here in the freezing rain and in the dark when they don't have to, isn't smart enough to be governor,' and she just walked off. He laughed and laughed and laughed. I bet you she voted for him.''

Amy Oliver, then a TV news anchor, remembers the scene (but little else) at the Clintons the night of the 1982 gubernatorial election. ''The Clintons were living over on Midland Street in a big old Victorian home that had a wide porch around it with a nice big swing. I was to be taking live shots from the front porch with the Clintons before they went to the campaign headquarters—it was a great stroke, you know a great assignment. Everybody was swinging and Chelsea was playing with the microphone, but I was suffering from this awful case of food poisoning. Here I am in this historic momentous occasion and I'm lying in the back of the truck throwing up. I don't remember what either Bill or Hillary said that night because I was so sick. I'm told I did an okay job and that I asked Bill some good questions; I just can't remember what I asked. I remember Chelsea grabbing the microphone. She was just a toddler then and I also remember she stood at the window looking out at us and waving. I remember Zeke, their big cocker spaniel, was jumping all over the place. And the bugs were bad.''

Zeke also made a lasting impression on the Clintons' Fayetteville friend Margaret Whillock. ''I remember their dog. The barking dog. The crazy dog that needed the psychiatrist. They lived a few blocks from us here on Midland Street and they had this dog name Zeke. Zeke ran all over the neighborhood and was just this wild cocker spaniel. He was one of the loudest dogs I've ever heard in my life. He would just bark and bark and bark and claw at the door waiting to get in to see Bill or Hillary. I'm not sure who the dog wanted to see. I decided that dog was nuts and he needed a psychiatrist. We all thought it was kind of a psychotic dog. It was always jumping around and it was a funny dog but they had it for years.''

Nor has journalist Gene Lyons forgotten Zeke. ''This dog used to get into the neighbors' trash. He was an incorrigible leash-law scofflaw. The dog was in constant leash-law violation. He was out all the time. He'd come visit then he'd go back home. Tear into the trash bags, that sort of thing, but he wasn't a bad dog. The first dog we used to call him. The dog was actually killed on

Broadway chasing a car down by the Governor's Mansion. There were no citations issued. Now there's one to get into.''

Whatever one thinks of Bill Clinton's politics and policies, it must be conceded that he knows how to get elected. Even his most relentless enemies grant that he is a capable stump speaker who can, on occasion, fire up the sleepiest crowds. In a state like Arkansas, where people still expect prospective governors to shake their hands, look them in the eye, and ask for their votes, Clinton's amazing facility for remembering names and faces was an invaluable part of his campaign arsenal.

To observe Bill Clinton in full-campaign mode is to watch a master politician—he can swing from down-home good ole' boyism to fact-driven policy wonk in a matter of seconds. His message is not just custom-tailored for every crowd; at times it can seem fitted to each particular person he meets. Most of the people who've followed him through his gubernatorial campaigns comment on his incredible stamina—perhaps Clinton's habit of grabbing quick catnaps, which he apparently raised to a fine art at Georgetown, can account for some of his seemingly inexhaustible energy. Bill Clinton can say he's going to sleep for ten minutes, close his eyes, and emerge ten minutes later refreshed and alert.

Clinton, like anyone else, can occasionally grow tired of the game, but it is obvious that he takes a real delight in one-on-one campaigning. In a state like Arkansas, where races are still won on the ground, at fish fries and in dim honky-tonks, Clinton's preference for the face-to-face encounter served him well.

Craig Smith accompanied Clinton on some campaign road trips. ''I remember one day, we went to this little town. It was nothing but a crossroads with a grocery store. He said, 'You know, this is the only grocery store so everybody within ten miles must come by here. If I stay right here, within two days, everybody in this little area will know that I've been here.' So we just drank Coke and sat there and talked to the folks.

''After the grocery store, we drove to Hot Springs for the Arkansas Derby and presented the trophy to the winning horse. Then we went to a lumberyard festival in another little town and at the end of the day, we went back to Hot Springs where someone was having a Derby party. The day began at seven in the morning and by eleven o'clock that night, I was just woffed. I was so tired but he had another party he wanted to go to. He was talking to all these people, just having a good time, and I'm on the verge of collapse. I sat there in the living room in a big oak chair and he'd come in every now and then and say, 'You doing okay? Well, I'm going to be out there. If there's anything you need, let me know.' I said, 'I'm fine. Leave me alone, I'll be just fine.' "

Former *Arkansas Gazette* reporter Mark Oswald remembers Clinton's energy while campaigning. "What really struck me is how tireless the guy is. We got on an airplane in Little Rock about five-thirty in the morning. He was late of course. The plane was supposed to leave at five-thirty but he got there about six. We went all day. Made about five stops. The last stop was a fund-raiser at a state representative's house in Helena, Ernest Cunningham's house, which we left around eleven or twelve. Myself and the state trooper who went with him and his couple of aides, we were just totally out of it by the end of the day and he was still sitting at a table chatting. We went back out to the airport and got on the plane, and on the way back he still wants to give a lecture on the German health care system and he was shouting over the roar of the engine in this small plane while I'm just trying to stay awake. The only rest he took that day was when Cunningham drove us out at one point to a spot on the Mississippi River, a real pretty spot where they were talking about maybe putting a state park. During that drive, he took a five-minute nap. The whole rest of the day he was going full steam and just kind of killed us."

Alyson Hoge, the assistant managing editor at the *Arkansas Democrat-Gazette*, recalls one of Clinton's campaign trips. "This was my first time out with them on the campaign trail because up to that point, I'd been covering Frank White. We were scheduled to hit a number of little towns I had never even heard of before. It was just a bizarre little trip because, first of all, Clinton was so desperate. Clinton sees a group of people standing on the side of the street so we all had to stop. He runs out and puts Clinton stickers on everybody. It turns out that they're a bunch of old winos who have no gainful employment. They're just hanging out and he runs up to all these people who are probably illiterate and don't vote and he's putting stickers on them. That was the way he was running his campaign. One of his aides commented that it was like a Chinese fire drill because all of a sudden, everybody runs out of their cars. So I wrote that down and put it in my story, which caused an uproar in the campaign. They wanted to know who had made the Chinese fire drill comment. We're with this campaign that's doing the best that it can to protect its image. In fact, he made one reporter who was sloppily dressed wear a sign to indicate that he was a reporter so that nobody would think he was a Clinton staffer.

"The other thing I noticed on that trip was his charisma. You could see the effect he had on people in the eyes of the teenage girls who came to see him. Their eyes would light up—you would think that a rock star had just come into the Walmart, not somebody as dull as a candidate for governor; people liked talking to him. And while he's not Mel Gibson, there are two things that he does. He remembers your name and he looks you directly in the eye. He shakes your hand and as far as you know, you're the only person in the room when he talks to you. There is a certain charm about it that you don't get from a lot of public officials. For example, I saw Winston Bryant, the attorney general in the Capitol cafeteria earlier this year. He was eating lunch and he could have been just any state employee. Clinton wouldn't do that. Clinton would be looking around to see who he needed to say hello to. If there was someone he could talk to, he'd put his arm around them and chat with them; he's just very personable."

Arkansas Democrat-Gazette columnist Philip Martin agrees. "I'll have to be honest and say that when you first meet him, there is something of a rock star quality about him. You meet the guy and he engages you immediately. He does make you feel like you're important to him. I can remember when we got in the van with the state trooper driving and there was this sort of familiarity that he had with his driver, a black sergeant. Bill would say, 'Hey man, how ya' doin',' and kick up his cowboy boots on the dash of the van. 'Look at these boots. How much do you think these boots cost?' We'd say, 'We don't know, Governor. How much did those boots cost?' and he'd say, 'Well I sure hope they don't cost more than ninety-nine dollars because otherwise I'd have to report them as a campaign expense.' He'd just banter. Five minutes after we were out on the road, we were talking about his appearance on the *Tonight Show* back in 1988 after his debacle at the convention and he was telling me about Joe Cocker's band. He said, 'Man, they were bad, they were just a kick-ass band, man.' You know, he really wanted to play with Joe Cocker rather than going out and playing 'Summertime' but he was afraid to ask. He was really in awe. On one level, his chatting seemed charming and on another level you wondered what this guy was doing. It was almost embarrassing the familiarity he assumed with you. I mean, I'm a fairly reserved person.''

Maria Henson, formerly a political reporter for the *Arkansas Gazette*, remembers being somewhat surprised at seeing a governor ''so casual with the press corps, really at ease with everyone and animated. It seemed like he was having a good time and whether he was or not, he seemed to enjoy everyone there. He really made an effort to speak and be jovial.''

Philip Martin says, ''He has a lot of confidence in his ability to win people. I think that Bill Clinton has every confidence that if he can get you by yourself, you'll be a friend and ally before it's over with and I think he trades those little tiny confidences with you that, wink-wink, 'hey, we're alike' sort of exchange.''

Flying with Clinton on one of his campaigns could be as hair-raising as driving with him. Alyson Hoge recounts: ''We were in a plane together and I was looking at Clinton and the next thing I see is, Clinton's eyes open wide and his hair is blowing back. Apparently the airplane's door popped open. We landed. They closed the door a few times. We found out that this plane has had the same problem before and then we took off again. While we're up there with the door open we were making jokes about it because it's either make jokes or get hysterical. I had this big yellow notepad and I wrote things that Clinton was saying like, 'Let's have a Bill Clinton memorial sales tax just so I can write a few notes about it and throw the notes out of the airplane.' Everybody is nervous but they're not panicking. Somebody says jokingly, 'This planes going to crash. We're all going to die,' so Clinton says, 'Ask for a two-cent tax increase then. Maybe even three.' ''

Maria Henson says, ''I've been on a plane with him that was going up and down. We were knee to knee and he just continued to do his work. Had his briefcase open and was doing his work and signing letters and it didn't bother him one bit that we were jumping up and down and around. Once we had to drive somewhere, because it was cloudy but it wasn't raining or windy and he spent a good twenty minutes haranguing the state police officer, 'Why are we not flying?' And that was a little disconcerting. I thought, 'Well, the guy said the weather's bad and we shouldn't take a plane up. It's just going to take us a little bit longer and we had to leave a little bit earlier than we had planned but no big deal. Nothing to get upset about.' But it was disconcerting how worked up he was over that. He was really annoyed, pretty angry as a matter of fact; and he wasn't pacified till he started eating a banana. He's not a morning person.''

Joe Quinn, KTHV-TV anchor in Little Rock, covered Clinton on some of the farther reaches of his campaign trail. ''One of my most vivid memories is of a day in a place called Nashville, Arkansas, a little town that once a year has a big fish fry to which they'd invite any candidate running for any statewide or local office. We had a wireless mike on Clinton that day and had been with him eighteen hours, starting at about five in the morning. We got to Nashville at about seven at night and he starts working the crowd. He's running against a Republican named Sheffield Nelson, a very well dressed, monied, articulate man with what a friend of mine used to call CEO polish. They're both working the crowd and it's hot. It's terribly hot. Well, Clinton shakes every hand in the park and then he waits his turn to speak and now it's 9:15 and starting to get dark out. The parking lot starts to empty and gradually cars are driving away into the darkness and Bill Clinton is still wandering around the parking lot talking to people. There's one elderly couple with their lawn chairs in their hands standing there and Bill Clinton, the governor of the state, has now spent thirty minutes with this one couple. Every car has driven away and the state trooper in charge of driving Clinton is kind of slumped over the wheel of his car. I've been on the road sixteen hours with him. My photographer's exhausted. So we're sitting there with the state trooper and he looks over at me and he says, 'You know if he doesn't have their vote by now, he might as well hang it up.' Clinton finally finishes with this couple and he comes running over and he says, 'Hey, ready? Let's go to the airport.' So we hop in the two troopers' cars and Clinton's just full of life. We're in two state trooper vehicles. Clinton and one aide are in front and the photographer and I are in the state trooper vehicle behind him. We're driving through downtown Nashville and we see a little Tastee Freeze hamburger place. Clinton had been unable to eat at the fish fry because he was working the crowd so the lead trooper car pulls into Tastee Freeze and my photographer says, 'Oh, please God. What are we doing now?' Clinton comes barreling out of the front car, and says, 'Hey, Joe, are you hungry?' I said, 'Well, I guess so, Governor.' I walked into the Tastee Freeze in front of him and the girl behind the counter says, 'Whoa, it's the guy on TV.' We're way out in the state. She says, 'I can't believe he's in here.' and I said, 'Girls, you ain't seen nothing yet.' And here comes the governor of Arkansas through the door to shake their hands. After I had ordered a hamburger, I went to a pay phone on the wall and I called my girlfriend in Little Rock to tell her we were running late. Clinton had finished ordering and was walking away from the cash register. I said, 'Hold on a second. Someone wants to say hello.' She was a huge fan of his and, you know, he spent fifteen minutes on the phone with her. We got back on the plane for Little Rock and he's still full of life. I remember looking at him in the parking lot with that elderly couple as everybody else had driven away and thinking, 'This guy has the energy level and enthusiasm to get to the White House.' I don't think that there was a politician anywhere in this country who could outwork this guy for the White House.

"I remember another night we were down in the southern part of the state and it was late. Again, we'd been on the road all day. It was a small entourage. Clinton came over to me late in the day and he said, 'You got enough tape?' and I said, 'Well, yeah. I've been shooting twelve hours. I've got a ton of tape.' He said, 'Would you mind if we threw the camera in the trunk for this next stop?' And I thought that was a little odd but I said, 'Sure.' We were near Hope but we were in an essentially still segregated county. You've got to understand Arkansas drinking laws. In a lot of those counties, whites with money drink at the local country club and there are really no nightclubs for the public. There was a club—I hesitate to call it a nightclub—a ramshackle old beat-up place out in the country, way out on a dirt road, where blacks danced and listened to great music. The sheriff drove Clinton out there to shake hands and work the crowd and I'll never forget it. It was this hot crowded place. Clinton has got his sleeves rolled up and he starts working this crowd in this club at the late end of a very long day. I was drinking beer standing off to the side and again that night I thought, 'Look at this guy's energy level. He takes the time to hit this county and not only work the power establishment during his stops today but now here we are at nine at night at this ramshackle old nightclub out in the woods.' He loved it."

Former state legislator John Lipton remembers the Bradley County Pink Tomato Festival. "Clinton really wanted to get into it with the people. So he said, 'I'll get into a tomato-eating contest.' Each person sees how much they could consume within a given time frame." (The governor was game, but he didn't win.)

John Reed, then a journalist at the *Arkansas Gazette*, particularly recalled "Clinton's 'preacher' style—a campaign asset, for sure.

Everybody knows he can go into a black church and preach to them and they love him and he's very comfortable. He can quote the scriptures. We went to a meeting of Pentecostals in Redfield, Arkansas, and there must have been two thousand people in this metal building. He talked for two solid hours and they loved him. He had most of them on their feet. Pentecostals hold up one hand if they like you and two hands if they really like you. They all stood up and were waving both hands. And he told those people, 'Thank you so much for inviting me because I really need this every now and then just to restore my soul.' He had just come from a few stressful weeks and I believe what he said was true. A lot of people make fun of religions that they don't particularly agree with, especially in these rural counties. Not Bill. He had respect and just genuine affection for people. That's why I like him. He likes people.''

Philip Martin recalls, ''When we went to this nursing home he talked about all the old people he knew. He charms old people so well. I mean folks in nursing homes just love Bill Clinton because he comes across as so boyish and he was a lot more boyish then than he is now. He was like everybody's grandson. And in these nursing homes he could remember all their names. He would talk to these people and say, 'Yeah, I remember you from here. Yeah, I saw your son, your son-in-law,' and it was incredibly amazing for someone like me who can't keep five or six faces straight in a room. I don't think he spent a lot of time thinking about doing it. I don't think he stayed up at night studying who would be at the nursing home. It's just amazing the recall he has for names and faces.''

Maria Henson, too, often found Clinton amazing. ''When I would travel with him, we could go into the smallest town, like Queen or Picket, Arkansas, and he would turn to his aide and quickly get a refresher on some names of the people who would be attending each event. He would make a few notes on napkins and that's all he would need to get up and deliver these wonderful speeches, basically the same speech everywhere. Even then, it seems like you could see the seeds of the speeches he would give when he wanted to become president. The whole thing about pulling people together in Arkansas and trying to help them work toward a common goal. Some of us in the press corps would joke that he had the same three-legged pig joke that he pulled out all over the state. We'd sit in the back of the room and mouth the words as he spoke them. I can't deliver it exactly the way that he did but basically there was a farmer who had a three-legged pig with a little wooden leg and he bragged about this pig to every-body who came to visit. The farmer would tell how the pig had saved him from a fire. People would be amazed and he'd say, 'Well, that's not all. The pig saved the farm from going bankrupt.' And the folks were amazed. But the farmer would say, 'That's not all. The pig saved the entire town once when the dam broke.' And they said, 'Well, gosh, it's pretty amazing that you have this pig but you never did explain why it has only three legs.' And the farmer said, 'Well, gosh, you wouldn't want to eat a pig this special all in one sitting.' That was the joke that he told all the time and people laughed every time he told it.''

In a more private moment on the campaign trail Maria Henson remembers ''just sitting down with him late one night when he brought up this whole thought about how somebody had got to really campaign and tell a story, the story of this country. What brings people together. Why we're in this together and why we need to ensure the future for our children because the American dream had always been built on the concept that children will do better than their parents had done. And as you can see, that was the theme that he carried into the campaign but at this point it was more from the heart. I don't mean to sound naive about this but I really was struck by his sincerity. I mean, nobody was around and it was as though he had really thought about this a long time and this was going to be this tapestry that he was going to weave no matter what happened from here. At that moment I was pretty sure that he would eventually run for president. I didn't think that he would win or could win because of the powerful people who were expected to get into the race later on and who would have money, which he didn't have.''

Jerry Jones, an attorney in Little Rock says, ''I met Bill when I was a senior in high school at a Democratic Central Committee meeting in Benton County, Arkansas, at the Rogers Holiday Inn. He was teaching at the University of Arkansas at the Fayetteville law school and was strongly considering running against an incum-bent congressman named John Paul Hammerschmidt. In high school I was involved in politics and at that point in time, if you wanted to be involved in Arkansas politics, you had to be a Demo-crat. So I was on the committee and he came and spoke and I was very impressed. He struck me as someone who would be able to run a very good race against a very popular and very good congressman who had historically taken care of his constituents very well. Bill was just overflowing with ideas about things that he wanted to do. He impressed me because, one, he was very, very articulate and two, he could connect. Most of the people in that room had never met him before. He'd look you in the eye and talk to you—not talk over you or below you. You could tell that he was really committed to running for Congress and to doing things for Arkansas. People might say it's easy to say this looking back but even then I knew this guy was going to run and run and run in politics because it was just in his blood to be involved in government. Even then he was a tremendous campaigner but he separated out politics from government and he had a lot of really good ideas about what he wanted to do in Congress.

"Later I traveled with him and drove around the districts, went to square dances to meet people and to the livestock auction in Madison County. We'd eat fried chicken picnics in county squares, stop in a little grocery store for a Coke and an apple." ("So, he liked junk food even back then?" I ask. "I don't know that an apple is junk food," replies Jones. "Oh, I thought fried ..." I am quickly informed that "fried chicken's not junk food in Arkansas.")

Reporter Jeff Stinson, formerly of the *Arkansas Gazette,* remembers "one night at the state fair, in 1989. He was going from booth to booth and then spending some time in the main exhibition hall talking about drugs because he was going into a special session in the fall of 1989 to ask for a hike in taxes to fund law enforcement to fight the drug war. There was one woman out there who hung around and afterward went up to him. She was in tears and began telling the governor that she had a son she just didn't know what to do with anymore. He had rampaged the house because he was on drugs. Clinton kind of brushed his aides and the reporters away and he went over and put his arm around that woman and talked to her. I'm a pretty good eavesdropper so I was able to hear him telling her basically that he understood that almost no family in Arkansas or any place in the country was left untouched by the scourge of drugs and that his own brother had problems with drugs. Roger's drug problem was well known throughout the state. He took the woman's name down and passed it on to an aide to see if there was anything that he could do. How many people, politicians or governors, in this day and age brush everybody away and take the time to put their arm around somebody and listen to their problems? Granted it's a smaller state but you just don't see it. Over the years I've covered six governors in four states before I ever met Bill Clinton and I have never seen that kind of personal time spent with people before. Basically, this guy can empathize with people and their problems better than any politician I've ever seen.''

Little Rock correspondent for the Memphis *Commercial Appeal*, Joan Duffy, recalls an incident on the Fourth of July 1991, several months before Clinton announced he would run for the presidency. ''We were in Nashville, Arkansas, at the town parade grounds waiting for the fireworks. There was a fellow there who was probably about nineteen or twenty years old. He was kind of a skinny guy with blue jeans and a T-shirt and long scraggly hair and a dirty old hat and he looked like a real hard-working kind of guy. Clinton was surrounded by a lot of people from town who were just kind of hanging with him and hugging him, but this guy was standing on the fringes of that group. He caught my eye because he was sticking with the group so I knew he wanted to say something but he obviously didn't feel comfortable coming real close. We were going back to the car and this guy stepped forward and stuck out his hand to Clinton and introduced himself and they started to talk and just a few words into the conversation Clinton kind of put his arm around him and walked him away so they could talk privately. Clinton spent a lot of time with him. They finished and said good-bye and we were walking back to the car when I noticed Clinton had tears in his eyes and he was shaking his head. He was smiling a little bit and he said, 'Boy, that guy . . . what a story. This is what I really love about this job.' The kid had been in high school when Clinton had come to make a speech at the high school several years earlier and Clinton had given his standard speech about, 'You can be anything you want to be. All you have to do is try.' The kid said he had had terrible problems with reading. He was dyslexic and he was going to drop out of school but that speech made him stay in school and get his diploma and he just wanted to thank Clinton for that inspiration. It genuinely affected him that an individual whom he had never met had been touched by his speech and he said that's what he likes about this job. 'You can touch people. You can affect them. You can make a real difference in their lives whether you know it or not. But away from here, away from the state level, it's all posturing and positioning papers. Sometimes I wonder if I'm giving up what I love most about this,' and I think he was really torn about whether to run for the presidency, whether he really wanted to win. I think he really wanted to run but wasn't sure he really wanted to win.''

Woody Bassett says, ''When it comes to meeting people I've never seen Bill Clinton nervous. Now he might have been nervous inside but he never showed it. One thing about Bill Clinton is that he genuinely cares about people. He has a good heart. He has an uncanny ability, too, to know when people are hurting, even if they don't tell him. There are a million examples, but I'll give you just one example. We were at a rally in Springdale in 1990 during his last campaign for governor. All these people were standing around after he got through speaking, wanting to shake his hand or to say, 'Hi,' and there's a girl, sixteen, seventeen years old standing off away from the group. I could tell that she wanted to talk to him and I said something to him and he walked over there and he ended up talking to her privately for fifteen or twenty minutes. When they finished talking, he walks over and hands me a piece of paper. He says, 'This is the girl's name. She's pregnant. She doesn't have a job. She doesn't have a family. She's just forlorn,' and he hands me this note and says, 'Look, this girl needs some help.' He wasn't looking for a vote. He's just got a great heart. There had been times when I would pick him up at the airport or we'd be in the car and I might not be in the best of moods and I wouldn't say anything but he always has this ability to pick up on that. He knows when people are hurting. He genuinely cares about people which sometimes makes it difficult when he's governor or president because he cares about everybody.''

David Matthews offers another example. ''I've told the story throughout the course of the campaign about his involvement with a young boy from Lowell named Aaron Pyle. I told this when I introduced him the first time I was up in New Hampshire. He was standing off to the side and heard me tell the story and according to the reporters who were observing he was moved by it but it's a true story. A young boy from Lowell, Arkansas, named Aaron Pyle has cancer. His father's a mechanic and his mother's a secretary. They're common people; they have no financial wherewithal or political influence. Aaron was at the Children's Hospital in Little Rock, which is across the road from the state Capitol. One day doctors told his mother that the little boy needed to get out and get some fresh air so she took him over to the state Capitol. They were making their way around and they came to the governor's office, which had a sign that said, 'Governor Bill Clinton. Please come in,' and so they did. While they were in the waiting room, it just so happened that the governor got up and was walking down the hall and and looked in and saw the little boy with no hair. He went back and cleared his office of the people that were in it and invited Aaron and his mother to come into his office. He sat and visited with them for about fifteen minutes, had the photographer come up and take Aaron's picture sitting in the governor's chair with the governor and all that. They were obviously impressed that the governor would take time to see them but never expected he would see them again. Two or three months later, they were back at the state Capitol for some other reason and they were in the rotunda. Apparently a legislative meeting was going on because, as Aaron's mother told the story, the governor was talking to a group of men when he spotted them all the way across the rotunda and left the men, came walking over, walked right up to Aaron and said, 'How're you doing, Aaron? Good to see you again.' Visited with him. Now they're really impressed. On election night in 1990, Bill Clinton is fighting neck and neck with Sheffield Nelson and Aaron is back in the Children's Hospital undergoing chemotherapy, very sick and they're trying to get him to go to bed. He won't go to sleep because as he says, 'I want to see if my friend Bill wins.' Well, his nurse heard that and told someone who told someone who told someone else and the next day a courier hand-delivered a note to Aaron Pyle from the governor that said, 'Dear Aaron: Thanks for pulling for me. I don't think I could have made it without you. I want you to know I'm pulling for you. Your friend Bill.' He really cares about folks without regard for what they can do for him.''

Some stories about Clinton seem dusted with the patina of myth yet are, nevertheless, true. Almost everyone who meets him is, initially, somewhat seduced by his presence. He has that indefinable air of power about him—a charisma that makes women want to be with him and men want to be him.

At least part of it is manufactured. Clinton is aware that when he drops his eyes this way and he cocks his head that way, he can exude boyishness; that if his voice breaks he will sound more sincere. He has tried to imbue his handshake with John F. Kennedy with torch-passing symbolism. Clinton's doubters take this as a sign that he is cynical and hollow, but self-awareness does not always signal duplicity. One suspects that the tenderness he sometimes displays is very real. When he says he cried when Elvis Presley died, those who know Clinton believe him.

Even to his enemies, Bill Clinton oftens seems more than an actor with a fresh haircut and a practiced smile; even amid the cheap suits and cynicism of the huddled-together press corps, one can sense an odd mix of awe and envy.

KTHV commentator and former journalist for the *Arkansas Gazette* Bob McCord says, "There is a legend about an early settler in Arkansas who traveled across the state and got lost. Eventually he ran across a hillbilly deep in the woods and they exchanged some words, but the hillbilly didn't trust the traveler and wouldn't give him anything to drink, wouldn't let him in the house, didn't even invite him to get off his horse so the visitor borrowed the guy's fiddle and he played a mountain tune on it—the fiddle song. Now the hillbilly had never been able to get that tune quite right so the minute the traveler finished it, the hillbilly invited him into his house, gave him food to eat, and a place to rest. Clinton is kind of like that fellow with the fiddle. He has a way of communicating some of the most prosaic, mundane things that makes them seem terribly important. Building friendships and making friends for an underdeveloped state like this is not prosaic and not mundane. His eloquence and his communication skills are so superior to most that I've heard. I'm sort of a fan of Clinton's."

George Frazier speaks of Clinton's special qualities. "I first met Clinton when he was running for attorney general and he came to my office along with a good friend of his, George Wright, Jr. I detest the word, 'charisma,' but he has an outgoing personality that just makes you feel like you've known him all your life. He's the kind of man who when he's talking to you, looks right into your eyes and makes you feel that you have his undivided attention. He has had that knack, that character I suppose, as long as I've known him and I've watched him as his stature in politics has increased. He maintains that same kind of one-on-one relationship. A good many men and women, when they reach a higher position in life seem to be talking down to you if you're in a lower echelon; their eyes are continually roaming the room to see if there's anyone else more important they should be talking with. Bill doesn't do that. Even now, when he goes down the line to shake hands with people, the person with whom he's in contact has his undivided attention. It's not an affectation with him. It's not something he's developed. When Bill Clinton asks you how you are, he really wants to know, and I think that sets him apart from a lot of politicians today. Bill Clinton will meet you in a crowd today, not know you from Adam. He will make sure he has your name, where you're from and so forth, and if you meet him four months from now, somewhere else, he will call you by name. He does not have to see you in context to recognize who you are.''

Longtime Clinton supporter Jim Walters too uses the word *charisma*. ''When he got ready to run for president, I told him, 'Look, you're forty-four years old. You have a tremendous amount of personal charisma. You reach out. The way you speak and the way you talk and your actions remind me a great deal of President Kennedy. You have a kind of Kennedy mystique about you.' He looked at me and he kind of laughed. I said, 'Let me explain what I'm talking about. You reach out to people. You talk to people. That's the way John Kennedy was.' ''

Managing editor of the *National Journal* Carol Matlack says, ''There's a specific event that I remember very clearly and this sort of fast-forwards to the 1982 reelection campaign. He had been invited to come and speak at this black church in a town called Earle over in the Delta. We came up to the church and the reporters were sent in ahead and then Clinton made his entrance a few minutes later and the place was just rocking. They had this organist who was singing 'Bill Clinton goes marching on' to the tune of 'Battle Hymn of the Republic.' Glory glory hallelujah. It was really a whole congregation, you know. It was a warm night and everybody was sweating and fanning and swaying and just the incredible adoration and the connection that he seemed to have with the crowd was amazing. I really had never seen anything like it. What was so striking was that Bill Alexander, who was their local congressman, had been speaking right before Clinton and he just sort of vanished right into the woodwork before Bill Clinton even came into the room. As soon as people focused on Clinton, it just eclipsed everybody else and it was just this very powerful emotional bond. I was struck by it because I've never seen anything like that before with a politician so that is one very vivid memory that I have. I remember talking to some of the people at the newspaper about it and just sort of marveling at why these people would feel this way toward him. There was this tendency toward a fairly cynical view of this common practice of black ministers getting walking money from the local party people and to think that whomever they anointed would sew up the black vote; so I was unprepared for that emotional reception.''

Longtime Clinton supporter Marlin Jackson also remembers the power of Clinton's pulpit oratory. "I offered him modest help when he ran for attorney general. We had what in most towns would be called Coke parties where you have Coca-Colas and the candidate comes in. The largest business in Paragould, Arkansas, is the Dr. Pepper/7Up bottler so we had soda parties there and maybe a big fish fry for him. Got seven or eight hundred people in a county with a population of twenty-eight or thirty thousand people. That's a very good group of people to expose a candidate to. I either took him or arranged for the proper community leaders to take him out over the county to the various voting precincts as he made a couple of whirlwind trips through the county.

"One event that stands out is when he spoke in our Methodist Church, which is probably the largest church in Paragould. Every October, we have a thing called Layman's Day on which the clergy steps aside and the lay people of the church plan the church program. We invited Bill Clinton to be Layman's Day speaker. I was asked to introduce him and I don't believe in spending very much time introducing someone who needs no introduction so I said, 'I have two fundamentally important jobs to do today as part of Layman's Day. One, I am required to tell you that my wife for the fourth time in our marital existence has succumbed to that dreaded disease called pregnancy.' (I had forgotten that the program was being broadcast and that she had not told her mother and father or my mother and father.) 'My other job is to introduce to you a young man who needs no introduction, our esteemed attorney general, Bill Clinton,' and I got a big laugh out of both of them. I didn't know what he was going to talk about and I didn't think he did because he had been scribbling ever since he arrived. He did a very good job. He did not dwell on politics. He talked about the family unit being the basic building block of civilization and how the dissolution of a basic building block of civilization affected us all. It must have made some impression on me because I remember it fifteen years later and I've heard so many public speeches and I don't remember very many of the others.

"He does a great job extemporaneously but if he tries to speak from a text, he would put the worst insomniac in the world sound asleep. I think if he's constrained to a written script, that he loses his effervescent enthusiasm. If he goes with the flow, if he wings it, listeners can hear compassion for people—farmers, laborers, Americans. His compassion for this country and this state and for

Hope, Arkansas, comes through but if you take that away from him, then he becomes Adlai Stevenson or William Buckley. By the time he gets into whatever it is he's going to say, you've already gone to sleep and it doesn't matter.''

Dick Herget says, ''The best speech I ever heard him make rivaled his State of the Union address this year, which I thought was monumental. It was a dedicatory speech he made at Arkansas State University, Beebe branch. It's a little two-year junior college that's right up the highway here and we were dedicating a new library and fine arts center in front of four or five hundred people, just country people out of the hills with the vast majority of the kids being first-generation college students. Many of the parents had never even graduated from high school and so to many of them, it's a big deal to have children in college. Clinton had prepared a talk and when he got up to make his speech, I could just feel this, he got the feel of the crowd and he saw the people in the overalls and the work clothes sitting out there and he made one of the most emotional speeches I've ever heard in my life. I mean, there wasn't a dry eye in the house when he finished. It was so touching. It was so personal. It was from the heart and it was classic Bill Clinton and I've never ever forgotten that. The group of people there in front of Clinton had absolutely nothing to do with his political career. There was nothing politically that they were going to do for him. This was a feeling of his own for this group of people and I thought, 'This man is extraordinary.' ''

Mark Grobmyer says, ''I can't remember Bill ever giving a prepared speech. To give you a great example, I took him to Washington & Lee University, where they have a mock convention that students put on. There are students from every state and it looks just like a real convention. I thought it'd be a good opportunity for him to speak. So we go there and Chuck Robb, I think, gave a keynote, and Bill gave the platform speech. Senator Robb helicoptered in from somewhere and landed on the golf course and he's got this leather-bound speech which he basically just reads. And the kids gave him polite applause. While he's talking, Bill said to me, 'Give me a few things . . . .' So I gave him a few ideas and he jotted down a few words on this piece of paper and then got up and gives this incredible speech. The thrust of it was, 'We don't have a person to waste,' sort of the Democratic platform. That's what he was giving was the platform speech. He said, 'We've got to make investments to give people better education, better training,' and he quoted one of his professors at

Georgetown who had explained that we're all in this together and we can't have different societies within one society, we've got to all rise and sink together. And until people understand that we're never really gonna' get moving. By the end of the speech, these kids were standing up. Now most of them wouldn't ever call themselves Democrats, but by the end of this speech, most all of them were giving him a standing ovation that continued for several minutes, and the kids invited him to come out afterward, they had a big party at this pavilion out in the country. So we went there and had a great time. Bill got on the stage and played the saxophone. The party didn't start till 10:30 so he goes out there just like he's a college kid again, gets up and plays, 'Summertime' on the saxophone, and the kids loved it. I'm sure a lot of them ended up being campaign workers.

"He loves students. He can communicate with them. As you can see on his appearances on MTV, he was in his element talking to those kids; he'll talk about anything, sports, music, movies books, or whatever."

Gwen Ifill, White House correspondent for the *New York Times*, also comments on Clinton's effect on young people. "I was with Bob Kerrey when he spoke at a high school, and he came across as totally flat and boring. The students were asking questions he couldn't answer like about the Seabrook nuclear plant—he didn't appear to know what it was. The next day, totally coincidentally, I returned with Clinton and he really connected with the kids in a way that Kerrey had failed to. I talked to the same students after the Clinton visit whom I had talked to after Kerrey's visit. They all were gushing over this guy with white hair as opposed to the young guy, just because Clinton managed somehow to connect in the way that he does."

Clinton connects; the charm is often magnetic. Former reporter Bob Wells recalls: "There's one incident that I always think of when I think of Bill Clinton. It involved a guy in the state house of representatives, a really fine man named William Foster who had been quite a supporter to the governor's education program. It was quite a crew. I really enjoyed covering those guys. Anyway, the city of England, Arkansas, Mr. Foster's hometown, built a new public library and they were naming it for Mr. Foster and they had this big dedication ceremony. So I drove down there to write a piece for the *Gazette*. Afterward, Mr. Foster wanted to take everybody to Cotham's, a little country store where a lot of people go to eat. It's not far from Little Rock and a lot of politicos would go there and hang out. So we went to Cotham's and we're all sitting at these big old long tables and Clinton was there and, of course, it was like he was holding court. He's got this overpowering personality. I was just kind of sitting there drumming my fingers on the table and not paying a whole lot of attention until he started focusing attention on me. He picked up on the fact that I was bored. It's like he had to have everybody drawn in. I felt that for a while there it was like 'Hey Bob, listen to this.' 'Hey Bob, let me tell you about this.' 'Hey Bob, what do you think of this?' He was trying to draw me in. There were ten or fifteen people sitting around this table and it just struck me how he had this incredible ability to pull people in and this incredible—I'm not sure what the right word is—need, perhaps, for other people. I mean, it wasn't enough that he already had fourteen of the fifteen people in the room listening to every word he said. He had to have all fifteen. He was just holding court and telling stories, political war stories and things. Jokes. Whatever. Because he's incredibly nice and incredibly charming, as a reporter, you had to work real hard to keep your distance.''

KHTV anchor Anne Jansen remembers, ''There's a part of Bill Clinton that's very small town, almost a little boy who loves a good joke, who loves a good time, who loves a good barbeque—you know, just sitting around with friends. That part of him is very legitimate and that's what I think has been very tough for him to give up but I remember that the last out-boundary campaign that I covered, on election night, was right down next to our station. It had been close because his Republican opponent, Sheffield Nelson, had come out with a tax-and-spend message three days before the campaign that just threw Bill into a tailspin. They really had to do some damage control to pull that puppy out. It was a long night but he ended up winning the campaign and we were trying to get him to come over to our station which was right next to his campaign headquarters to do an interview. We were still on the air. It was one o'clock in the morning and I'm standing outside of his campaign headquarters looking in while he finishes talking to all the workers who had been so dedicated. I'll never forget that image. He was dog-tired but he talked to every single person and there were probably two hundred people there who all had worked their fingers to the bone so he could get elected. He was not going to leave until he had spoken to every person individually to thank each one. He knew them all by name. That's the type of one-on-one that people don't forget, that I think is very good politically in terms of winning elections but I also think in his case is sincere.''

Former UPI correspondent Steve Buel finds Bill Clinton's energy and presence almost superhuman. "He doesn't turn his charm and energy on and then turn it off. I mean he's not the kind of disingenuous politician who is charming while the cameras are rolling and then shuts it down. Dale Bumpers, for instance, the senator from Arkansas, is very charming and cordial when he's on, but the moment that that's done, he's reserved and not a particularly ebullient guy. That's not the case with Clinton. Clinton is exactly who he appears to be.

"I covered one of the campaign swings through the Midwest and then on to North Carolina one night, nine days before the election. We had arrived in Winston-Salem, North Carolina, after a grueling day of campaigning that had begun in Michigan. It was 11:30. We arrived at the hotel and Clinton was mobbed. I stood around and kind of watched him work the crowd for a few minutes and then I put the candidate to bed and went to the gift shop looking for a copy of the Sunday New York Times. The gift shop was big as gift shops go—about the size of a large living room and I'm in there looking for a Sunday New York Times and suddenly, behind my back, it felt almost like the air pressure in the room changed. I just can't describe it other than it felt almost like there were too many electrons or something. I turned around and saw that the Secret Service had cordoned off the gift shop and was guarding the door to keep people out. They had done that because Clinton had come in. He's looking at the shelves and browsing and it's 11:30 at night. It's been a tremendously grueling day of campaigning. I probably had to get up the next morning at seven and my guess is in order to do his preparation, he probably had to get up at least at five in the morning and quite possibly much earlier. So he's been at it nonstop for eighteen hours and my butt's kicked, but he is wired, walking the edge of this gift shop picking up magazines and flipping through them and picking up Sidney Sheldon type novels and picking up North Carolina tourist curios and it's like he's eating the wall of this place. He's just picking the stuff up and browsing through it and it doesn't satisfy his need for stimulus. I think that says a whole lot about Clinton that is essential to his character. First of all, for me it was a nice visual confirmation of what I'd always thought about him, which is that this is a guy who feeds on information and on contact with humans. He is the ultimate stimulus junkie; at 11:30 at night when most sensible humans would be ready to hit the sack, he needs more. He's almost like one of those Japanese monster-movie characters that the more people it eats, the bigger it gets. At some point he looks over at me and he says, 'Hello.' I've known him as a reporter for ten years and covered him closely when I worked at the *Arkansas Democrat* so he knows me and he says some gratuitous sort of thing like, 'Hi Steve, it's good to see a friend out here,' one of those things that you know is political talk but you also hope is true. I said, 'Hello, Governor,' and we exchanged some platitudes back and forth and then he turned back to the wall and kind of kept looking at what he was looking at. At this point I've been covering him earnestly for about a month and I haven't been able to get close to him. I haven't really been able to ask him any questions. In spite of the fact that I knew him better than almost anybody on the campaign trail, I'm just one of a couple of hundred hangers-on with no interaction, so this is my big chance to talk to Bill. He has made the first move and he's called me a friend and this should be my grand moment. Instead I buy my newspaper and flee. There was no question in my mind about doing anything other than fleeing because in spite of the fact that it would have been great to talk to him—I had eight million questions that I would have liked to have asked him and I had failed in attempts to interview him for my alterative news-weekly and for the whole chain of newsweeklies across the country and for UPI—it was so uncomfortable being in the room. Because of the watchful presence of the Service and his obvious energy level, it was just like I said before, there were too many electrons in the room or something and it was the sort of thing that a normal human almost couldn't bear. It felt like an intrusion to even want to talk to him after that long a day, so I fled the room immediately, and then when I got outside, I asked myself, 'What am I doing?' ''

Starr Mitchell recalls "playing the mountain dulcimer at the celebration of Arkansas's 150th birthday in 1986. There's this big stage at Riverfront Park, and I'm playing my music and I can see a sea of people, as far as you can see there are people, just people, people, people. When I'm through I join all the other performers on stage and Bill Clinton comes out and stands at the podium. I am no more than three feet behind him when he begins his speech, a long speech, probably thirty-five or forty-five minutes. There's a part of me that loves this kind of thing and I can see that he loves this kind of thing too. All the people, the charge he gets from that many people.''

Adam Pertman, political reporter for the *Boston Globe*, concluded, ''Lots of pols, right, left, and center, depend on rhetoric over substance to make their point because at some point early on, you have to appeal to people. Otherwise they're not interested even if you've got a strong message. I think we've all learned that in politics but I would put it a little differently. I would say that he has a charisma in person that doesn't come through in words or even on TV and that was the sensation that everyone got. It's partly delivery and partly just something that flows from the guy—this rock star quality that a lot of people came to ascribe to him. Crowds just wanted to see him, wanted to hear him so I would ascribe it more to that. He has presence. I'm not sure what gives a person presence. I mean, we've all known individuals who have it, both friends and people we've never met before who can walk into a room and take over. To a large degree, I think you're born with it. Now what you do with this birthright is another question and he clearly understands that. I don't say this dismissively or derisively. He knows how to use it.''

UALR Professor Art English comments on Clinton's assets as a politician. ''I think the personal traits are those that have made him so effective as a politician. He has an ability to make the speech and imprint upon people very, very well. He has a tremendous personal warmth, an ability to really make people feel tremendously at ease, to make them feel very important. He looks people in the eye. He's extremely articulate, extremely bright and nonetheless is able to make the transition to all kinds of different perspectives whether he's addressing political scientists or talking to farmers in the agricultural counties.''

Former editor-in-chief of the *Arkansas Democrat* John Robert Starr finds some of Clinton's personal traits more apparent than real. ''He got elected attorney general because the field was weak. If the field had been stronger he might not have made it. But he ran against a weak field, and got elected attorney general, ran against a weak field in 1978, and got elected governor. If you look at Mr. Clinton from a distance you're going to believe he's sincere. He exudes sincerity. He's just as phony as a three-dollar bill but he does exude.''

Ernie Dumas says, ''As to whether he is sincere I think he does care. The people who are close to him believe he's a pretty deep and compassionate person, and I think he is. He's also a very calculating politician. He's a politician through and through but I think his great motivation still is not personal but to do wonderful things for people."

Sam Bratton agrees. "Because he is really good with people and really does care about people, he really thinks that he can make a positive difference and I think that comes across. It clearly comes across in his dealings with individuals and I think it comes across in some televised media sorts of situations but I think that the biggest key to his success is that he's genuine to his soul."

Talk show host on Little Rock's KBIS radio Bill Powell considers some of the limits of Clinton's sincerity. "I guess the thing about Mr. Clinton that I've noticed since he became governor, was his great ability to promise and his not very good ability to fulfill his promises. One of the things that first turned me against him was that he never stopped running for governor. It gets very tiresome listening to someone self-servingly tell you what a great job they're doing twenty-four hours a day, three hundred sixty-five days a year because they're campaigning for their next election all the time. As governor, quite frankly, he showed his ineptness. He is a great campaigner but not a very good governor, in my opinion."

In Arkansas, everyone knows Bill Clinton was never punctual. It became a statewide joke—Clinton never showed up at the scheduled time, he was always at least twenty minutes late and more often an hour or so behind. Most people tolerated Clinton's tardiness with good humor; they knew he was late because the governor could not pass up an opportunity to talk to a few more folks or shake a few more hands. But others saw an unattractive arrogance in Clinton's habitual lateness. Of course people would wait for him because he was the governor, just as rock-and-roll fans might wait several hours for a concert headliner to take the stage. That didn't mean that they liked it, or were amused by it. Some even thought Clinton's willingness to make others wait betrayed a certain personal insecurity—at the very least it was thoughtless.

Clinton's seemingly perpetual campaigning created what Maria Henson calls "Clinton time." She says, "He had people driving him around on his early campaign back when he ran for Congress. Somebody else was in charge of getting him there so he would leave when he was good and ready to leave. We called it 'Clinton time,' which means he was late everywhere he went but also it was funny that Clinton was going to get there in style. I mean, his trooper was going to drive eighty miles an hour if it took that. I remember we had to go to Jonesboro and it was really hard to keep up with him—that state car he was in, the Lincoln, was fast and it was so hard in fact, the poor guy from *USA Today*, Richard Benedetto, was in some kind of dinky little compact, got left completely behind. He had to find his own way into Jonesboro. He arrived so much later than everybody else because he couldn't keep up with the eighty-something miles an hour that we were driving through the Delta.''

State Senator Nick Wilson also comments on Clinton's tardiness. ''Problems were brought about by the fact that he can't stay on schedule. If you can stay on a schedule and see people when you supposed to see them, then there would be no need for him to be insulated, which is what his staff thought they should do.

''He's never on time because he's never had to be. He's never been in business. He's never made a living. I'm not talking badly about him. I'm just stating the facts. He's spent a lifetime in politics and his life is centered on shaking people's hands and making speeches. If you shake hands and make speeches and that's what you do, there's no end product. If you don't have to accomplish anything to bring in the dollars then you tend to fall into the habit of being late and once other people's time becomes your time and if they're willing to wait on your schedule, then you don't have a schedule anymore. I'm occasionally late a few minutes but if you treat other people's schedule as yours habitually and get away with it, then it creates problems and this is frankly one of the biggest problems he has. If he maintained a schedule, then a lot of his problems would go away.''

Senator Jay Bradford says, ''The thing I think is interesting is that he doesn't have any categories that he places people in. The person driving a tractor on a plantation is just as important to him as the most prominent wealthy person and I know that's true because I've seen it too many times when I've been out with him. He'll say, 'Let's go in the kitchen of this cafe before we leave,' and he doesn't do that just for political reasons. He wants to do that because that's what he feels. Whenever we'd go to a meeting he never would leave. He's always the last person to leave. He'd stay late and talk to whomever wanted to talk. Everybody would be tired and the driver would be sleepy but it didn't make any difference who was there. He would take just as much interest in people who couldn't help him as people who could.''

Former Little Rock mayor Lottie Shackleford also attributes Clinton's tardiness to his interest in people. "I used to point out to people that if you're at an event and you wait for him thirty minutes or forty-five minutes, he would still be there an hour after the event ended. That means he's going to be an hour late at the next stop so people started to understand that a little bit. Whether you liked it or not, at least you knew it wasn't as though he was late because he was holed up trying to get his rest. He was out there trying to allow as many people as possible to get to know him. It's almost as though he has this insatiable need to allow people the opportunity to make that judgment for themselves. I think he wants people to know him for themselves and not the way somebody else describes him. In my view that is a driving force that allows him to really get to hear the people."

Max Brantley, editor of the *Arkansas Times*, notes, "In fact, that's part of the reason why he is always late, which to me is one of his most aggravating and inexcusable habits. To me, it just speaks of a tremendous self-centeredness that keeps other people waiting but most often he keeps other people waiting because he's stopping to shake one more hand or have one more conversation. I mean, he will talk to anybody about anything and for at least a brief period of time make you think that you're the only person in the world he's talking to.

"He has this habit of looking you straight in the eye. He crawls into your soul for maybe a minute or two, and then he's looking over your shoulder for the next guy in the room that he's going to do the same thing to. His attention span is kind of short but he's able to do a lot in that period of time, whether it's trying to win over a potential voter or study a piece of policy."

Anne Jansen says, "What I remember most about covering him is that he was always late. Late to everything. No matter where he was supposed to be. No matter the size of the group that was waiting for him. Clinton is one of those people who was distracted by people and by stories and by things. I mean he's like a kid in a candy store about the environment around him. He'll see something and if it gets his attention, he's gone. There's no clock in his head. It's part of his makeup. He couldn't change it any more than you could change your shoe size. I mean, it's just part of him.

"People who have dealt with it all the time expect it and adjust their lives accordingly. I remember as an anchor, we were to have a live interview with Clinton and I bet my coanchor a bottle of wine that Clinton would not be there before the opening of the show and he was the lead story. Well, he walked into the newsroom as the music was playing. He had ten seconds to spare to get to the other studio and get clipped. I won a bottle of wine on that one. Some people would get frustrated with it but I don't think he really cares. That's just the way he is.''

One reporter who asked not to be named says, ''He has a hard time controlling himself. You can apply that context to so many things with him. Now Clinton knew that he should not talk about Ross Perot. He had no percentage in criticizing Ross Perot. Early on before Perot came back in, before the convention, Clinton knew that the less he talked about Ross Perot, the better it was for him, and yet he could not stop himself from responding to the questions. You could see that same lack of self-control in his lateness.''

Arkansas Senator Jay Bradford observes that, ''At breakfast or lunch meetings if there happened to be rolls on the table, while he was discussing an issue, somehow he'd finish every roll or biscuit on the plate after everyone else had finished. Some people smoke and some people drink. Well, he would eat, so if you put anything in front of him he would eat it and not even realize he was doing it. I think that's one reason that during the campaign, he started gaining weight. It's just a reaction.''

Steve Barnes says, ''He's a compulsive eater and his weight would just balloon. I think food is his booze. Once he was meeting with several of us in the Governor's Mansion conference room and they'd set out snacks and coffee. He's sitting there munching this plate of muffins and everybody in the room was joking about it or winking at one another. He picked up one fruit muffin after another. But some of his staff people were very concerned with his image and in rather a huff, Joan Watkins [Clinton's press secretary] reached over and took a muffin out of his hand like a mother snatching it out of a child's hand. And he just turned and looked at her and sulked in his chair for the rest of this meeting. When he's chastised by somebody who's close to him or that he trusts, I guess either he figures he deserves it or he just doesn't want the confrontation.

''About two weeks before he left for Washington Clinton had stood up about three hundred people at the state Capitol and the choir had sung every number it knew. Clinton was running about an hour late and a friend of mine who happens to be a producer turned the corner and there was Clinton and his mother. She had her finger in his face and both were red and she was chewing him out, telling him, 'You can't do this to people.' There stood the next president of the United States, the president-elect, being bawled out by his mother. My friend said, 'My God, what I would have done for a camera.''

CNN executive producer Sol Levine says, ''I most remember a conversation with him when we were on this twin-engine turbo prop fifty-seat plane, flying between Detroit and Chicago. He came back one night to get coffee. The coffee was in the back and I asked him a question about his repeated proposal for urban investment banks like the one on the south side of Chicago. He proceeded to tell me where that idea came from. It started with a United Nations or maybe it was an IMF program in Pakistan. He told me all about that and how that worked. In the meantime, the plane landed and people began to get off. Then he starts talking about what the banks could do in cities. The bottom line is we talked for about twenty minutes and then we landed and he continued to talk and I had by this time stopped asking him questions. He continued to explain to me, in detail, things that were now far beyond my comprehension in terms of how banks operate. I mean, I'm not a banker. I never took any courses. Everybody else has gotten off the plane except for me, Clinton, and Dee Dee, who is standing behind Clinton and basically sort of shaking her head at me like it's my fault that we're running late. I couldn't really gesture back to her because I was standing right in front of Clinton. It was all sort of funny because, as I thought afterward, this is why we're late all the time. This is it right here. I really believe very deeply that he is into the details and into the policy and he really cares about this stuff in ways that recent presidents haven't. In a way, it was neat to be covering somebody who was that into it. Imagine asking Ronald Reagan about the details of how he would put together urban development banks. I bet he couldn't tell you how it would work or what the model in Pakistan was.''

For the Record

As governor, Bill Clinton was an able administrator who occasionally had to give too much to a stubborn and very conservative general assembly. Often during his days in the Arkansas statehouse Clinton's proposals were more progressive than many in the state thought prudent. It is to his credit that he won more battles than he lost, in a state that desperately needed to be dragged into the twentieth century.

By far his most important battle was education, and it was in this field, most concede, that Clinton made the most progress. Part of this was no doubt due to his appointment of his wife Hillary to oversee a fifteen-member committee dedicated to redrawing public educational standards for the state. In a state where high school football was a major cultural force and high school principals were almost invariably drawn from the coaching ranks, some of the proposals made by Hillary's task force were bold indeed.

But Clinton, at least in his first years, took on some of the state's large utility interests and sought to bring jobs to Arkansas. His successes, while real, were never quite as spectacular as advertised, but when one considered the general obstinance of the Arkansas General Assembly, his results were remarkable in their own right.

Regional reporter for Gannett News Service Paul Barton found Clinton "a lot of fun to cover. The guy lives life on the cutting edge in terms of policies and the types of things that he was trying to enact in Arkansas. I give him credit for being a fairly progressive governor. I don't think he's a saint or anything but he was a progressive governor in a state that needed one. I do think he has a tendency to blow his accomplishments a little out of proportion but he was a pretty progressive governor overall."

Former state legislator Preston Bynum considers Clinton's record as governor. "Education would have to be one of his best accomplishments. The longer he served as governor, the more he accomplished. Health care was another concern that he had. He probably is not as business friendly as maybe I would have liked for him to have been. I think there were some wonderful accomplishments in the highway construction area. Gasoline taxes were passed. I think that we could have taken that a step further. We should have had a series of turnpikes or fused bond issues or other methods of financing additional highway construction.

"I think that he had a real record on protecting the environment and maybe the scales tilted too much in favor of the environment although i'm not sure that I know exactly what balance should have been struck. But I think the state is far better than it was before Clinton—I think he did an outstanding job. He had a vision for the state, the timing was right, and we had a period of unprecedented prosperity in the nation and in Arkansas too. It was a successful time for a lot of our companies, for the state, and for him.''

Betsey Wright says, ''The biggest contributions he made to Arkansas are education and the economic development turnaround. The economic development infrastructure that we put in place has really helped insulate the state from a lot of the recessionary impacts that the rest of the country has suffered. The environmental package that was passed in the 1990 legislature is one of the best in the country in terms of protection. I think that the contributions that Bill made in terms of setting a moral tone and putting women and minorities in the cabinet had a ripple effect. You'd see the private sectors making women and minorities members of boards and partners for the first time. It was a wonderful tone for the state. It was very exciting to see it and those aren't things you manage, they just happen. We'll see it happen nationally.''

Marlin Jackson adds, ''I have to say that his total support of my efforts as bank commissioner was the high point of the highlights. He had an unrelenting, virtual obsession on two or three particular points, one of which was education. I began my adult career as a schoolteacher so he and I had a common interest that gave me an inside into the fact that he was not just interested in the status quo or in getting teacher salaries up. He was truly obsessed with a fundamental reform of the quality of education in Arkansas. The other obsession is a close parallel and that is the economic development. He was obsessed with providing hope for the next generation of Arkansans. I guess the third aspect is his very inordinate and, I think, very unusual but very genuine feeling about individuals. People were not numbers to him. His people were not simply staffers; if they had a problem in their family, it affected him profoundly. I think those three things probably are highlights.''

Former Arkansas senator Max Howell points out that ''when Bill Clinton was elected governor our state's general revenue fund was about 750 million dollars, maybe 800 million. When he left, it was two and a half billion dollars. It takes a fantastic salesman and someone who knows what he's talking about to do that. I was concerned with mental health at that time. I was very active when I got back from the war in 1946 and had been point man for a lot of veteran legislation. I was concerned with college opportunities for returning veterans and professional schools and advancing the state colleges and things of that nature. We didn't have vocational education capacities. We had several state colleges and one university and Bill Clinton appreciated my concern for education and understood that it was important that we finance education and he supported those needs.''

Mike Trimble thinks that "Clinton's education reforms are his biggest contribution. I don't think the teacher's test was that big a contribution but the educational standards were, and nobody should take that away from him. Because of Bill and Hillary, if kids in a school district don't correctly answer a certain percentage of their test, then the whole curriculum gets reviewed. It was a massive change politically, a very brave thing for him to do.

"He got a lot of mileage out of the teacher's test and some people don't think it was quite as courageous as all that but he still seemed to get a lot of squawking. I mean it seems like nobody would object to improving the standards, but once again, his detractors say, that's why he's so good at what he does. He knew, they say, that there would be a lot of squawking from the Arkansas Education Association, the teacher's organization, but according to his critics he also knew that it (the criticism) wasn't anything that could really damage him politically and that he would give the appearance of running against this monolithic teacher's union.''

Ernie Dumas, too, rates education "Clinton's biggest accomplishment as governor. That's what he's best known for. He changed attitudes about education in Arkansas. Somebody has said there was a kind of poverty of spirit in Arkansas and not much value had been placed on education. That was really the most profound problem he had. People really didn't care if their kids got a good education. They wanted them to learn how to read and write but some thought that if youngsters got a good education, they'd go off to some other state . . . you didn't want your kid to get too good of an education. I think he changed those attitudes just by harping on it so much. Education became valued.''

Former Clinton staff member Mahlon Martin agrees. "In the early 1980s, everybody was critical of the education system and critical of the people in it. Many were almost indifferent to the role education would play in a small state like ours, a rural state, in terms of our future. Yet after the 1983 initiative and even up through the time he left, there was just a whole different mind-set around education. People were still critical of some of the things that went on in the system but they really embraced education as important. The changing of this mind-set was as important as anything he did.''

Professor Roy Reed says, "Education has to be right at the top of the list of his accomplishments. Now there was an example of what the guy can do when he's focused and motivated. That campaign from beginning to end was brilliant. You can write a textbook on how to do a political piece of work and use that as an illustration. And it didn't happen in a hurry. It took a long time, months, maybe a year."

Lloyd George states that "Hillary passed the education bill for him. He could not have gotten that bill passed without her. She took six months and toured the state and went into every county and a hundred schools and personally sat down with the people and addressed it on TV and on the radio and in the papers. It went on month after month. She was doing real get-with-the-people's work and you get results that way. She had the time. Bill didn't. She put in a lot of time being with the people. She did a hell of a job."

Arkansas senator David Malone agrees. "Hillary was actually out there having the public hearings and listening to people talk about what they wanted and meeting with teacher's groups and administrators. She traveled the state and he kind of stepped back and let her get the standards together and come up with a consensus. I know that he participated in the process because at dinner table meetings and things like that, there was a lot of discussion about which way should we go and what should we do and how can we raise these standards, but from the public standpoint Hillary was out in front. She was the one leading the group. He stayed completely out of it until the education standards committee had made their recommendations and it then had to be sold to the legislature. Then he stepped back in and seemed to take over."

Meredith Oakley takes a dimmer view. "They needed to build Hillary's popularity which was much lower than his and so they created that position for her. And, of course, she shone, as she was destined to do in that position. That was a prefabricated issue. Bill Clinton has always been running for the White House."

John Robert Starr has much to say about Clinton and his education reform bill. "In 1983 some members of the legislature were encouraging Clinton to go for a one-cent tax increase for various purposes. Some of it would have gone to schools but a lot of it would have gone to other things. And that's the first time I think I ever offered him any advice. I called him and said, 'Don't let them do this. We need all this money for education. If you do it now you can't get anything else for education. Just tell 'em no, no tax increase, which is the way it worked out. That's how I got into the ball game. And then, I didn't read anything about Hillary's education program that I didn't agree with. When Hillary came in with a program, I agreed with the program in total and supported it in total. Probably made as many speeches for it as he did.

"Honesty is the word. Hillary is an honest person where Bill is not, Hillary is courageous where Bill is not, Hillary will look you in the face and tell you the truth whether it's what you want to hear or not. Bill will try to figure out what you want to hear and that's what he's going to tell you. He'll try and tell you what you want to hear to the extent it will further what he wants to do and win you to his side. A totally worthless human being.

"On the education program, the one-cent sales tax of 1983 that started the education program has been so thoroughly sold. That's the only time in my life I ever saw people demanding a tax increase. Clinton went out there and screwed up so bad he barely did get it through. He let the lobbyists get to him. He let Ray Thornton, former chief lobbyist for higher education in Arkansas, get away with a third of the money for the colleges, which wasn't in the plan that I supported. The plan I supported was to get the money for the public schools in 1983 and come back and raise the income tax in 1985 to take care of the colleges. Now, we couldn't do the colleges in 1985 because, in the first place, they got a third of the money in 1983 and the hell with them, and in the second place, the Arkansas Education Association was fighting him so bad in 1985 over the teacher testing that saving the whole program took all the energy that it had in the legislature and we couldn't get a tax increase for higher education in there.

"There were two other small taxes that he tried two or three times to get through on the last day, and he couldn't so he just abandoned those two taxes. Now that was several million dollars, maybe ten, fifteen, twenty million less for the program. So he called to tell me that he got it through. I said something to the effect of 'Boy, that's great, we've got the sales tax and this and that' and he said, 'Well, I didn't get the other two.' He'd cussed me out a couple of times in the past but this time I cussed him out. I said, 'You sorry, worthless, no-good son of a bitch, you should have stuck in there. You could have got it if you had the guts and fought for it. You're on my list forever. The hell with you.' He didn't have a chance to say anything but I called him back later that afternoon. I realized that this guy had really pushed, had really fought a good fight and he'd come up with an education program; Jesus Christ, let's start over again. It was the greatest day of his life and I'd treated him like that. I called up the Governor's Mansion and told them to tell him I'm sorry. I guess they got the word to him because he called the next morning and I told him that I was sorry I'd said it but that I had meant it at the time.

"By 1990, he's farting around making speeches all over the country, so I said, 'If I support you I want you to promise me that you won't run for president, you won't go out of the state making any speeches at all until we get this education program straightened out. Now if you agree to those things, I won't trash you. I will write favorably about you. If Sheffield Nelson comes up with an education program I'm going to support him, so you haven't got any chance at all if he comes up with an education program. If he endorses your education program and improves on it, then I'm going to support Sheffield. But if he doesn't, then I will support you. So that was our agreement. And so in 1990, he does file to run for governor. He says he left the governor's office intending to say he wasn't going to run. He told me that—it's not secondhand, that's not speculation, that's not what somebody else heard. He told me that. Apparently he hadn't told anybody else, not even Hillary, but maybe only Hillary knew what he was planning to do. But he says he left the office planning not to run and talked himself into running again while he was making his speech saying he wasn't going to run. That's what he says. I had conned Sheffield and Clinton into agreeing to do a debate on education. Not an ACLU debate or a League of Women Voters debate but a debate solely on education of which I would be the emcee. I kept telling Sheffield, 'Sheffield, get yourself an education program.' 'I got one,' he said. 'No, you haven't. You don't even know how to spell education.' And it became obvious at this debate that he didn't do it. So the next day I called Clinton and said, 'Sheffield's out and I'm gonna' bid for you but I still don't want to endorse you unless you get into trouble. You're not in any trouble now and I don't think you'll get into trouble.' On the Friday before the election Sheffield began to run ads. Clinton absolutely panicked. He went up to the bank at Berryville and borrowed a hundred thousand bucks that he didn't have to counter these ads. He spent money effectively because he saw that he was dropping. He called me on Sunday morning and said, 'I need you to endorse me.' He said he was down nearly 50 percent. I said, 'Bill, you haven't lost that much.' Seven o'clock in the morning on a Sunday I came down to the office and wrote a column endorsing him.

Even though I didn't want to, I kept my part of that bargain and I expected him to keep his part too. And what did he do? He went out and got a four thousand dollar raise for teachers so he could buy the support of the Arkansas Education Association. Did nothing at all to improve education and took off to start running for president.

"I think he cares about the reading level of school kids as long as it doesn't interfere with his personal agenda. If he were to see a poll tomorrow saying that the people wanted the public education system abandoned, that 99 percent of the people wanted to abandon public education, he would run there. He's what Jim Johnson calls the kind of a leader that finds out which way the crowd's going and then runs around and gets in front and says, 'follow me.' "

Arkansas, of course, is not exactly a southern state, although it was part of the Confederacy and some of the same issues of race and rights apply. Bill Clinton claims his first political impulses were related to the civil rights struggles of African Americans in Arkansas, and it is easy to see how a man of his generation could have been profoundly affected by events in the fifties and sixties.

It is as sad as it is true to note that there are still some people in Arkansas who hate and fear Clinton largely because black voters supported him in extraordinary numbers—typically Clinton would garner more than 90 percent of the black vote in his gubernatorial races. Critics of Clinton's record on civil rights issues state that he was more interested in appearances than substance, that he took no particular political risks, and that Arkansas still has no states civil rights law. Still, his appointment of unprecedented numbers of blacks to state boards and commissions as well as to high-profile policy-making positions continued to have the dual effect of providing positive role models and encouraging black political fealty.

Bill Powell asserts, "It's just this misidentification that he puts forward of himself as the champion of poor people and of black people. He hasn't really done anything for anybody. He calls himself a champion of education. When he took office, we were forty-ninth, forty-seventh, forty-eighth in every statistic. We're still forty-ninth, forty-seventh, forty-eighth. The only difference is it's costing us five times more now than it did then and we're not getting any bigger bang for the buck. We're getting a lot of lip service, and very little implementation."

Memphis *Commercial Appeal* reporter Guy Reel disagrees. "Ultimately his heart is in the right place even though he may not go about things the right way. He may be calculating and manipulative, but he's ultimately calculating and manipulative for the right reasons. The end he's trying to achieve is to help the downtrodden and the poor as opposed to being calculating and manipulative to aid the rich and the powerful."

Brownie Ledbetter says, "We had a lot of hope for Bill, particularly in lifting the pall of racism that hung over all our political efforts. I mean, it's been the touchstone for the whole nation, but it's still a difficult issue and Bill's openness and understanding of that issue was important to me. Racism is one of the issues that over the years he's cared the most about. He's accused of being slick and all those things, but racism is one thing you can't accuse him of. He's very committed and very sincere."

Cal Ledbetter, professor of political science at the University of Arkansas at Little Rock, agrees. "It was quite important to him that he appoint blacks and women to high positions in Arkansas— particularly blacks and politically he really didn't need to do so. The Arkansas population is only 16 percent black so you could be elected without the black vote, but he put women and minorities in high-ranking positions, not just in ceremonial slots."

Mahlon Martin speaks from personal experience. "I was the first black whom Clinton appointed as director of the Department of Finance and Administration and it took a lot of courage to put a minority in as fiscal officer of the state, because the power associated with that position is amazing particularly in our state government and that was a real risk. He also made a commitment to appoint a black to every major board and commission in the state government. They are very coveted positions and he took some really progressive steps in doing that. Often, things like these appointments happen strictly for the purposes of political window dressing. It wasn't like that with Clinton and that was part of the reason why I felt good about traveling with him. I never felt that he looked at me as a minority and, certainly in terms of some of the decisions I had to make, I never felt that I was a token. I felt like I was there because I could do the job. You can see that he's trusted in the minority community by the votes he's gotten from minorities. He's never gotten less than 80 percent and often gone as high as 90 percent."

Lottie Shackleford agrees. "It's how he relates to all kinds of people. From the very first time I met him many, many years ago he was comfortable, and you don't always have that comfort level with people of different races. It's not just black-white with him—you don't ever get the sense that he is patronizing or placating. He has a genuine concern for you as a human being. Another thing that struck me about him the very first time I met him was if he doesn't like something you say, he feels comfortable telling you. He'll say, 'You know, I don't like that hare-brained idea,' and he doesn't worry about disagreeing with you because you're black. I like that about him. I mean, it's not something that he has to think about or plan. It just comes naturally for him. If you're in his presence, you don't have to feel that this is a person who is sort of uncomfortable but trying to be comfortable or trying to reach for the right and appropriate things to say. You don't get that feeling with him because he's not that way.''

Phoebe Wall Howard, formerly a reporter for the *Arkansas Gazette*, recalls, ''In August of 1989, the paper sent me to England, Arkansas, to do a story on the community swimming pool which was a privately run public pool, meaning the city was leasing it for a dollar a year. There were no black members at the pool even though one third of the city's population was black. I wrote about how the memberships were $125 for families, $75 for individuals, and I quoted people in the community. A young black teenager said the signal they get is, 'If we want to swim on a hot Arkansas day, we can just go to the bathtub,' and then I quoted a member of the pool who said, 'Blacks make whites feel uncomfortable, more uncomfortable than whites make blacks,' and this was said by a high-school teacher. She said, 'I'm not prejudiced but there is a limit. I feel a little uncomfortable being around them all the time. They could get government money and go where they don't have to pay.' That story came out in August of 1989 at the end of the swimming season. The following year, the situation stirred itself up again and we heard that the Ku Klux Klan was coming into the community and meeting in homes and sending out pamphlets. It's interesting what happened next. In April of 1990 Clinton went to England, Arkansas, without notifying anybody. He went privately and met with people in their homes after hearing about the KKK letters. The press didn't find out about his visit until after the fact. He himself discussed security with the police. He set up everything himself and did it all behind the scenes so it was very interesting to see how events transpired. Later the community heeded his recommendations and set up biracial committees and basically dealt with a lot of racial issues that had never been dealt with before. It was very interesting to see how that whole thing evolved.''

The New Yorker's Washington editor Sidney Blumenthal says, ''When I was at the *Washington Post,* a black writer at the *Post* named Herb Denton died. He was a very close friend of a friend of mine and I knew him too. I liked him a lot. Herb Denton grew up in Little Rock and his funeral was going to take place there so I called Clinton and told him about the funeral. He went out of his way to show up and to talk to the family. I don't know exactly what there was in it for him. He said to me, 'Well, I think I know that family,' and he was very interested in what church the mother had gone to and where the father had worked. He was very interested in sort of figuring out what someone was like based on their background rather than, in Herb's case, his writings. Herb had been quite a distinguished correspondent in Lebanon, for example, but Clinton was more interested in this other aspect of Herb's life, the part that he could touch personally, that he could feel.''

Lottie Shackleford notes, ''If you've been attending a convention or you're having a meeting with him he always wants to talk about how things went with whomever hangs around afterward. 'How do you think people received it? Did they understand what I was saying?' That's always on his mind. He says things like 'When the banquet is over, come to the Mansion.' He did this with the Little Rock Nine. The nine blacks who integrated Central High School in 1957 had a thirty-year reunion in 1987, which was the first time all nine of them had been together since they had left Central. Clinton was formal during the course of the celebration but then later that night, at the Mansion you could just let your hair down, people played the piano, that kind of thing. At about midnight or 1:00 A.M. everybody else is trying to get to bed and he still wants to have just a friendly gathering. He has courteous warmth. What still strikes me most about him is his true genuineness.

''If you wanted to put just one little thing in a capsule that told what Bill Clinton did for Arkansas, I'd say, 'Helping to instill self-pride among Arkansans.' ''

As governor of Arkansas, Bill Clinton was not always on good terms with what, at times, could be a nearly regressive general assembly. Preferring compromise to defeat, Clinton was often able to get some of his programs through the body, but the legislators and lobbyists almost always exacted their price. Clinton was, by any outside measure, a fairly effective governor; however, his triumphs were invariably more modest than the rhetoric that preceded them. Clinton staked out the high ground on education reform and advocated an ambitious restructuring of the state's tax system. His job training program passed in 1985. In 1988, he took before voters a referendum, a code of ethics for legislators, a measure that angered lawmakers and injured his ability to work with the legislature.

Bob Wells gives Clinton a plus on the lobby disclosure bill. "When Nick Wilson was president pro tem of the Senate, he was constantly giving Clinton fits. For example, a couple of times both the governor and lieutenant governor were out of state, and Nick had stationery and cocktail napkins printed up with his name as governor. He came down and fired half of the staff and took over his office just to harass the guy. Clinton wanted to pass a bill that would disclose all the gifts legislators were receiving all the sources of funding they were getting from different lobbyists. During the special session, Wilson basically held the governor's lobby disclosure bill in what was just a show of ruthless raw power. It was incredible. The House overwhelmingly passed this bill and you looked out there and saw people like Doc Bryant, who's a paid employee of one of the most powerful lobbies in the state, the Arkansas Poultry Federation, voting for the lobby disclosure bill. You know these guys knew good and well that they could put on this act. They could say they're for lobby disclosure knowing full well that the state Senate—in particular, Nick—was going to kill it at the other end of the building and it was never going to go anywhere. I went down to the Senate end of the building when the bill was in Nick's committee. There was a TV camera there and Nick starts ranting, 'So this is the way it's gonna' be. Let's get the TV camera over here.' They were four to four on the committee and there was this one senator from Hot Springs, Bud Canada. He just basically looked down at the table and said he was undecided. Wilson leaned over and glared at the guy and said 'Are you going to vote, Mr. Canada?' And Canada's sitting there with the TV cameras on him and the fate of the governor's lobby disclosure bill in his hands and Nick Wilson glaring at him and his hand kind of lamely goes up siding with Nick. The bill was bottled up in the committee, and it ain't going anywhere so this whole session proved to be a disaster. That same day Clinton suddenly appears in the House chamber. I think maybe we'd had a few minutes notice. He addressed the House and made this incredible speech on this important bill and how names were called and they had responded and were with him. He was adjourning the special session and he was going to take this thing to a public vote. He would have a referendum on this lobby disclosure bill and travel the state to drum up support for the bill and he would go to these guys' districts and tell their people that they were with him. These guys stood there clapping but with their eyes glazing over and thinking, 'Oh, my God.' They had played right into the governor's hands. All of them. Because that little episode that Nick pulled in that committee showed everybody how those lobbyists had that whole place in the palms of their hands. It was incredible the way that thing was bottled up in that committee. Clinton's gut political instincts and his timing was incredible. My lead in the *Gazette* the next day said if he had been a Hollywood director he couldn't have found a better moment to yell, 'Cut.' Basically when he went up there and made that speech, he totally rewrote the next day's headlines. Instead of, 'Governors suffers another defeat and Nick Wilson bottles it up,' it became, 'Governor taking initiated act to the people. A referendum to the people.' ''

Former reporter Scott Van Laningham remarks on Clinton's style with the legislature. ''At the very end of the legislative session, they have what they call the revenue stabilization act which determines how they divide up the state funds. There was a last-minute fight over the division of those funds and that threatened to hold up the adjournment of the session. I'm sure you've heard that it is not at all unusual for him to come out of the governor's office and go back and forth between the two chambers when something was going on. In this case, he basically jogged back and forth between the two chambers, meeting with the day legislators in each group and basically hammering out a compromise that one could live with. A lot of folks think he compromises too much but I guess I'm one of those who think that a large part of politics is about finding the middle ground, and that's what he did. You could just see him going back and forth between the groups.''

Charlie Cole Chaffin thinks that ''his relationship with the legislature was really very good. There are a few people who were always against Bill Clinton in the legislature and that's probably because of the type of people they represented. Bill Clinton was hands-on, very, very active. If I needed something from him and he wasn't really very agreeable, I would send somebody down there like Senator Beebe, who'd say, 'Charlie is really mad at you. Charlie is really aggravated about something,' and the governor would call me down to see what the problem was. We'd talk about it and a lot of times I'd get what I wanted. He was accessible any time day or night. Bill Clinton is famous for his late-night telephone calls but I also would call the Mansion late at night and he would return my telephone call that night. He was hands-on. Very accessible.''

State Representative Myra Jones says, ''I was elected to the city council in 1976, the same year that Bill was elected attorney general. Bill was always very receptive and talked to us about our issues but when I ran for the legislature, that's when I really began to have a closer working relationship with him. He has a way of empowering people. He talked about that a lot in the campaign but I felt that as a legislator, he almost empowered each and every legislator to feel that they're a part of the team. Everything was hands-on with Bill. We would be in a committee room that had one of his bills and he'd be popping in and out and he would tap members on the back, whisper in their ears, make deals sometimes, I'm sure. You'd get phone calls sometimes late at night about a bill he might have up the next day and what it would take to pass it. I realize now that we were very spoiled because he was the only governor who did that. Although we have good leadership in our present governor, it's so different. I didn't realize how spoiled we were. He'd be running between the House and the Senate. The aides couldn't keep up with him he was running so fast. He'd be popping his head in and pulling you out. Getting the votes. It was very, very hands-on.

''One of the really key things that he did was put his package on our desk the first day with a note that said, 'Sign on as many bills as you want and I'll cosponsor them. If you want some changes made, submit it in writing and have it in my office by Monday. I will consider them.' So he always kept an open mind. He was willing to compromise if you had a better idea or something that you thought could work better. He was willing to change. But because of this he always had ten or twelve sponsors on every one of his bills. He did very well that way.

''I think he had a very warm relationship with many individuals in the Senate and the House. We played cards every Wednesday night. He loves to play hearts. We always would send a note down to the governor to let him know where we were playing Wednesday night. One night he came in black tie from a function where he'd given a speech. He didn't even eat his dinner; he just came right over so he could play hearts. And he wanted to win. He didn't like it when he didn't win. He liked to shoot the moon and worked hard at doing it and generally he did win.''

Charlie Cole Chaffin comments. ''Contrary to what many people believe about legislators, we don't carouse all night. Once a week, we played cards together and there is a number of us who play bridge and a number who play other card games. Governor Clinton played hearts and really liked to be with us in that social kind of situation so probably a dozen of us would go over in jeans and play cards. We had two or three tables of cards going and he had a wonderful time doing it.

''He was definitely a regular player. Sometimes he'd be late if he had to go speak somewhere first but I remember the days after some card games when some of the guys would just be bleary-eyed and they would say, 'The governor wouldn't leave. He played cards all night.' He was having such a good time that he would play till two or three o'clock in the morning.

''He was really competitive if he was playing with people who knew how to play well but he also would teach newcomers. He'd say 'what you really need to be doing is this,' but then he might just pick up their tricks.''

It is not for nothing that Paul Greenberg, perhaps the most astute long-term observer of Bill Clinton, dubbed the governor of Arkansas ''Slick Willie.'' Clinton, at times, seems to take pleasure in carefully wording his statements so that their letter may be preserved while their spirit is trampled. Some think his slickness is at least in part due to his dysfunctional family life, that he genuinely wants to convince his opponents and win over his enemies. Others suggest that Clinton's key instinct is for political survival. Many note that it is wise to pay close attention to not only what Clinton says but how he says it, for he often allows himself more than a little wiggle room.

News reporter Brenda Blagg sees Bill Clinton, the governor, as essentially a consensus builder. ''The main thing I can tell you is that he worked hard. He always worked very hard and if you didn't agree with what he did you still couldn't slight him for not trying to get done what he thought was right. He is very much a consensus builder. That's what he likes to do. He doesn't like to

A young Bill Clinton (standing, seventh from left) attends a back-yard birthday party in Hope with most of his kindergarten class. Mack McLarty is seated just to the left and in front of Clinton.

Clinton, far left, plays saxophone in his high school jazz band.

Hillary Clinton wipes away a tear as her husband announces he will not seek the 1988 Democratic nomination for the presidency.

Bill Clinton with his long-time friend—and political ally—Diane Blair, in January 1989.

Bill and Hillary visit with Betsey Wright days after she resigned as the governor's chief of staff in 1989. Wright had held the position since 1983; she'd be back in 1992 for his presidential campaign.

Hymning it up with the Reverend Billy Graham during the evangelist's crusade in Little Rock in September 1989.

All photos courtesy of the <u>Arkansas Democrat-Gazette</u>.

make anybody mad and, of course, in the process of trying not to make anyone mad, he makes somebody mad every time.''

Syndicated columnist and *Arkansas Democrat-Gazette* editor Paul Greenberg wouldn't call it consensus building. ''I've never got the impression that Bill Clinton would deliberately take a stand if he knew it would cost him a political election no matter how strong his beliefs. Much of what he did was about getting elected. It was persuading people to like him and to agree with him. That doesn't necessarily mean that he didn't believe in what he was pushing.''

Kathy Ford calls it being wishy washy. ''A good friend who has known Bill forever was watching a documentary on Huey Long with me. Huey's mannerisms and speech and his oratory style reminded both of us of Bill. We were comparing the two when my friend said, 'You know, the only difference between Huey Long and Bill Clinton is that Huey Long carried his balls in a wheelbarrow and Bill Clinton carries his in a baggy.' Well, I think he was trying to say that balls are analogous to guts. It's a comment on his being wishy-washy.''

Lib Carlyle notes, ''I have never worked with any individual who was more organized. Who cares more for people. Who has such a big heart that he wants to bring everybody in and make them part of whatever he's doing. He does this to his detriment. It's so difficult for him to make decisions sometimes because he does not want to hurt anybody's feelings. He's very sensitive to people. He cares very deeply about people and being elected president hasn't changed him a bit. I think the characteristics are great to have in an individual but I think sometimes people accuse him of waffling as they say and this may be why he does: He is so sensitive that he just doesn't want to hurt anybody's feelings if he can avoid it at all.''

Mahlon Martin says, ''It didn't happen to me but I've been in meetings where other folks thought they had an agreement with him and it turned out they didn't. One thing about him is he comes across as being compassionate and very understanding and more often than not, when people would come and talk to him his empathy and compassion were misread as approval. So, often they would leave with an impression that he agreed to do something he hadn't agreed to at all. There are people who felt they had a commitment from him when, at least in my presence, I think he was expressing concern rather than agreeing. He would say, 'I understand.' Very seldom do I remember him telling someone,

'No way. Get out of here.' So people left more often than not thinking they had his ear and that he was committed rather than believing simply that he understood their problems. Also, I learned that the environment is constantly changing. As a result of that, even sometimes when one agrees to something, the environment can change to the point that the agreement is no longer appropriate.''

Bill Wilson says, ''Like him or dislike him, one of the most impressive things about him is that he actually kept a handle on just about everything happening in state government. He understood the issues on both sides and listened to both sides. And I think he's gotten a bum rap from people who claim that he told them he would do something and didn't do it. I think his willingness to listen and quote what your position is then leave it without making a decision was misinterpreted. A lot of people's fond hope turned his empathy into promises a lot of times. I never knew him to make a promise that he didn't keep, and I am suspicious of people who accuse him of it.''

Columnist Max Brantley looks at a larger context. ''You have to listen to him very carefully. Looking back I wish that we had employed videotape a whole lot more during the years we covered him. I know there were times when he would say something to me on one topic or another and I would have understood him to have said one thing when the next day he would say something different than I'd understood him to say. An awful lot of times I would give him the benefit of the doubt saying, 'I don't take very good notes. Maybe I heard him wrong.' Now seeing him in the national spotlight where everything is videotaped, I can see I was right. He was fudging. He calculated his statements very carefully and he seems to be ad-libbing while in fact, he very clearly understands precisely what he's saying most of the time. He builds consensus by moving positions very incrementally as he talks to a wide range of people from press to advocates to opponents to supporters and out of that evolves what eventually is his position. Sometimes he gets there and sometimes, he doesn't. It's kind of interesting.''

''State Senator David Malone thinks that Clinton's ''changing his mind is political. I think it's an effort on his part to try to accommodate everybody that he can and try to bring everybody into the decision-making process. Say he talked to legislator A in the morning and told him one thing, then he talked to legislator B in the afternoon and he had more information, he'd learned something else. He's willing to change based on that and I don't think it would have troubled him to have legislator A and B in the room and to explain to them that 'I've changed slightly from ten o'clock this morning to what I'm feeling now.' He's always generating and assimilating new information so I'm looking at it in a positive light. I always thought that he was trying very hard to come out with the best possible policy but it did generate a lot of jokes and a lot of internal laughter when legislators would say, 'He seems to have changed his mind from the time I talked to him this morning when he told me this.' "

CBS *Newsnet* reporter Regina Blakely says, "If there's anything Bill Clinton can do, it's talk, and that is why sometimes he's not very effective in getting his message across. You would think the talker would be a good communicator. Sometimes that's not necessarily so. Friends of Bill Clinton have said he is not the thirty-second sound bite man, and he's not. He can talk to you as much about a book that he read last night as he could talk to you about the details of a health care plan and he tends to go on and on. He opens himself up to criticism because sometimes he says too much. One day he will say X, Y, Z, and the next day he'll say X and Z and leave out Y and everybody wants to know where the Y is. Is that a change in policy? Did you mean it the first time? George Bush had the same problem. George Bush would ramble on incessantly about this, that, and the other and not complete sentences and sometimes the press would get frustrated with that. Clinton, because he is able to talk on and on just about any subject, he sometimes sets himself up. The next time he talks about that subject, you want to know why it's not as complete as the first time he discussed it."

Professor Art English speaks "as a political scientist, and my first impression of Clinton is that he's extremely smart, and probably the most articulate politician I've ever heard. He can conceptualize policy ideas very well, and he's extremely impressive when he's working with people. The flip side is his indecisiveness of which a part is due to his overstudying things."

Ernie Dumas recalls some consequences of Clinton's indecisiveness. "Clinton came up with this bill to give a 100 percent tax credit for a donation to a college or university, which was nice because you could give a college a thousand dollars and endow the Ernie Dumas chair in journalism, and it wouldn't cost you a penny, because it would just come off your taxes. So everyone passed the bill, and it was up to the governor. The Department of Finance Administration said to him, 'Governor, you can't sign this thing because it'll be every inducement in the world for everybody to give tons of money up to the limit of their tax liability to the colleges and universities, and they'd just say "Well, rather than give to the state police and all that stuff, why not just give it to the college and get all this recognition?" Everybody could just endow chairs and scholarships and whatever and it wouldn't cost them a penny. This thing may cost many, many billions of dollars a year.' So Clinton decided to veto it. He called up Joe Bell after the session closed and the legislature had gone home. We were in the closing days of the session that passed seventy-five to one hundred bills a day and just dumped them in the governor's office. The governor then has twenty days after the session to act on these bills if it reaches his desk in the closing days. He's working feverishly against the deadline. He gets this bill and vetoes it and then he calls Joe Bell and says, 'Joe, look, I just want to notify you I'm vetoing this college tuition tax bill.' And Joe says, 'Well, Bill, you can't do that. Remember when four or five months ago, I brought some college presidents into your office? We talked about this thing and you said that if we passed it you'd sign it.' He said, 'I did?' 'Yes sir, you said you'd sign it if we passed it.' Clinton had already vetoed the bill. The state troopers, the security, had taken it out of the Capitol and put it in the mail slot in the House door because the next day was the deadline. And so he hung up and began agonizing. 'I told those college presidents, I've got to keep my word.' It's never been verified exactly how they did it, but they never denied that they did it this way. He had the state troopers, go out to the Capitol and rake around under the door with a coat hanger until they got that bill out and then they took it back out to the Mansion. The governor's stamp doesn't say 'veto,' it says, 'disapproved', and then he signs it. At the Mansion, Clinton took his pen and blacked out his stamp and put his initials on the side. In the middle of the night he sent it back out there and the next morning it was approved. We didn't find out until days later what had happened. Apparently Joe Bell told people and they were laughing about it. We decided to go check out that bill and see what it looked like. He had scratched it out, so we took a picture of it and put it on the front page. And so then of course, the Department of Finance says, 'Governor, this is catastrophic. In a few months people will start writing these checks to the colleges and universities and the tax revenues will plummet.' The colleges and universities immediately sent all these letters. They were doing this massive mailing saying, 'You can get a 100 percent tax credit if you can donate up to a certain amount. It won't cost you a penny, and you'd be helping your university.' The Department of Finance convinced the governor that this was a bad mistake, so then he called a special session of the legislature to undo the bill, to repeal the act. So the legislature were summoned in a special session to do that. That anecodote kind of sticks out because it was such a funny story. We had a good time with it. Clinton of course was red-faced about it.''

Bob Steele asserts that "his biggest weakness is not that he waffles or that he wants you to love him but that he's indecisive. He will not make a decision until he's studied it from every angle known to man.''

Newsweek political correspondent Eleanor Clift, however, says that "his behavior is classic child of an alcoholic. He wants to please everybody.'' Clift explains: "He frequently has what seem to be contradictory impulses. Reduce the deficit but spend money on investments. Cover everybody but have money left over for the deficit. Contradictory goals can be accomplished to a certain extent but not as easily as he sometimes portrays. They do reflect his need to try to bring everyone to the table, which is not necessarily a bad quality because government in the end is about compromises. It's just that he's frequently a little too transparent doing it. It looks like he doesn't have any principles. That's the problem. I think he does but sometimes it doesn't look so great. He is passionate about some issues but he's a master of digression. He wants to do it all and he has a hard time harnessing everything into a single achievable goal. That's where Hillary comes in. She's much better at that. He doesn't know where the boundaries are in an issue. He wants to do it all.''

Pam Strickland, former political reporter for the *Arkansas Gazette*, considers the psychology of his behavior. "He wants to be loved. Not liked. He wants to be loved. He may have enormous confidence and a very well developed ego but on the inside there's still a part of him that doesn't want to make anybody mad at him. He probably is a little neurotic and maybe a little paranoid. I've learned a lot through my own personal experiences about dysfunctional families and addiction and you can see that he bears the wounds of having an alcoholic stepfather, which is something that he's never really talked about.''

Kit Seelye talks about the effects of Clinton's childhood.

"Given the circumstances of his childhood, which I think was really difficult especially for a really smart kid in this backwater town with this horrendous stuff happening in his home, I think he needs to control situations. I think he talks and monopolizes things to feel in control. I also think a part of him is the 'policy work.' We all heard about the reporter [Sol Levine] who had an interview up in the front of the plane with Clinton and then he came back sort of staggering from all the details.

"I remember an incident that illustrates Clinton's compulsion to please. A pro-life guy was posing outside of his hotel as an autograph seeker. This guy handed Clinton a pen and said, 'Can you give me your autograph?' At the same time, he had hidden under a newspaper a fetus that he thrust at Clinton. Once Clinton saw this he just turned away. Got in his car and then realized he still had the guy's pen. He got out of the car and gave him his pen and said, 'Here's your pen back.' Most people in that position would not even think about the pen or would throw it on the ground in disgust but there's a side of Clinton that so wants to please other people that he would hand this man back his pen. I found that really mind-blowing."

In *She Stoops to Conquer,* Oliver Goldsmith has a character offer this advice: "We must touch his weaknesses with a delicate hand. There are some faults so nearly allied to excellence, that we can scarce weed out the fault without eradicating the virtue. All his faults are such that one likes him the better for them." Some of Bill Clinton's foibles are endearing, others are enervating. Most of Clinton's critics have found his record not without its blemishes. Ernie Dumas says, "In Arkansas powerful groups have enormous influence in the legislature. The poultry industry, for example. The trucking industry, which absolutely controls western Arkansas. Hardly any member of the legislature would vote in a way that the poultry federation and trucking industry would object to. Everybody had their own opinion about whether Clinton gave in to the legislature too easily. He frequently gave in. Sometimes he waged a good fight. I think he was able to define where things were. He didn't want to be defeated so if the outcome didn't look good, he didn't take on the fight."

Mara Leveritt criticizes how Clinton handled (or didn't) a First Amendment dispute. "Our publication ended up fighting the state of Arkansas all the way to the U.S. Supreme Court and, of course,

Clinton was indirectly our opponent there. Now at the time, the [*Arkansas*] *Times* was a monthly magazine, and because of a fluke in how the tax law on publications was written back in the thirties, this kind of general interest regional magazine was not included as exempt. Every other type of publication was specifically named as exempted. We weren't specifically exempted because nothing like us existed when tax laws were written. The attorney general and the state tax revenue office decided that we would be taxed, making us the only publication in the state that was being taxed. We said that was not fair. We made several calls to the governor's office to say, 'Hey, you guys, let's just be reasonable about this.' And, of course, Clinton could have stopped the process at any moment with a phone call. He neither returned our phone calls or did anything about it, so we took the thing at great expense to us and to the state, to the Supreme Court. The Supreme Court ruled in our favor and the state then had to pay our attorney's fees as well. It was a very expensive proposition for Clinton to say nothing at the time. We didn't understand why he didn't just return our calls and let us talk to him. Maybe there was some good reason that he didn't but it ended up being a costly blunder. You would think that anybody who appreciated the First Amendment which is what the court ruled on, on the face of it would have seen that this is not an issue worth pressing but he never interceded so we had to fight all the way.''

Meredith Oakley strongly objects to Clinton's ''government by litigation. He did nothing about the welfare of children in this state, regardless of how anyone wants to portray it, until we were sued in federal court. The Department of Human Services was negligent in that it was not providing adequately for its clients. He knew of this well in advance and still left it until he was sued and then he suddenly called a special session to appropriate some money to pay the legal bills. Clinton's adminstration relied on delegation and litigation. If a problem developed he would form a task force or a study commission and they would study it for a year or two before coming up with some ideas. Some ideas would be introduced but most would not be. And then if the problems were so severe that any change made didn't improve the situation, well then, he would wait to be sued. We spent millions of dollars on lawsuits in this state simply because the executive branch and the legislature did nothing to heed the warning signals. And sometimes those signals were huge.

''One lawsuit dealt with the negligence of state agencies toward children and families particularly. We had foster children dying of abuse, cases of sexual and physical abuse in this state that caseworkers knew about and ignored. What was going on with the children of this state was a state tragedy and he did nothing. In the column I write, I am a very strong advocate of children's rights. And child abuse is just one of the things I periodically write about. I am passionate about it. Old folks, animals, and children should not be treated abusively. I wrote a column after the Daniel Toric case, the little boy who was returned to an abusive situation and only taken away from them permanently when criminal charges resulted. They jammed the little boy's leg into a bucket of scalding water and he lost his leg below the knee. People are doing time for this. I just let the passion flow in this column. I received an awful lot of input from the public, people who were experienced with the system. I had discovered what many people already knew, that the caseworkers were not only underpaid but that many were suffering from burnout. There were supervisors who were not supervising, children who were being permitted to stay in abusive situations with the knowledge of authority because caseworkers were helpless to do anything about it or were just too damn busy or too damn burned out. I found a system that was failing the children. He got a copy of the report during a session of the legislature but nothing was done to address these problems. "First we had to have a blue-ribbon panel," he said. In July, while that panel was still meeting, he got sued by one of the children's groups in California. So while Bill and Hillary were bleeding for the children of Arkansas, the children of Arkansas were bleeding. And nothing was done about it.

"The people of Arkansas, through this newspaper, told him chapter and verse, here is what you need to do to solve this problem. Months later a blue-ribbon panel came out with the same damn recommendations. Not verbatim, of course; they probably didn't have access to the report. The same recommendation. Nothing was done. Then we got sued. The state paid tons of damages.

"He knew what to do and didn't do it. There was a problem here and he ignored it, but he sure as heck had time to go flying around the country working on becoming president. And now I've got all these reporters coming in and saying, 'Please tell me about the wonderful things Bill and Hillary did for the children. I understand she's real big on children's issues.' While Daniel Toric was losing his leg an eighteen-year-old girl in south Arkansas was dying from anal rape. All these things were going on.

"I am not sure either one of them cares. I am saying that they care like all intellectually superior people care. They are, in their minds, intellectually superior people who have to take care of the unfortunate. You have to care about the great unwashed. That's what I'm saying about Bill and Hillary Clinton. Doesn't make them bad people."

Political science professor Gary Wekkin believes that, "Clinton was good for the state but wasn't everything he could have been. We're talking about a superbly endowed politician and a superbly endowed publicist. I felt that his stewardship was lacking because of the amount of time that he spent pursuing his own political interests."

Bill Bowen says "the public service is what drives him. He has little zest for acquisitiveness apparently. Give him a roof over his head, a Big Mac, and a little decaf coffee and let him run and wear shorts to work and he's happy."

Craig Smith points out that "everybody writes about McDonalds and how he goes there because he likes their coffee. Actually we didn't eat at McDonalds very often. He loves to eat at Taco Bell."

Paul Berry lived with Clinton for five months in the mid-seventies in the Plaza Tower apartments in Little Rock. Cooking for Clinton was no great challenge. "I did the cooking but the cooking mainly consisted of trying to keep bologna in the refrigerator and some bread. It was during those times that I learned of his affinity for peanut butter and bananas. A peanut butter and banana sandwich was one of his favorite things. I got him his own jar of peanut butter because he didn't necessarily use a knife to eat peanut butter directly out of the jar."

Jimmie Lou Fisher comments on Clinton's taste in food (and lodging) when he was on the campaign trail. "I don't want any sexual connotation out of this at all, but all the 'George Washington Slept Here' signs would be nothing compared to Bill Clinton's record. If we had a sign that said, 'Bill Clinton Slept Here,' probably 55 percent of the homes in Arkansas could post it. He didn't like country clubs, he much preferred a fish fry out on the riverbank or sitting down to some corn bread and salt pork than he would a fancy filet mignon. And everybody loved him for that. The boy does love to eat. The first restaurant that he and I stopped at was usually a barbecue or fast food place. He likes all kinds of food. I've never heard him say, 'I don't like that.' He's one of the few people I know who eats the entire apple, seeds, core, and all.''

Joan Duffy recalls, ''The first time I traveled with him was either in 1989 or very early in 1990 and it was when there was still a serious question as to whether he would seek another term as governor. We pulled into a McDonalds. He ordered a fish sandwich and was kind of aggravated because they made him wait for it and he was grumbling about 'They call it a fast food restaurant,' and that kind of thing. I told him if he was going to order something weird like a fish sandwich, then he needed to wait so shut up and wait. He ate like a pig too. I was going over my notes getting ready to interview him when I heard this sound from the front seat. I almost opened my mouth and said, 'Chew with your mouth closed' but I didn't. He just kind of chomps and talks and eats apples, core and all, and licks his fingers and is pretty much a pig.''

James Merriweather says, ''He does a lot of smacking. The last time I rode in a car with him, he ordered two of his favorite sandwiches and he just had a gleeful time eating as he rode from making a commencement speech back to Little Rock. He definitely had a good appetite.''

Newsman Mark Oswald also comments on Clinton's appetite. ''He gives the impression of being a big kid in a way. I'm trying to think of a good way to put it. Watching him eat sometimes, reminds you of how a kid eats. One of our reporters once had a tape. Clinton had given a talk in Conway, which is about twenty miles from Little Rock, and our reporter got time to do an interview with him in his limousine on the way back. The tape was great because they stopped someplace where Clinton liked the sandwiches. It wasn't a chain restaurant. It was some kind of a local joint that made great sandwiches and Clinton got two. On the tape you could hear our guy asking questions and then Clinton chomping through his sandwiches with his answers. We got a kick out of that.

''He was notorious for his appetite. I can remember one time, down in Pine Bluff, there was a high-tech bio-tech plant that was going to reopen so there was a press conference down there. It was a scorching hot day in the middle of the summer but they had a big tent set up with lots of food. I remember it was the day that Clarence Thomas was announced as Bush's Supreme Court nominee and we had already picked up that Clinton had been at

Yale the same time as Clarence Thomas, so I needed to hang around the little ceremony to try to ask him about it. He just gravitated over to this giant food table so it took me a while to get to talk to him.''

Another reporter who traveled with Clinton during the 1992 campaign says, ''One thing that amused me—and this is not really a fair example but of course we all knew his reputation and would make jokes like, 'Is the fork lift with the governor's lunch here yet?'—I just remember one afternoon, he was working his way back to his limo, through a bunch of citizens. I was with his crew and as we went around his car I glanced down through the window and saw a couple of cheeseburgers wrapped up sitting there on the backseat just waiting for him. I thought, 'Boy, if he could see that, he would forget about those 150 voters and make a B-line for the car,' but hell, if I could have had a couple of cheeseburgers waiting for me on the bus, I would have loved it too.''

Bill Lancaster particularly remembers Clinton's popcorn. ''I would see him at the movie theater a lot. He would always order double-buttered or triple-buttered popcorn and I had never seen that before. I asked him one time, 'How does that work?' And he said, 'Well, I'll show you.' They would fill the popcorn bag about a third of the way and then they would just load it down with butter and add a third more popcorn and then load it down with butter and pour on the top third and load it down with butter so he had triple-buttered popcorn. When I think of Saturday nights at the movies, I always think about that triple-buttered popcorn.''

Evaluating Clinton's career as governor, former Senator Ben Allen says, ''I served under Clinton all the time he was attorney general and while he was governor, of course, and it was a different, different experience. I served under every governor since Faubus and his was a totally different approach to the government. He was tenacious. He worked at things day and night during a legislative session and hell, he didn't think twice about calling me at midnight or at six o'clock in the morning. He was very effective with the legislature in Arkansas because he was so tenacious. He would stay with you until you worked out the deal. He would give and he would compromise, which I didn't tend to do, and he would just stay with the legislative problem like a dog with a bone. He'd shake it and stay with it and give and take until a job was done. We went to the Far East together for a couple of weeks some ten or fifteen years ago and he was the same way in hustling business for Arkansas. He'd get up at five o'clock in the morning and meet with the Japanese president or the president of Sanyo corporation or whomever that morning and he'd have another meeting at ten o'clock and another meeting at noon. He'd have another meeting at three and another meeting at dinner and then drink sake with someone until they would just give up. He was that tenacious."

For John Lipton, Clinton is less like a dog with a bone than like a cat. "There's one thing about Bill Clinton, he's just like a cat. You can drop a cat thinking he's going to hit on his back and he always lands on his feet. Never sell the man short. His greatest strength is his ability to personally communicate. His weakest trait is to be naive enough not to get good grass-root support and advise.

"Bill has a vision but there's a difference in having a vision and having the capability to carry through to the end result of that vision. He's a friend of mine, but if I have to say that he has a shortcoming, it's not in recognizing a problem, it's in carrying through and monitoring so that whatever solution is put in place is actually working. That's great but if you're going to be a visionary, you better have detail people to carry things out and you better monitor what you put into place."

The gap between Clinton's vision and its reality is filled, as many see it, with empty promises or insubstantial symbols. Bill Powell says, "I think that Clinton is a marvelous campaigner. He is the consummate politician. And most of the callers to my radio show don't like him because he doesn't tell the truth. He cannot in his own mind tell the truth. Before he was elected, in 1990, he promised the school teachers four thousand bucks. He gave them two hundred dollars before the election and promised them four thousand dollars if elected. Most of them haven't got it but guess who they voted for? Count every member of state government, take all of the people who work in the bureaucracy in the Arkansas state government. Take all of the commissions that he's appointed, and there are literally hundreds of them. Take all of the high rollers here in this state and their employees. There's a company right here in town where a friend of mine works who doesn't like Clinton, and wouldn't vote for Clinton, but he contributed to Clinton's campaign, because if he didn't he wouldn't have a job. Take a look at the 326,000 people he excluded from the tax rolls. Whom do you think they're going to vote for? I can sit down and, just with my meager imagination, give 450,000 to 500,000 votes going into every election. Without even thinking about it. I've watched Dick Daily at work. I've watched Bill Green at work in Philadelphia. I saw Carmine DeSappio in New York City. I know what a political machine is. They could all learn from Bill Clinton. He could put together a great political machine. That's a plus if you want to get elected.

"He cares only about getting elected. If he cared about people, if he cared about you, would he want to diminish what you could earn? If he really cared about you, would he be trying to get in your back pocket, to redistribute wealth? I think anybody who adheres to Keynesian economics cares not about people but only about power. Clinton is symbolism over substance. He's committed to what looks good and what sounds good this week. What can we do to make people think we're doing something. Symbolism over substance, always."

Paul Greenberg agrees. "My impressions of Clinton during his first campaign for governor? Very smooth. A kind of margarine-like political substance. He seemed sincere but he didn't seem to have much to be sincere about, since there didn't seem to be much substance to him."

Meredith Oakley finds the Clinton years hollow ones for Arkansas. "I think he improved after the first year. Do I think he became a good governor? No, I don't. When we get through with the hyperbole and the punditry I think history will show that there was very little substance."

Ed Gray, the book editor for the *Arkansas Democrat-Gazette*, also has reservations. "I like him. I have to say I do. There are a lot of things I don't like about him. He says things to get elected. He probably means them when he says them. But nonetheless, he's a slick politician and that side of him is almost revolting."

Eleanor Clift considers the gap between political expectations and realities. "I think his biggest sin is over-promising. I do think that he believes he can achieve what he promises. Even in the White House, they say that they have to convince him that he can't pay for everything out of the savings for reinventing government. He is a born optimist.

"If you measure his accomplishments by his promises, he's a failure but if you look at the accomplishments in isolation, he's brought us a long way on health care, on civil rights and for the gay people in the military, and I think pro-choice. I think he's done some good things but nowhere near to what the expectations were. It would have been inevitable for any Democrat after twelve years. Candidates are pressured to make specific promises and those pressures were greater than ever.''

Regina Blakely says, ''Bill Clinton will ask for the world but will settle for a country. He knows that's how the process works so he's going to ask for the entire world and then he's going to negotiate down but hold on to the things he really wants. You saw that in Arkansas and I think you're seeing it on a national level. Some see it as capitulation and losing whereas I think in the long run, it's all probably a strategy on his part.''

Achievements are relative. And some are less tangible, as Professor Roy Reed points out. ''More than any governor whom I've known in my lifetime he fought this self-image, as Hillary put it one time, this poor ol' Arkansas opinion. He and Hillary fought it simply by example. It was clear early on in his governorship that this was a guy bigger than Arkansas. He was always going around the country and even around the world. He was always being quoted and speaking out on the national issues. He began to make Arkansans think, 'You know, one of our guys is accepted out there in the big world.' ''

David Matthews believes that Clinton's ''greatest contribution, bar none, was that he got us out of the shadow of the Little Rock desegregation case and he made us believe that we didn't have to be last in everything. He just exuded hope and excitement and promise and realization that we as Arkansans were not inferior beings, that we could do whatever we wanted to do and that's his greatest contribution. You can't comprehend what it's like to have grown up in a state and to travel around the country and say to people, 'I'm from Arkansas,' and see the look in their eyes. 'This guy must be a bigot. He must be ignorant. He must be a hick.' Arkansans had a terrible self-image, and he changed that.''

Bob McCord speaks of Clinton's accomplishments. ''I've been covering governors here a long time and Governor Clinton is one of the best. Clinton promised early on that he was going to bring jobs to the state. That he was going to improve education and that he was going to try to heal some of the racism and the animosity that we had here in Arkansas since 1957 and I think he's done all three certainly better than any governor I have ever seen. Arkansas leads the country in industrial job growth. The dropout rate in Arkansas schools has been reduced tremendously. The curriculum has been improved. He appointed more women and more blacks to jobs than any governor before him so those are three things that he said he would do and, by George, he's done them. Not many governors can say that.

"He's also given Arkansas a good image which is terribly important. That's why I'm a fan of his.

"There's no question that he shifts and changes. He's a conciliator of the highest order and many people see that as a weakness. He keeps his options open; he's reluctant to commit. There are instances when I think he's gone overboard. I think he's overdone tax favors for industry, the grants, the concessions, and the tax laws. But he's accomplished what had to be done and what he promised that he was going to do. So I don't understand the hollow man theory, I really don't.

"If you take away the Rhodes scholarship, Clinton is typical of his generation. He talks too much. He eats too much. He likes rock-and-roll music. He's fascinated by stars. He vacillates. He didn't want to go to Vietnam. He grew up in a one-parent household for all practical purposes. Saw his mother abused and stopped it from happening. Plays the saxophone for God's sake."

At a dinner for radio and television correspondents two months after his inauguration, President Clinton flashed the self-deprecating wit many of his friends find so appealing. Referring to the Bush administration's attempt to dig up dirt on his Oxford days, Clinton quipped that when he first met John Major, the British Prime Minister told him, "You don't look a thing like your passport photo." A few days later, at a dinner for newspaper columnists and Washington bureau chiefs the president was equally ingratiating. But soon, his relationship with the White House press corps dissolved into a kind of anxious, barely civil, distrust. The offices of Press Secretary Dee Dee Myers and then Communications Director George Stephanopoulos were declared off-limits. One of the main reasons David Gergin was called in to replace Stephanopoulos as communications chief was to help repair the Clinton administration's frayed relations with the press.

Most of the folks who had covered Clinton in Arkansas found this somewhat puzzling. Clinton had always taken pains to cultivate members of the press, and even if he was not always accessible, he was almost always cooperative when cornered. He spent years cultivating some national reporters—Gergin, a Republican who left *Newsweek* to join Clinton's team, was an old friend. Rare was the reporter who came into personal contact with Bill Clinton and did not feel, on some level, courted. Sometimes the air of recruitment was thick enough to make some of us uncomfortable.

But then Clinton wants to win everyone over, to convert the planet person by person. He is a world-class schmoozer, and the crowded room is his natural habitat. And when the cynicism of the press meets the studied earnestness of Bill Clinton, odd things can and do happen.

Rex Nelson, political editor for the *Arkansas Democrat-Gazette*, speaks on Clinton's relations with the press during his gubernatorial years. "The first contact that I really remember is kind of an interesting experience. When he was governor during his first term I was the sports editor for the daily newspaper in Arkadelphia, a paper called the *Daily Siftings Herald*. I was covering the state high school basketball tournament. A little town called Okolona had one of the most highly recruited guards in the nation that year. His name was Ricky Norton, and one night during that tournament he was being heavily recruited by Kentucky. Joe B. Hall was coaching Kentucky at the time. He was there, and Eddie Sutton, the coach at the University of Arkansas, came down to the game. Governor Clinton attended the game with Sutton, sat with him the whole game, and went to the dressing room with Sutton and Norton. At the time, Nelson Catalina, the assistant coach at Arkansas State University at Jonesboro, was a friend of mine. He's now the head basketball coach there. After the game, Catalina came out livid and I said, 'What's wrong, Nelson?' He said 'Well, the governor ought to be the governor of all the state, wouldn't you think?' and I said, 'Oh, yes I agree completely.' He said, 'We're a state school just like the University of Arkansas, right?' and I said, 'Yeah.' And he said, 'The governor shouldn't play favorites.' I said, 'I agree.' He said, 'Well, he's in there with Sutton trying to recruit Ricky Norton to come to the University of Arkansas and we're also in the battle for this kid. I don't think it's right.' So I went back to Arkadelphia and wrote a sports column in which I said exactly that. The governor doesn't have any business picking sides and picking the University of Arkansas over Arkansas State University. He needs to stay out of sports and stick to politics. A few days after that I got a letter from Clinton. He had handwritten the letter with a felt-tip pen, and it was a long letter too. Chelsea, his daughter, had just been born. He said he was home babysitting Chelsea that night at the Governor's Mansion and had read my column. The letter, which was almost a little tacky, showed that he had a tremendously thin skin. It made me mad in fact. It started something to the effect, of 'I know you might find this hard to believe, but I was just there to watch a basketball game.' Well, I came back and wrote another column that said, 'If he loves high school basketball so much, why hasn't he been seen at any games in Little Rock? There were games all year he could have gone to there. He was obviously invited to the game by Sutton to help Sutton recruit Norton.' You'll hear so many tales around Arkansas like that about Clinton's first term. The governor with a thin skin. The governor who really ticked people off when he should have been cozying up to the press. He did make me mad with that letter and it did show an extremely thin skin I think for a governor to take the time to write a hand-written letter to a sports editor of a small-town daily newspaper, something you wouldn't think he would normally be reading.

"You would expect a John Robert Starr as managing editor of the *Arkansas Democrat* or an Ernie Dumas at the *Arkansas Gazette* to be getting letters from the governor which they did, but I was just sports editor of a tiny daily newspaper in Arkadelphia. I mean, why is the governor even taking time to recognize my existence? It made me feel good. Let me contrast that to an incident that occurred in 1983. By that point, I was editor of the Arkadelphia newspaper and I was invited to lunch with the governor at the Governor's Mansion. I was told it was an off-the-record lunch for journalists from smaller papers. This was the new Clinton. The old Clinton in his first term would write a handwritten letter and blast me. The new Clinton would have you to lunch, off the record, so instead of asking him questions, it was mainly him asking me and these other small-town editors, 'What do you think about this? What do you think I should do? How do you think I did? What would you have done if you were in my shoes?' and he was obviously playing to our egos. It seemed like he cared and he was genuinely interested in what we thought.

"Personally I've always liked him. I think he has a short fuse and a temper, but so do I. They took all of our pictures standing with the governor at the off-the-record lunch almost as if it's a campaign appearance instead of a media opportunity. Three or four days later, I got this photo of me and Bill Clinton with a handwritten note on the bottom of the photo saying, 'Thanks for all of your help, Bill.' I think those two incidents summed up the change between Bill Clinton in 1980 and in 1983.

"Now a few years down the line, by the time I was in Washington working for the *Arkansas Democrat* as their Washington correspondent, he was a master at schmoozing with the media and making people think he really cared. National media types would fall all over themselves to go cover or go talk to the governor of the state of Arkansas. I remember one incident in particular, it was a National Governors' Association meeting and Joe Klein, who at that time was at *New York* magazine, came up to Clinton and Clinton made the point of saying, 'Joe, I just read your article on whatever it was, X, Y or Z, and I thought it was wonderful. I thought this point was good, that point was good.' It was obvious Clinton had actually read the article but also he was playing to Klein's ego, was already cultivating him, and by the time he would run for president, Klein would be at *Newsweek*, one of the major publications in the country, and would be one of the nation's most influential political writers. Now, you have a hard time finding *New York* magazine in Arkansas but Clinton had it and had read it and used it to cultivate Klein. I remember that incident, I found it extremely instructive. I also remember several instances when Clinton would come to town and he would have had appointments until late at night but he would call and invite me and Maria Henson, who was the *Arkansas Gazette* correspondent in Washington, to breakfast the next morning. Now most people would have been in bed resting from the night before but Clinton was never one to waste time. He was making every second count and meeting the *Arkansas Democrat* and *Arkansas Gazette* Washington correspondents for breakfast. He was bad in 1980. He was already getting good in 1983, and by 1986–1988, he was a master at schmoozing the media and using his time wisely by making every second count politically.''

Of Clinton's off-the-record editorial sessions with the press former managing editor of the *Arkansas Gazette* John Hanchette says, ''He was very smart because to find out what both papers were thinking, he would allow them to have some of their editorial sessions in the Governor's Mansion three or four times a year. You'd go over there and he'd have breakfast with you and, of course, he loves to talk policy and stuff but when you start talking with him, you end up being interviewed by him. He'll ask you questions and he'd turn it into a debate on some subject but by doing that he'd find out what was on the mind of the editorial writers and he'd learn what was going to be in the paper. He was very clever at that. And, of course, everybody liked to go the Mansion and get to fire questions at him. The editorial writers always seemed to want to leave before he did. He would sit there and talk to you for as long as you wanted to talk. He still does that today. He's famous for putting off appointments until he's finished with one. He was talking about a matter of state policy but he got off on so many wide-ranging subjects and talked so much about national and international issues and his work with the National Governors Association and how he knew other governors that it struck me right then that the reports that he had national ambitions were true.

"I guess my first impression was how easygoing he was. I've talked to a lot of governors. They always seemed to be more formal and less comfortable talking with reporters. You start talking with him and a thought goes through your mind, 'Gee, this guy is sort of an average Joe and I can relax.' That's what everybody says about him. He started talking to me. He asked about my background but obviously already knew it; I had mentioned that I had covered Bob Graham who was governor in Florida for many years and he launched into Graham stories. When he sort of let out a little breath of air, Hillary broke up this particular session because Chelsea was going off to school and wanted him to review her homework. This ritual later became famous because he used to do it on the campaign plane. She'd fax her homework to him.''

Doug Smith, now associate editor for the *Arkansas Times,* also attended Clinton's breakfasts. "When I became an editorial writer, he would regularly invite us all out for breakfast when he was proposing to have a new tax program or something and we all would sit around the Mansion and eat a very big breakfast. He does like to have a good breakfast. Clinton would try to sell you on his ideas and he knew that some of us would be skeptical about them. The *Gazette,* for example, was always reluctant to endorse raising the sales tax unless there was no other way to accomplish some needed goal and so he would explain, 'We looked at trying it through an income tax or a severance tax but it just won't work out.' He was very good with numbers and explaining all this stuff. He was very slick at that and he would try to explain to you why this other proposal wouldn't work and why his plan was in fact the only one. He would generally listen to us but I don't think we influenced him. [Ernie] Dumas, in particular, would sometimes argue about things. These were fairly heated discussions because neither liked to admit they were wrong, but I don't think anything got changed. One of the press' problems with Clinton is that a lot of people thought in the beginning, 'This guy's really going to listen to me and I can be like an adviser in really helping set the course of the state,' and I don't think he really did listen to the press all that much. He was mainly presenting his ideas and trying to neutralize any opposition that might be building up out there and I didn't hold that against him. That's the way he operated.''

John Brummett has had his ups and downs with Clinton. ''Before I became a columnist when I was a state Capitol reporter, I wrote a page one analytical piece about how he had mishandled a certain matter affecting the highway tax bill which he ended up vetoing. This was in 1985. He vetoed it, but sort of as a scam because as he vetoed it he wouldn't fight the override. It was so transparent that I wrote a little analytical piece. He called to say that he thought I was on target and he had mishandled it and he thought it was a good article. Usually, most of the calls were of the other variety when he didn't like something.

''After his address in Atlanta at the 1988 National Convention I made several references to how he tried to blame everybody else for his bad speech. I wrote that he shouldn't run again in 1990 and that Hillary ought to run instead. Sometime after that he was giving a speech to the senior Democrats of Arkansas and I was in the audience. I made eye contact with him and noticed he was writing on the back of an envelope, writing on the flap, drawing arrows all over the place and I thought, 'Well, I guess that's how Clinton writes his speeches' you know he's terrible at preparing text, he's just outlining some remarks. After the event was over, he shouted for me and I came up and it was a note to me. Upon seeing me there, he decided to tell me off and this was a note about the various things in columns that I'd written recently that were wrong. He had arrows going through the flap, #4 continued back side. He said, 'You're just being unfair and unfortunately you'd prefer to write without contact,' because he prefers to have contact with people who write about him. And he also said, 'Hillary knows better than I what makes people like you tick.' And I thought that was interesting. I think it reflects a general truth about that couple. Clinton has the poorer judgment and depends on Hillary to make a lot of his judgments for him especially about people. He told me once that she's the most brilliant and compassionate person he's ever known. He said so in sort of a defensive tone because, well, the conversation got started when he said, 'I understand from some of the campaign people that you don't like Hillary.' He pressed and I said, 'Well, I think she's kind of cold and rigid.' He then, not angrily but in a spirited way, told me why I was totally wrong. He said I had no earthly idea how wonderful she was. I think it's interesting that he talks about her brilliance and compassion.''

Ernie Dumas remembers calls of the other variety. ''I remember one call in particular. I had just gotten to work so I guess it was about 8:15. The phone rang. 'Hello, this is Bill Clinton. What do you mean writing this?' And I forgot the full commentary but there was some bad language in there. 'This goddamn piece of shit' or something like that. He went on and on for what seemed like a couple of days. And I said, 'Wait a minute, wait a minute. What are you talking about?' He said, 'This editorial.' I said, 'What editorial?' He said, 'The one about higher education.' I said, 'I haven't written anything about higher education.' 'You haven't? You didn't write that thing this morning?' I said, 'No. I didn't write that.' He said, 'Who did?' I said, 'It was Jim Powell. Governor, let me switch you to Jim Powell.' 'No,' he said, 'I don't want to go through this again. I've gotten it off my chest. I feel pretty good now. I don't want to get mad again. Are you going to tell him what I said?' I said, 'Yeah.' So then he warmed up and he just talked another thirty minutes about everything under the sun. He has flashes of temper but it's a very momentary thing. As far as I can remember, I've never known him to hang up without kind of smoothing it over. He gets it off his chest and then its as if it never happened; he's just as warm as he could be.

''I was at the art center one night at a reception that my wife and I went to. Clinton was shaking hands with everybody and as I came through he grabbed my hand and he wouldn't turn it loose. I had this crowd behind me and he just held on to my hand and told me how much he'd disliked some of my recent editorials. I was arguing with him but really basically trying to get loose. I was a little embarrassed about the people standing around. Although he was speaking in a little voice that they couldn't hear, they could probably see from his face that it was not just a pleasant conversation. Later we wound up spending what seemed like an hour with Bill Clinton there around the shrimp bowl. Most people had left and he was just talking with us about what Ronald Reagan was doing to this country. He was saying that he's just destroying the middle class and that he did great harm to the poor people . . . the usual stuff about rich people but never anything else about our earlier conversation. That little three- or four-minute conversation was forgotten. I also remember getting mail from him. He would rip out editorials and write all over them, grab an envelope, address it himself (you could barely read his handwriting) and ship it off to you. It may have had nothing to do with him. It may have been an editorial on food stamps or Afghanistan. If you'd been writing about something or another, and he found an article in *The New Yorker* or the *Atlantic* or something, he'd ask somebody to photocopy it and he'd send it to you and write a little note. 'This has got some great insight. What do you think about this?' He would send those things to everyone from time to time. That's what he does.

"In about 1985 I wrote a column about his education program that said, 'Well, sure Bill Clinton's done some pretty good things about education but actually there are other governors who have done even more.' Two days later I got an eleven-page letter— eleven pages, single-spaced—to the editor responding to my column and so I sent it back with a letter to his press secretary, Joan Roberts, and asked her, 'You want this thing serialized or just a special edition?' "

Reporter Guy Reel recalls an hour or so with Clinton. "We went into Diego's (a Little Rock restaurant) to have a couple of beers, Scott Charton and I, and the governor walks in with his family, Hillary, Chelsea, and I believe Virginia might have been there too. Clinton obviously is there to have a good time with his family but he sees me and Scott at the bar and walks over and gladhands with us and has a beer with us and the people at the bar for I'd say a good hour just totally ignoring his family. We thought that was funny just because it was obvious to us that the only reason he was doing that was because we were reporters and he'd thought it might help his relations with us and didn't really care about his family. That was my impression of that event. You could see that Hillary didn't look happy but she never looked that happy. She always looked like she was steamed about something."

John Reed considers Clinton's apparent accessibility to the press. "I first met him in 1984 at the Little Rock Hilton. He was going there to speak to a statewide meeting of African Americans. It was a very religious group, one of those civic groups, a fraternal order, where they all get dressed up, and he spoke to them. As usual Bill Clinton was very comfortable with an all black crowd and was very good. He carried the day. I was there just because my father was there to meet him. I was hanging around in the lobby and as Clinton is wont to do, he shook hands with everybody in the lobby which made him late going in but nobody seemed to care. As a political reporter for the *Gazette*, covering the cabinet and Bill Clinton's administration, one thing I found was that you had this contrast between a man who is so accessible to the public and a political figure who is, at other times, extremely inaccessible. He's always been very good about controlling his message. All those times you would just run into him in the hallway and get a great hallway interview seemed so spontaneous but I realize now, in retrospect, they probably were not. He knew exactly what he was going to say, what he was going to get on the news. He knew that those newspaper men and their notebooks and the TV guys with their cameras were out there and that they would come follow him and he would get his message of the day across.

"He was a great one for roaming the halls. Some people thought that kind of behavior was demeaning to the office because past governors had always done their business from their offices and if they needed to talk to a legislator, they'd send for the guy and the legislator would go to the office. Clinton was the exact opposite. It seemed like he was always here. I have a vivid image of Bill Clinton sipping coffee from a styrofoam cup and leaning on a door and just watching the action, kind of doing what his lobbyists were doing as well. Just making sure his guys were inside and weren't going to take a walk on him, that he was there to answer questions if there were any.

"He was open when he was ready to be open. It's only now that I realize that his accessibility was planned. But let's say there's some story developing that's not so favorable to him, such as when Larry Nichols got fired. Now his staff could just as soon not have that come up and a stone wall would go up around his office. You just could not get to him. We attributed it to Betsey Wright. Prior to Betsey Wright, he had a press secretary named Joan Roberts who was very good and very fair but also very tough in controlling access to him. These strong women realized that left to his own nature, to his own devices, he'd be an hour late to every event because he would sit there and talk and talk and talk and he would be too accessible. (And he was accessible once you actually made physical contact with him. He would take the time to answer your questions in amazing detail.) He's the wonk, I think is the new word they have for him. He's a stark contrast with Reagan who'd wave and walk by with his dog and he would never answer a thing even though you could actually make eye contact with Reagan. I mean, if you actually got to Clinton, he would open up and give you just about all the time you wanted. One time when he called me back on the phone I was just amazed. I didn't realize how unusual that was at the time. It was a Sunday night and it's pretty sleepy around a newspaper on a Sunday night. Something happened that day and I had to get a comment from him and I thought, I'll never get a comment from Bill Clinton on a Sunday night but I called the Governor's Mansion and left a message anyway. Twenty minutes later the phone rings and it's Bill Clinton on the phone. I realize now that it was all planned and they knew that they could probably control Monday's news cycle, but to be fair to him, I think he honestly enjoys that give-and-take. I think he really likes reporters.''

KARN radio talk show host Pat Lynch reveals another way that Clinton controlled messages. ''I've been interviewing Bill Clinton since 1983. He is a brilliant person. I like him enormously. I even support his policies. Many times when interviewing Bill Clinton I always had the idea that I hadn't gotten much in the way of answers. And for the longest time I blamed myself. Then I saw his first interview with Dan Rather and I knew it wasn't me. Clinton, at one time, was just shameless about jamming the phone lines and planting his own calls. In other words he'd produce his own enemies. He'd know what the negative question was, but he'd plant somebody to ask it in a specific way so that he could frame his answer and be in charge of setting the agenda. He's not the only guy to do this so we developed a strategy. When we have these people in, they fill up the call board first thing, and we just take the calls, answer them, put them all on hold, and then when we get ready to take calls, we just hang up on all of them and start over again. We'd just blow off the whole bunch of them.

''Clinton is very, very smart and he's very personable. And there is a genuinely decent person inside. He is so political and he is such a capable politician that it's a little scary.''

Former Little Rock TV journalist Tom Atwood says, ''I just remember that after I talked to him the first time and we shook hands, he said, 'What's your name?' I said, 'Tom Atwood.' And he kind of looked at me and said, 'I'll remember that.' I kind of thought, 'Yeah, sure you will.' But he does remember names and that's one thing that's amazed me about him is it seems like he can remember everybody's name. I've covered governors in three states and he was by far the most open, most accessible governor or politician whom I've ever covered. He only ran away from me once and that was in 1988 when he was considering running for president and I think he was just really fed up with all the questions. On this day, Cuomo had dropped out. Clinton was coming into the Capitol and I said, 'Governor, Mario Cuomo dropped out. Does that change your plans at all?' He said, 'Look, I can't talk to you right now. I've really got to go up and find out about this.' But all the other times, he'd never run away from questions. He might dodge them but he would always stand there and take it. We were really pretty easy on him. Clinton was always better in terms of response if you provoked him a little bit. I mean, just ask a pointed question and he seemed to like it. He would like the back and forth. He generally would give a better response and get right to the point. It never really seemed to bother him to be asked those pointed confrontational questions but it did bother Hillary. I once asked what I thought was a pointed question and she said 'I can't believe you asked that.'

"One of the worst moments of my career involved an interview with Bill Clinton. It was the night of the primary election in 1986. He had just defeated Orval Faubus in the primary, the governor's race. We were at his campaign headquarters at about ten o'clock and he had come out to give his victory speech to about a thousand of his supporters. To give you an idea of how intimate things were in Arkansas in terms of how politicians were covered, he was up on the platform but there was not one mike that fed sound to everybody—the reporters literally stood right next to him and held their own mikes. I was standing on his right and Chris Phillips, a reporter from channel 7, was on his left and other reporters were around him and we all held mikes to pick up the sound. He had started to give his victory speech and he was thanking everybody and it really was kind of a boring speech when in my earpiece, I heard my producer say, 'You know, this is really pretty bad. We need to get moving here. Let's pin-cushion him.' That's a really weird practice that we used to do there. It's where you take an earpiece, what we call an IFB and, instead of me interviewing Clinton, you would say, 'Governor, I've got our anchor and he'd like to talk to you,' and you stick it in his ear. The other stations are sort of taken out of the interview because it's your anchor asking questions. Other viewers can't hear it. It's a real competitive thing and there's a dog fight every election to try to get that exclusive interview but I hated the practice because I just thought it was much better for everyone to just ask him questions and just let everybody have access.

"So it seemed real inappropriate to me and I didn't like it

anyway and it was in the middle of his speech. This was not a news conference or even an interview. It was his acceptance speech before his supporters so I just stood there. A couple of minutes later, the producer came back on and said, 'This is really boring. come on, stick it in his ear.' And I was thinking to myself 'It's not right.' I didn't do it. The next voice I heard was the news director and I do remember his words. He said, 'Atwood, if you want to keep your goddamn job stick it in his goddamn ear.' And I'd only been in TV for a couple of years and I thought, 'Well, it's not worth getting fired over.' So, I waited for him basically to take a breath and then I reached for my earpiece. The plan was, our station had Orval Faubus so they planned to have a split screen with Orval Faubus and Bill Clinton. I was to say, 'Governor, I've got Orval Faubus for you to talk to.' As soon as I reached for my earpiece, Chris Phillips from channel 7 reached for hers and she was much better at it than I was because she had done it more, so at the same moment in time, we both had our thumbs in Clinton's ears and the crowd gasped and the newspaper photographers' light bulbs went off pop, pop, pop, and that was the picture on the front page of the newspaper the next day—Clinton with his eyes wide open and two thumbs in his ears. The bottom line is, she knew how to do it. I had never done it before. She got hers in. Mine fell out and they got the interview. It was disastrous and I was kind of embarrassed about it anyway. After it was all over, we were kind of cleaning up and Clinton was still there shaking hands. I went up to the governor and I said, 'Gee, I'm really sorry about that,' thinking that he might kind of slap me on the back and say, 'Oh, it's okay, Tom,' but he just looked at me and said, 'Yeah, that was really weird.' It really was. He never mentioned it again and I don't know if he even remembers it. I just thank God that the front page picture of him with two thumbs in his ears is a tight shot so you can't see whose thumb it is.''

Former KARK news director Bob Steele recalls, ''I had a political reporter named Tom Atwood who's fantastic. The guy's at Nashville now and he covered Clinton all the time at the legislature and they liked each other. The primary election night came, and Atwood's at the campaign headquarters with Clinton. My competition has a woman reporter named Kelly Mitton who is beautiful. So Clinton gets through with his speech and then of course everybody rushes the podium to try to get in questions. Well, Kelly gets in there and just kicks Atwood's butt. Question after question after question and I'm going, 'My God, I can't believe it. He's getting his ass kicked, and he's usually so good with this guy.' The next day I call a friend of mine inside of the Clinton inner circle and I said, 'You know, we got our ass kicked. I can't believe it. Is he mad at us? Why didn't he talk to us?' and she said, 'You sent a *man*, Steele,' like I'm an idiot, and it just hit me. 'You're kidding me. It's that simple?' and she said, 'Yeah, Mitton looked fantastic. He kept telling her how good she looked.' I'm going, 'Oh God.' So when the general election came round I called an intern who was knock-down gorgeous into my office. I said, 'Listen, I'm going to ask you to do something but I want you to know why I'm doing this. It's a very sexist thing to do but apparently our governor is attracted to females and I don't know if that's true but I want you to wear a yellow dress and it's better if it's low-cut and you can say no. This is not an order. I'm just asking you to be an assistant to Tom Atwood on election night. If he needs an interview, help escort the interviewee over and bring him Cokes cause he'll be all wired up.' She said, 'Sure.' Election night comes. Clinton goes right to us. I mean like a goddamn magnet.''

KARK anchor Margaret Preston also remembers the competition to get Clinton's ear. ''I think one of my biggest kudos was in Little Rock on election night in 1988. The crowd was humongous and we were trying to get to him. I ran out of microphone chord. He was speaking on behalf of Dukakis. It was my job to get the governor's reaction as the election returns came in because he and Dukakis were friends. I grabbed him by the sleeve to try and pull him over to my microphone but he was very much interested in talking with the people in the crowd first. He knew that it was my hand on his coat sleeve and he looked at me and he kind of smiled and he just gently pulled away as if to say, 'You know, I can't do this right now. My primary obligation is to the people who are here.' Well, he finally did have time for us. He got up on the podium which was elevated, and I got pushed off. I fell off the stand and somebody pushed me back up. Another reporter slipped an IFB in his ear and when I saw that it just freaked me out because every reporter's wish is to be the first one to have someone like the governor respond to your question and I thought I'd lost him. He'd never hear me and I had a question prepared. When I saw that happen, I just kind of lost it and I just started screaming, 'Governor Clinton, Governor Clinton. What about blah-blah' and he turned and he looked at me because I was screaming his name so loud I think. And he said, 'What Margaret? I can't hear you.' and he pulled the IFB out of his ear. It was like, 'I won.' I think he did that because he does tend to be more attentive to people who are in his presence than to tune into something as remote as someone talking in his ear. Everybody back here was watching both our coverage and our competitor's coverage and so they knew immediately what had happened. They saw him pull it out of his ear. They knew that the other station had lost all communications with him and he turned to me and he said, 'What Margaret? I can't hear you.' It was great. I loved it.''

Nor will Preston forget the first time she covered Clinton. ''I think the first time I met him in person I was just a junior in college. I was studying photojournalism. It was during the summer. I was pregnant, very pregnant, and it was my first photo assignment. It was just a regular news conference with the governor and I was really excited because it was a big deal to me. I got there and I was trying to remember all the textbook stuff, all the different angles. One of the things that I was taught was to get different perspectives. He was sitting, so I got on the floor to get an upward perspective. I got down there and I couldn't get up and I was at his right arm, very near him. He kept looking at me and he interrupted the news conference and he asked, 'Are you all right?' and I said, 'Yes I'm fine.' He said, 'Can you get up?' and I said, 'Yes,' but I couldn't. And he said, 'Do you need some help?' and I said, 'No, I'm really fine.' I wasn't a journalist, I was a student, and all the major TV stations and all the major radio stations were there and all the newspapers were there and I'm sure they were wondering who is this person, but he was very kind. I sat on the floor for the entire news conference until everybody left.''

Bob Steele views Clinton from a different angle too. ''In 1990 we had a huge flood. I knew he must be running for something because he came down and stood in the rain next to the river on a lifeboat to get on the *Today* show. I mean, the guy would do anything to get on the air, but he was wearing a suit at this big flood in Pine Bluff. The reporter down there, Melinda Dunston, was in jeans, dressed appropriately for the story and here's the governor in a suit. It looked stupid, so after she brought the video in I called him and I said, 'You know, it's just a little TV thing but you should dress appropriately to the story and anytime you go into a flood or a tornado, a dedication of a park or something outdoors—don't wear a suit. It looks dumb.' He never wore a suit again in a flood. I said, 'Remember Lyndon Johnson in Vietnam?

He didn't jump out of the chopper in a suit.' That's my little contribution. Anytime you see him at a flood or a major catastrophe notice what he's wearing. If he's got a suit on, he's forgotten my advice.''

Governor Clinton was no power dresser. He was no snob, either, when it came to things sartorial. Clinton wore what was handy and what he liked. The governor's wardrobe elicits considerable comment. Former housemate Paul Berry says, ''The Bill Clinton I've known most of my life has never been what I'd consider a power dresser at all. He's not meticulous that way and I guess that's a little bit of the sixties influence in his style—it wasn't quite as important to have on your Brooks Brothers three piecer.''

Clinton's style in sports attire is also sometimes wanting. Berry relates, ''One day, my phone rang and it was my buddy Mickey Cissell who is also a friend of Clinton's. We made plans to play golf the next day. We agreed to meet at two o'clock at the Little Rock Country Club. Well, about one o'clock the phone rang and it was Governor Clinton. He said, 'What are you doing this afternoon?' I said, 'I'm meeting Mickey Cissell at two o'clock to play golf,' and he said, 'Can I play too?' I said, 'Yes, but on one condition.' He said, 'What's that?' and I said, 'That we don't talk about any of your governor's stuff,' and he said, 'Oh, okay, okay.' I ran out there. I didn't have any golf pants so I just played with my suit pants on. I bought a golf shirt. I had some shoes and clubs in my car. And here comes Clinton; he gets up on the first tee and I look over and he's got some kind of golf pants on that aren't quite right. It's that Clinton style. You can see through his golf pants and he doesn't have on bikini underwear, but he's got on some wild kind of underwear.

''I looked at him and I said, 'God bless him, Mickey, look at the governor,' and he said, 'Yep. Here we are trying to have a relaxed round of golf and we're gonna' have to look at him in those flimsy golf pants and that loud squirmy underwear all the way around the golf course.' He blushed and we had him on roller skates the rest of the afternoon, but he got me back as a matter of fact. I wasn't dressed properly either and he started giving me hell about wearing pin-striped George Raft gangster pants. I guess I shouldn't tell that story because presidential undergarments are probably not newsworthy. But we were giving each other the devil and that's one of the reasons why I enjoy his company. Whatever his office has been, when we get to the golf course and there's no one else around, he's one of the guys, because he's always been one of the guys.''

Jimmie Lou Fisher says, ''He shared a lot of the duties at home. I remember going over to the Mansion for an interview because he was trying to figure out which staff position I should have. He was getting ready to go to work and having trouble finding a matching pair of socks out of the dryer. He was not a clotheshorse. He always just bought suits off the rack. And you know, a man of his size was not easy to fit off the rack. So it wasn't so much his choice in clothes that was bad, it was just that they weren't tailored.''

Joan Duffy says, ''He's kind of a dork and I'll tell him so to his face. I'd make fun of his haircuts and his high-water pants. Once I saw him in Baton Rouge for a meeting of Louisiana's Democratic party, and he had on a nice suit. I looked at him and said, 'Nice suit.' He said, 'Well, I've had this suit for a while,' and I said, 'That's how I can tell if you're running for president or not. When you wear those high-water pants, I figure, uh-uh. You start wearing a nice looking suit, I figure, any day now, he's going to announce.' He laughed and then the next time I saw him in Baton Rouge, he had on the ugliest pair of high-water, too-tight, seersucker pants and I said, 'Oh, scratch you from the list.' Then he got a haircut one time and I said, ''Ooh, did you pay money for that?' and he got all offended and said, 'Well, it's not a bad haircut,' and I said, 'It's pretty ugly.' It looked like he stuck it in a pencil sharpener. Sometimes he'd take it and a lot of times he wouldn't know it was a joke and you'd have to tell him, 'Excuse me, it's a joke, get it?' 'Oh, okay. I get it.' ''

Pat Lynch saw Clinton's haircut differently. ''One of my most vivid memories of Bill Clinton was in the Snyder Corporation men's room. I was washing my hands and he was standing at the urinal. I looked at him from the back and he looked just like JFK. This was while he was still governor, and I thought it's remotely possible that this man using the urinal right now might some day be president of the United States. Then I thought, 'Nah.' ''

Lynch recalls another occasion: ''It would probably have been August of 1990. I was going into Juanita's Mexican Restaurant. I was opening the front door and a guy down the street, kind of a grungy-looking guy with a cap on his head said, 'Hey, Pat. Hey, Pat.' He's waving at me and I just want to go inside and have a drink and eat. He comes closer and I can see that this fellow in a baseball cap and just covered with sweat is the governor of Arkansas. I concede to being nearsighted—quite nearsighted—but he must have really given himself a tremendous run that day because it didn't look much like him. I just about snubbed him. I was thinking 'Here's another yahoo trying to take up my time.' Doggone and it turns out to be Bill Clinton.''

Bill Bowen says, "His staff loved him. Mike Gaulden said one time, 'If I didn't love and respect him, I wouldn't be interested.' I've never seen such affection. They never talked behind his back. They might criticize the way he looked—somedays he'd need a haircut—or joke about his clothes. Until he ran for public office, his suits looked like they'd been hanging on a nail. They looked terrible.

"He has an absolutely voracious appetite. He would eat quite often and he would get through an enormous plate of spaghetti and tomato sauce. He never ate at fancy places. He was a meat and 'taters kind of guy. And he was very much an off-the-rack kind of guy. I think he took pride in it. Like Sam Walton said, 'I never bought a suit that wasn't off the rack.' He bought a suit when we thought he was running for president back in 1987. Somebody tipped off John Brummett and he wrote this whole column saying that Clinton's definitely running for president because he bought a thousand-dollar suit. That's the last time I saw him in that suit. He never put on another nice suit after that."

James Merriweather comments on Clinton's taste in ties. "He was always admiring my neckties and my suits and I told him, 'Well, you should get some nice suits.' He said, 'Well, people expect the governor to be more mundane.' As it turns out, he still wears those blue and red striped ties from time to time and I always advised him to stay away from those. They're supposedly power ties but I always told him it wouldn't hurt him to get a paisley or two. He wished that he was able to be a snappy dresser but he thought that being governor, he should just stick to the more basic kind of things."

Craig Smith recalls one occasion when Clinton evidently chose a less basic kind of thing. "He wears some loud ties. We were in New York, Al From, Clinton, Kiki Moore, and I and he was fixing to do some editorials for the *New York Times* and the *Wall Street Journal*. We were all getting ready to go to our first stop, the *New York Times*. He walked out of his room wearing one of his louder ties and Al and Kiki came to me and said, 'You cannot let him wear that tie. This is the *New York Times*. You've got to say something to him about the tie.' I said, 'Governor,' and he said, 'What's wrong?' I said, 'Do you really want to wear that tie?' This was in 1991 when he was thinking about running for president. He said, 'I'm not going to let a bunch of handlers tell me how to dress. Come on, let's get out of here,' and he walked out. Al and Kiki were on the other side of the room just rolling and they're saying, 'Look, he has to take the hit on this one.' One of the guys at the *New York Times* said, 'Clinton, that's a pretty flashy tie you got on.' So later in the day Clinton asked me, 'You think this tie is a little bit much?' I said, 'Well, you know, it'll be fine for now but. . . .' It was not a pretty day.''

Gwen Ifill, too, remembers Clinton's "one vanity"—ties. "The first time I met him he was governor and I remember him having big hair, big lapel suits with sharp lapels that it seemed to me couldn't possibly have been made in Arkansas, and big flowery ties. When he ran for president, he had to give all of that up. He had to cut his hair and wear more conservative suits. The only thing he ever complained about was his ties. He really hated having to wear 'funeral ties,' which is what he called the red and blue striped ties that his media advisers told him to wear. The minute the campaign was over, he went back to wearing wild ties again."

Chuck Carroll was Clinton's tailor in Little Rock. "When he was governor, he was a good customer of ours. We're a real traditional store. He is the kind of a man who looks good in a traditional cut. He's gone into the more European look, Italian suits. I had a discussion about him last summer with Chris Shalley who is the costume designer for *Evening Shade* and *Designing Women*. He asked me what I thought about his clothes and I thought and I still do that they don't look very presidential.''

Running or Not

By early 1987, there were widespread rumors that Clinton would seek the Democratic presidential nomination the following year. With Ronald Reagan's eight-year reign about to end, Bill and Hillary Clinton—and many of their supporters and staffers—thought 1988 would be the year for the Democrats to return to the White House. In early July, the speculation increased when it was revealed that the Clintons had bought a condominium in Little

Rock for Hillary's parents. The supposition was that Chelsea's grandparents would move to Little Rock so they could take care of Chelsea while Bill and Hillary were on the campaign trail.

On July 6, Hillary Clinton promised that her husband would announce his decision in the next two weeks. All signs were that the race was on. But eight days later, Bill stunned supporters—and many journalists—by announcing in a press release that he would not run. The Clintons had scheduled a news conference for the next day, and it had been widely believed that Bill would use the event to announce the formation of an exploratory committee for his campaign. Ray Strother, a well known Democratic consultant, was already in town planning media strategy.

Friends of the couple remained convinced that Bill was planning to run for president in 1988. And they still don't know what happened to change his mind at the last moment. Gary Hart of Colorado had been forced out of the race following the Donna Rice affair, and some feel that questions about Clinton's alleged marital infidelities would have hurt his candidacy and, in the process, destroyed his future political viability. In any event, a teary-eyed Clinton told the press the main reason he had decided not to run was because he did not want to subject his daughter Chelsea to the glare of the campaign.

Clinton later said the decision was a "tug-of-war" because 1988 appeared "tailor-made for my candidacy." Later he would say he "knew in his heart" it wasn't his time. Earlier in the year he had said if he did not run for president in 1988, he might never have another chance. But Bill said during his July news conference that he no longer believed that to be the case. "If I get another chance, I'll be 110 percent," he said.

When asked what role potential questions about his personal life played in his decision, Bill said he had decided how the couple would handle questions about his personal life but declined to discuss it further "because I'm not a candidate."

"I think there are worse things than going to your grave knowing that you lived putting your child first," Bill said. "I need some family time. I need some personal time. Politicians are people too."

Former Associated Press Capital Bureau Chief Scott Charton recalls the night when Clinton changed his mind. "He called a big news conference in 1987 and everybody expected him to announce he was going to run for president. The night before, Clinton staffer Bev Lindsey called the AP bureau. I took the call and she said, 'I have a statement to read to you.' Bill Simmons had the presence of mind to get on the phone and say, 'Talk to me,' to make sure it wasn't a hoax because he knew Bev very well. She read a very simple statement from the Governor's Mansion that said he would not be running, and they couched it along the lines of 'we didn't want to put everybody out if people had made travel plans.' The fact is most of the media were already there anyway. The announcement was to be the next morning. Most reporters and national press people had gotten into town that night so the statement sounded kind of feeble. Clinton got up the next day at the news conference, which was held in an elaborately lighted ballroom at the Excelsior Hotel, and he talked about how he didn't want to be away from Chelsea that long. Well, everybody knows that he adores Chelsea. That's been shown and his reason sounded plausible. Many people were wondering at the time, 'Is this the real reason?' And of course when he came back and ran the next time Chelsea was a little bit older and he said then 'I think she can deal with the rigors of the campaign a little bit better.' But there was a lot of questioning that night. I remember getting a tip that Clinton and his senior staff including Bev Lindsey were going to dinner at the Capitol Hotel, a little private dinner to thank everybody who had been helpful to him. This was the night that he had pulled out and before the next day's announcement explaining why he had done it. I believe John Brummett and I were the only reporters to have gotten the tip. That was kind of a weird night. Nobody really understood why Clinton was doing what he was doing. Why would you have an elaborately staged news conference if you weren't going to announce your candidacy? I went that night to a place called the Flaming Arrow Club, a restaurant in Little Rock, and Clinton was the talk of the Flaming Arrow that night. None of it was published but there was much speculation. I heard one state senator saying to another senator, 'They must have found a living bastard child.' Everybody was assuming, 'Gee, there must be more to this.' ''

A media person who wishes not to be identified recounts the story of another telephone call. ''No question about it—he was going to announce that he would run for president. The story there is that he got a phone call from the *New York Times* that said, 'We understand that you are screwing a judge in Arkansas. Is it male or female?' The story is allegedly true. I don't know what they had.''

John Reed remembers that ''it was a very emotional day and

Clinton gave a wowser of a speech. He gave his reasons for not running: his family life, the fact that Chelsea was only seven or eight. I remember my editor, Max Brantley, walked over from the hotel where he made his announcement to the *Gazette* building. Max came away a goner. He said, 'Wow, what a great speaker.' We reporters were thinking, 'Max, no big deal.' We're a cynical bunch. I think we all pretty much figured Clinton thought the timing was wrong."

John Brummett says, "He's a very emotional person and I think maybe he looked at his daughter and said, 'What am I getting into?' And he also thought about the Gary Hart problem. He just woke up one morning and said, 'I can't do this. Gary Hart's going to kill me.' Jay Bradford tells a story about being in Clinton's office and talking about some state legislative issues. Clinton was staring him in the face and he suddenly says, 'You know, I think if we admitted that there've been problems in our marriage, it wouldn't be a big deal.' It had nothing to do with their discussion—it was a complete non sequitur. He was obsessing on the question. I think he also knew if he sat down with Hillary and they worked out a joint response that they could go on and in the end they did."

Mara Leveritt remembers "being at the press conference. Hillary was standing at his side. All the national media were there so his decision not to run seemed to have happened that morning. His decision was made so Bill was under control but Hillary clearly was not.

"There was a lot of speculation about why he didn't run. I was very curious about that too. The rumors of womanizing were afoot and a lot of people thought that he was afraid of it all blowing up in his face at that point. Crusty old reporters like myself had a hard time knowing whether to buy this line that he was backing off for Chelsea. There were also stories about a significant financial backing that he had expected that had not come through at the last minute."

Political consultant Darrell Glascock speculates. "This is only conjecture because I have no inside information but I think the night before the announcement they were sitting over at the Mansion going over all of the things that he eventually would be hit with in the 1992 campaign. They just weren't prepared to take on those issues at that point. I think he went to work immediately getting ready for the next cycle. My personal opinion is that when he got ready to run in 1992, he cut a deal with Hillary and the deal was, 'If you'll just stand by me, stay with me, we'll win this thing and if we win it, you can have all of the influence, all the say that you want.' I truly believe that's what happened. After all, Hillary likes power as much as Clinton. When you get down to it, I think she wants the power more than he does. He wants the adulation and the nice things that come with power but he doesn't crave being powerful as much as she does.''

Joan Duffy thinks that ''he had problems with the past that he hadn't dealt with. He had to make arrangements for them. After the Gary Hart business it was obvious that it was going to be an issue that year.

''Clinton has a past. I think any politician who is running for president, if he has any sort of problem in his past, needs to figure out what to expect. Does he have some previous girlfriend who's going to talk? Is there some illegitimate child out there? If he had half a brain, he would contact women whom he had affairs with and question whether they would talk. And I do think that Chelsea had something to do with it. I think he was genuinely concerned about Chelsea. I think it weighs heavily on Clinton that Chelsea is an only child. He has talked about it time and time again. He's mentioned it to friends of mine who have children or who've had a baby. He's said, 'Don't let them be an only child. It's such a lonely life.' I think it weighs very heavily on him that Chelsea has no siblings and no cousins. She has no children in her generation who she's related to and I think that affects her. I think she is a very mature young lady, sometimes even a little adult. I think the fact she didn't grow up with children her own age in her family may have had something to do with it. Even so it's hard for me to believe that you would decide whether to run for president based on that reason and that reason alone.''

Paul Barton places Clinton's decision not to run in a larger political context. ''For the most part, I think he benefited in Arkansas from a very youthful press corps that perhaps did not assess him as completely as it should have. Some things came out last year that maybe the Arkansas press corps should have been on top of and I include myself in there. The womanizing rumors were always there. You heard whispers constantly but I think the attitude of the press corps was that it was going to take pretty damn solid proof before anybody would even begin to ask him about that. In the second half of 1987 after he had dropped out of the presidential race and amid the Gary Hart controversy, he was maybe a little more nervous than usual about certain questions.

Also sometime in the fall of 1987, after Ginsberg admitted he smoked pot, we started having these questions about this new generation of politicians and whether they had smoked pot. We put that question to Clinton's office and he came back with the response that he was not going to respond to 'have-you-ever type questions.' That continued to be his response to a lot of stuff that he ultimately had to deal with head on in the presidential campaign. When Dan Quayle's draft record was examined the Arkansas press corps started putting questions to Clinton and you could see his unease and how that issue vexed him even then."

Scott Van Laningham says, "I was surprised when he didn't run in 1988. I think we were all convinced that he was going to do it. The best explanation I ever heard for that came from Hillary right after the announcement that he was not going to run. I remember talking to her and I think the question was, 'How did everybody get misled?' And she said, 'Well, what you do when you're trying to make the decision, you have to proceed as if you're doing it. You have to decide, can I raise the money? Can I put together the organization? Do I have a message that the people would be receptive to and in the process of going about those things, you are sending off the signals that you are running but then, even after you go through all that, there comes a point where you say, "Okay, do I want to do that now?" ' And when they sat down, they decided the answer was, 'No, not now.' Looking back on it, he was right. That wasn't the time."

On July 20, 1988, Bill Clinton became a national joke. Clinton's nominating speech for Michael Dukakis at the Democratic Convention in Atlanta bombed. The televised speech was overlong, and it followed a fiery address by the Reverend Jesse Jackson. During the speech, the convention floor whips prematurely drove the crowd into a "We want Mike" chant. Some Clinton loyalists thought the Arkansas governor was set up by a spiteful Dukakis who was angry that Clinton had failed to endorse the Massachusetts governor in the early days of the campaign.

Ramsay Ball, a Little Rock real estate developer and writer, was at the convention as a delegate for Paul Simon. He later wrote in *Spectrum* that "Dukakis's people read (Clinton's speech), whooped, and said, 'By God, this is the best. Read every word.' Now, a day later, the Duke's campaign is putting a little distance between itself and Clinton. The governor's people are even having a hard time rounding up passes for the convention, which is the ultimate sign of estrangement.''

But Clinton recovered beautifully from his disappointing speech by agreeing to go on the *Tonight Show with Johnny Carson* a few nights later. Carson had skewered Clinton in his monologue for four nights straight after the convention, but the Arkansas governor showed some pluck, playing saxophone with the studio orchestra as they swung through a creditable version of George Gershwin's ''Summertime.''

Hillary Clinton discusses Clinton's ill-fated speech at the Democratic National Convention. ''Michael Dukakis asked Bill to give that speech. He told us he wanted Bill, in effect, to introduce Dukakis to the country as a fellow governor. There were not going to be any other speakers. Bill passed all of his drafts by the Dukakis people. The day of the speech, he was called three times by the Dukakis people asking him to add things to the speech. They said there was no reference to Dukakis being the commander-in-chief, so they wanted some reference to that. There was no reference to Dukakis's compassion—they wanted something in there about that. And they wanted Bill to mention some specific people. So, they knew about the speech. They approved the speech. They made it even longer by having him add their comments. We saw Dukakis at around five o'clock that Wednesday. He loved the speech. He thought it was exactly what he wanted. Now, we get to the convention center. If you've ever been to a national convention, one of the things that is just par for the course is that the people running the convention want you to pay attention to what goes on at the podium. This is important. They have the lights lowered in the convention hall so that people didn't mill around and talk with each other. They focus their attention on the stage. That's what they did for Ann Richards. That's what they did for Jesse Jackson and that's what they did the next night for Michael Dukakis. As we were going up to the podium I said to the woman who was leading us up. 'Are you sure that the lights are going to go down?' She said, 'Well, I suppose so.' I said, 'Well, would you double-check for me?' And she came back and said, 'Yeah.' So Bill started his speech. The lights did not go out. The Dukakis campaign people were not telling the delegates to listen. In fact, in several instances, they were telling their delegates to yell every time Bill mentioned Dukakis's name, which was often since it was a speech about Dukakis. The Democratic National Committee people, who actually run the platform, had not been told that Bill was going to talk for seventeen minutes. Something was wrong in the signals that were given. I don't want to speculate on what that was, but it was clear that what Dukakis had told Bill to do, for whatever reason, either was not communicated to the compaign people who were running the floor operation or it was communicated and, for reasons unknown to me, disregarded. I sat there knowing that there was something really, really wrong, because if the lights had gone down, if the crowd had been quiet, if the speech had been given the way we had been told that it was supposed to be given, it would have done exactly what we thought it was supposed to do and what Bill had prepared for it to do. Because the lights never went down, because the whips never kept the crowd quiet, because the crowd was yelling and screaming, the TV people said, 'Well, he's speaking too long—this is boring the crowd, turn it off, pull the plug,' which was a total surprise to us. And I sat there thinking, 'What would I do if I were Bill?' Bill had told Dukakis he'd give the speech, so he gave the speech. It was one of the most agonizing moments of my life because I knew that we had been misled and I couldn't figure out why. I couldn't understand what the problem was.

"He was able to redeem himself on national television with Johnny Carson because he didn't rely on anybody else to do it for him. He did it himself. That was a lesson we learned real well."

Betsey Wright recalls Atlanta in nightmarish detail. "Dukakis had staff fiddling with the speech for days so I don't know what Dukakis did or didn't touch. He clearly let it be known to Bill that this was the way he wanted the speech given. When we got out of there, Hillary's first instinct was that Bill should go back to the hotel. My instinct was no, he needs to walk the streets and talk to people and get it off his chest and she said, 'Well, you're probably right,' so we walked the streets going in and out of the restaurants and bars nonstop trying to talk and explain and listen. Then we got up early the next morning and went back over to the press hall. It was hard. He knew it would be very, very hard and painful. He is better at ad-libbing as opposed to giving speeches because his soul doesn't show if the speech is prepared. In the campaign, he really began using speech writers for the first time and he almost never had used written speeches before. He certainly didn't use speeches that other people wrote. You can tell the speeches in which he's ad-libbing and doing his own thing because his soul shows and it's his greatest resource. It kills me for him to have to rely so much on written speeches but part of that's because you have to weigh every word in terms of impact on the economy and national relations and all that kind of stuff but he's always been a much better extemporaneous speaker. The hole that night was the problem though. It had nothing to do with Bill's ability. It was a sabotage as I call it in my most paranoid moments. The whips kept telling people to keep talking, keep screaming. They wouldn't tell people to be quiet like they did for other speakers. I was up on the platform and I could see the whips' insisting, 'Keep hollering' or 'Holler "Mike," "Mike," "Mike" ' while he was trying to talk. I mean the whips almost destroyed him and he just kept trying to go hoping at least maybe the TV audience was hearing it. Oh it was awful. It was awful. It's been very hard for me to believe it wasn't deliberate. I tried to get them to dim the lights because people would have gotten quiet but they wouldn't do it.''

George Jernigan, too, remembers a shaken Clinton. ''He gave his speech, his famous speech. And it was a disaster. I was a delegate to the convention and our delegation was sitting in the balcony about as far back as you could. There was an empty chair by me and after it was over, all of a sudden he came and sat down by me. I'd had a copy and was reading through it. We'd all commented just looking at his speech. There's no breath in these half-page paragraphs. We were all shaking our heads. And he said, 'How did I do?' And I said, 'Would you sign my copy?' I still have an autographed copy that he signed. And then the press descended on him. I didn't tell him how he did. I mean if I'd told him I'd have said, 'Terrible.' He did not know that he had done poorly because from up at the podium all conventions are busy and I think he thought he was coming over well. But he didn't have that rhythm, he didn't have that beat. And the speech was long. Then the press came down, and from the tone of the questions, you could just see the color going out of his face.''

Sidney Blumenthal says, ''At the Democratic Convention of 1988, he delivered a very lengthy nomination speech for Michael Dukakis. I ran into him afterward and he was extremely upset at its reception. He was in control but talking very rapidly and his eyes were wild. We talked for a while about how he was attempting to do what he thought would be best for Dukakis and that he was trying to do what the Dukakis campaign wanted him to and it had not turned out so well. He had wondered if anyone thought it had been okay. He was seeking positive comments but not finding any. This is a small incident but it shows that this was his big moment—his first time on the national stage—and I think he was very anxious that his career at that level may have been ended but it obviously wasn't."

On March 1, 1990, Bill Clinton filled the rotunda of the state Capitol with five hundred supporters. They came to hear whether or not he would seek a fifth term as governor. They were curious and attentive. Nobody knew what his decision would be. One legislator, state Senator Jerry Bookout of Jonesboro, called it the best-kept political secret in Arkansas in decades.

"I must confess that one of the reasons I have been reluctant to face this day is the fire of an election no longer burns in me," Clinton began. "The joy I once took at putting on an ad that answered somebody else's ad, that won some clever little argument of the moment, is long since gone."

But as the crowd, convinced that Clinton would not seek another term, let out a collective sigh, the governor of Arkansas continued: "I've listened carefully to my friends and counselors around the country, but mostly just here at home. Some say, 'Leave while you're on top. Walk away from a nasty political campaign.' Others say, 'My God, you're only forty-three years old. Surely you're good for one more term.'

"In spite of all my reservations about the personal considerations, I believe that, more than any other person who could serve as governor, I could do the best job.... We know there is always the problem of arrogance of power, and we are bending over backward to be as humble as we can in this campaign.... In the end, I decided that I just didn't want to stop doing the job.

"I don't think anyone but Hillary Clinton knew," said state Senator Lu Hardin of Russellville. Hardin had called his own news conference to announce a gubernatorial bid in the event Clinton decided not to run. He had to settle for telling reporters he would run for a third term in the Senate. Like many another young Arkansas politicians, Hardin was frustrated by Clinton's stranglehold on the governor's office.

Tom McRae had not expected to run against Clinton in the Arkansas 1990 Democratic primary. "When Clinton first announced the press conference, I was betting he wouldn't run and quite frankly, I don't think he made up his mind until the very last minute. There's a story that was told to me, I won't say by whom, but by someone very close to Bill who said that he was invited to his announcement and when he and Clinton talked that morning, Clinton said they were going to close it down. The story is that he started his speech with the idea of not running and changed his mind two-thirds of the way through his speech. If you go back and look at it, you can see the point where he switched. I said, 'What's going on?' because Hillary clearly at that point didn't want him to run. The story is that a former governor really said, 'Unless you're sure to lose, run again, because there's no life after politics.' I don't know whether it's true or not. It makes a wonderful story.''

Clinton's Republican opponent in 1990, Sheffield Nelson, points out two major issues in that race. ''Bill has continually said what people wanted to hear in spite of the fact that he didn't plan to do half of it. They learned that in Arkansas time and time again. When I ran against him in 1990 the two major issues that I hounded him on were number one, that he would run for president if reelected and number two, that he would raise taxes. He raised taxes the most any time in history, twenty million dollars, and he ran for president. He had promised unequivocally that he'd do neither.''

Pat Lynch comments on Clinton, the people of Arkansas, and the 1990 race. ''Only 30 percent of everybody in Arkansas hated Clinton. I mean, 70 percent of us like him. Clinton really, really stayed too long at the dance here. I'm sure he had to be sick of it. I wish more than anything else that I had my tape of an interview I did with Hillary Clinton. Back in the gubernatorial race of 1990 I asked Hillary as the opening question for my talk show, 'Mrs. Clinton, your husband has been, with the exception of two years, governor of Arkansas since 1978. Tell me, are you as sick of him as the rest of us?' And she took my head off. She said something like, 'You know, Pat, that's kind of a dumb question.' She went on to elaborate on how people were with Bill Clinton for leadership but there was also such a thing as followship and that if people wanted to try to follow him, that he had a great deal more to do for the state yet and how devoted he was to us and of course her answer was very colorful.''

Former KTHV reporter Susan Rodman recalls the night Clinton was elected to his fifth term as governor. ''After his last gubernatorial election once Sheffield Nelson had conceded, everybody wrapped up their pieces and we all went to a little pizza joint called Veno's. It's a little dive. Beer and pizza, that's all they serve. And it had been a long night and so we were going to get something to eat and have a few beers. We knew that some of the campaign people were going to be there. Well, Clinton pops in and just starts partying with everybody. He had just won the gubernatorial election and instead of doing whatever you would think they would do, he and Hillary went to Veno's. He was carrying around pitchers of beer and pouring beer for everybody. Hillary left earlier but he stayed and at around four o'clock it was just us sitting around talking about old times. He was not drinking. I better throw that in. I never saw Clinton drink any of the beer.''

Tom McRae favorably reviews Clinton's last legislative session. ''It's a great irony but in many ways, his most effective and honest legislative session was his last and that was because it was the first time that I saw him really willing to take political risks. I don't think that even as a new governor, I could have accomplished what he accomplished that legislative session.''

John Lipton talks about some of those accomplishments. ''I ran for speaker of the house and was elected speaker designate in 1989, which allowed me two years time to begin to work on a program for 1991 through 1993. I put together a pretty interesting program which we shared with Governor Clinton that was based on a consensus view of the hundred members of the Arkansas House of Representatives. We did the largest highway program in the history of the state of Arkansas. We funded education and teachers' salaries and were deemed by the educational association as the best education session in the history of our state. We addressed rural medical care and ways of financing doctors in rural areas. We got working on the medicaid program. We adopted major environmental laws and for the first time water quality legislation was passed. I could go on and on about these items. We had ten in all, and all of them passed. Clinton was beginning to feel that maybe he was going to run for president but was having a problem because he had made a campaign promise that he would be a full-time governor, that he would serve all four years. Yet we had accomplished in the first two years of that term more than we could have expected to accomplish in all four years. He actually asked me one day, 'Johnny, what else is there left that we really need to do?' and I said, 'Governor, this is the end of the 1991 session and we've done it all.' ''

Professor Art English observes, ''I think that he was rejuvenated after his reelection. The last couple of legislative sessions had not really been very good ones for him. He had been trying to implement a broader base of taxes and he was always being blocked in terms of creating jobs. He had a lot of visionary sort of ideas that he put together in some respects but it never really seemed to be a coherent package for the state. Maybe because he thought he was really going to run for president in 1991, legislative sessions in his last term were very, very successful.''

Regarding Clinton's twelve years in the governor's office, Rex Nelson believes that when ''you put the scales out there and weigh both sides, I think they would probably come down in Clinton's favor. He's extremely bright and extremely intelligent and we could have elected much worse men to office during those twelve years. I would say that Clinton probably did more good than bad but if he hadn't had such huge national ambitions, he could have done so much more.''

One of the strongest complaints about Bill Clinton throughout his reign as governor was his frequent absence from the state. Clinton was forever seeking ways to build a national base; early on it seemed clear that Arkansas was too small to hold him. Some people thought it impaired his ability to govern effectively—others thought he served the state well as an ambassador-at-large.

Sheffield Nelson comes down on the negative side. ''He totally abandoned his number-one job, that being governor of Arkansas, and left it to others. A full-time chief executive working in the areas of education and industrial development, the social service area, working with human services and so forth, could have done a much better job. The state would be much better off today but for the fact that we supported Bill Clinton's six-year run for president. A ship simply cannot run without a captain. Somebody half as capable as Bill would have done a better job as governor because they'd have put 100 percent of their effort into it. We would be a better state today if we'd had somebody in charge of the state during that period of time.''

Pat Lynch agrees. ''I said he should resign. I said he's guilty of an illegal exaction of living in the Governor's Mansion and collecting a salary while he wasn't governor. I said that he was disabled and ought to be removed from office under the disability clause. He hadn't been here in months; if the sitting governor could not serve he should be succeeded.''

Clinton's out-of-state travel caused him some very public embarrassment. His then-Lieutenant Governor Winston Bryant relates: ''The angriest that Clinton ever got at me was when Nick

Wilson was co-chairman of the Senate and third in line for governor. Up until that time Clinton and I had a very informal arrangement. If he was out of state, they'd call me in. I would simply be on notice although I'm sure there were a number of times when he left the state for a half a day or a day that I was not called in on. In any event, Senator Wilson was causing a problem for Clinton so Clinton's staff sent a memo down to me that I would have to record in writing every instance of Clinton leaving the state. So I said, 'That's fine, you let me know in writing anytime Clinton's going to leave,' and so they did. A year went by and the press somehow got wind that we had these memos recording his absences and they wanted to see them. It came down to the fact that they were public documents and we had no right to hold them. I released them. They showed that Clinton had left the state well over one hundred days that year—almost a third of the calendar days. I don't think he neglected the state by traveling but he was incensed at the fact that the press got hold of that record."

Retired state Senator Knox Nelson did not think "it was upsetting to members of the legislature that he was traveling so much the last few years. I think that there was a desire or willingness among the members of the general assembly to make that sacrifice for him so that he could seek this office because we thought it would be good for the state so we were willing to do that. I encouraged him to run. He talked to me about it and I said, 'Governor, as long as I'm in the Senate and you're trying to seek this office, I'll do everything I can to help you.' which meant keeping government going and not letting it get out of control."

To charges that Clinton was absent too often Joan Duffy responds, "By the time he was running for president, he had been in office for so long, he had people in place whom he knew well and trusted and the place basically ran itself. It's not a very centralized kind of operation like Louisiana where the governor has a lot more power and a lot more authority. Clinton worked well with the legislative leaders at the time. He may have had trouble had he not had as strong a president pro tem, lieutenant governor, and house speaker at the time. The lieutenant governor was Jim Guy Tucker and the president pro tem of the Senate was Jerry Bookout, a very close friend of his. The speaker at the time was John Lipton who was also very close to Clinton. Lipton and Bookout especially were very much behind his presidential race and very supportive of him both personally and politically. They viewed his running for president as not only good for him and the country but also for Arkansas. I mean they just saw great potential and supported it. Had he not had the support of those people, the state's problems could have distracted him a great deal.''

Lloyd George dismisses the charge of absenteeism. ''The fact that he was out of the state so much doesn't mean anything in this day and age. With fax machines and telephones you can govern Arkansas from Alaska now. It doesn't make any difference just as long as you can be reached all the time. Look at our president. He runs our country and half the world and he can do it from *Airforce 1*. He doesn't have to be sitting in the oval office anymore.''

Charlie Cole Chaffin agrees. ''When a guy calls him at midnight it doesn't matter if the governor's sitting in the Mansion in Little Rock or if he's sitting in Hollywood, California. The phone sounds the same and the issues and the words are the same. Whenever he was leaving the state, he contacted everybody that needed to be in close touch with him. I would never fault him on that.''

Sheila Bronfman points out that midnight calls were not merely figurative. ''If the phone rang after midnight, you almost could be assured it was Bill returning a call. Sorry never entered into it. He was up. Isn't everyone? Half the time I had to try to remember what it was I'd called about. I used to keep a notepad by my bed on the days that I would call about something so I could remember why I'd called. He's famous for those late-night calls.''

Ernest Cunningham too got his share of them. ''To give you an example of how energetic the guy is, when I was speaker in 1987, he'd call at midnight and at one o'clock in the morning and want to talk about the bills of the next day. He'd call every night. That he woke people up never bothered him. Occasionally he'd say, 'You know, I tried to call you last night and I got a busy signal.' I wanted to say, 'Well, some of us have to sleep sometimes.' But I never did tell him I was taking the phone off the hook.''

In October 1991 Governor Clinton broke his promise to serve Arkansas for a full four-year term. This did not surprise Sheffield Nelson. ''In reality he was running for president from day one. The same holds true going all the way back to 1988 when he made his aborted run for president. He planned to give up the governorship to be the Democratic nominee. Of course he fell by the wayside when three or four popped up who were stronger than he was. When he ran for governor in 1990, he knew very well that he'd be running for president in 1992, but he looked the people in the eye and forcefully told them—very convincingly told them—that he would not run for president. He had to be sitting governor. He had to be able to pull those strings that he could only pull as governor in order to bring a tremendous amount of Arkansas money to him through utilities, insurance companies, and others who were beholden to a chief executive who would still be governor for two or more years if he lost the presidency. The utilities and insurance companies in Arkansas provided a tremendous amount of the campaign money either directly or indirectly. Trace it back and you will find the bond houses, the insurance companies, utilities, anybody who had to count on something coming out of the state of Arkansas, whether it be financial or support from the governor's office, kicked in their help. And what doesn't show on the balance sheet is the soft money, the people traveling at their own expense to campaign for Clinton when he badly needed help in states like New Hampshire.''

Darrell Glascock also believes that Clinton had been planning to run for the presidency in 1992 when he ran for governor in 1990. ''He kept telling me that he wasn't going to run but I didn't believe him. When Jim Guy Tucker ran for lieutenant governor, it became very obvious to everybody that there had been a deal cut. Jim Guy had announced he would run and had already spent a couple of hundred thousand dollars running for governor. So the deal was obviously, 'Jim Guy, I'm gonna run for president. Why don't you back down and run for lieutenant governor. If lightning strikes, you're governor; if it doesn't, you're lieutenant governor for four years and I won't run again.' The deal had obviously been struck.''

A deal had been struck, according to Bill Bowen, but not by Clinton. ''Jim Guy had announced in early March that he would run for governor. Time really was getting short. My good friend Ben Allen and I felt that Bill needed to announce because he was going to have a tough campaign, probably against Tommy Robinson who was very much alive and well, and he did not need to fight Jim Guy Tucker too. We went to Bill to see if we could get his permission to get Jim Guy out of the race. He gave us the green light, and we pursued Maurice Mitchell, Jim Guy's former law partner, and we argued that Jim Guy could not win against Bill, that Bill was going to rough him up and scar him and make him spend a lot of money just to lose. Jim Guy reexamined his commitment and decided to run for lieutenant governor where he'd be an absolute lay-down shoo-in.''

Lloyd George recalls a 1991 meeting with Clinton shortly after the Democratic Leadership Conference. "I went out to the Mansion to meet him and he had just gotten back from the Democratic Leadership Conference and he was absolutely dumbfounded and amazed. He said, 'I can be elected president.' He talked to me for one solid hour and I didn't do anything but sit there and listen. He was excited. He was on cloud nine. He told me about all the governors he had spoken to, how they all commented on the nation's dissatisfaction, the dissatisfaction in every state and the condition of the country. He said, 'I know what they want. I know what they need.' He said, 'I can be elected president if I just get my message across.' He even convinced me after talking to him for an hour. I said, 'Let me know how I can help, Mr. President.' "

As John Lipton sees it, in 1991, the time was right for Clinton. "I will never forget the conversation. Some of the big name Democrats, the big guns so to speak, the ones you would have thought would have been out there actively seeking the Democratic nomination were pulling out. They were beginning to say, 'Not now, next time.' Bill Clinton said, 'What do you think?' and I said, 'If you stay on another two years in the governor's office, the Democrats will be coming out of the woods to run for president. Coming out of this session with all these accomplishments, your chances might be better now than they'd ever be. This might be a no-lose situation. You will be credible enough to at least get name recognition. You'll find out if you're a player in the big camp. What better time to do it than now?' And he said, 'Well, what would you do?' and I said, 'Governor, I'd pray about it and I'd consult my family about it. I'd go for it because I believe the people of Arkansas will understand your breaking that commitment. The Republicans wouldn't but your supporters would accept your decision.' "

The Fourth of July holiday became a prelude to Clinton's presidential campaign. Says Jane Fullerton, Washington correspondent for the *Arkansas Democrat-Gazette*, "There was an incident that sticks out in my mind that occurred before the campaign that was kind of a prelude to the campaign. Governor Clinton made his traditional foray around the state to go to various July Fourth celebrations. It was a real interesting day because his theme for the day was to ask people, 'Gee, will it be okay with you if I run?' It was interesting to see him in operation that particular day. I had not covered the state Capitol as intensively as during a legislative session and that was one of the first times that I saw him really up close and saw how he interacted with people, particularly people that he is familiar with like those in Arkansas. It was a real eye-opening experience.''

Joan Duffy also recalls that holiday weekend. ''I had this great trip with him on the Fourth of July weekend in 1991. Every Fourth of July in Arkansas the politicians make the picnic-and-parade rounds so they asked me if I wanted to go along with his entourage and I said, 'Yeah.' Four or five of us went on this little plane. We attended the opening of the National Civil Rights Museum in Memphis and ended up in Hot Springs with the fireworks. It was a long day but it was very interesting because he opened up on that trip about what he was thinking and what he was going through. He talked a lot about Chelsea and that was the first time that I really believed that she was a major reason why he didn't run in 1987 but it was very interesting to listen to his thought process. It's not that he thought he was going to win then because nobody did. Everybody thought, 'Go ahead and run and Bush will get reelected because he's so high in the polls and then you're all set to run the next time.' But he didn't think that. He told me 'Nobody gets two shots anymore. It doesn't work that way anymore. This is it. I either run and I either make it or I don't but this is it.' He said, 'If I wait four more years, Chelsea will be in high school. She'll be a senior in high school and she could stay here with friends or family or whatever and finish out high school here and then go off to college and have a relatively normal life. But if I do it now,' I think the exact quote was, 'If lightning strikes and I win, she loses me.' He's very, very, very concerned about that because he lost his own father and he talked a lot about that on this trip. He almost indicated he really didn't care if he won or lost. It was the contest he was interested in. It was bringing the issues in front of the nation that he felt so passionate about. It bothered him that Bush and Dukakis never talked about issues. All they talked about was who looked silly in a tank and all that waving the flag. It really pissed him off that they didn't get down to talk about the issues that were affecting his state and every other state. That's what he wanted to do—improve the debate. It's not that he didn't care if he won or lost but that wasn't the main purpose. But he knew he only had once chance and he said, 'My father died when he was twenty-nine. I've lived so many years beyond my father. This is all gravy for me.' It was almost as if once he'd surpassed his father's lifespan, it was all a gift that he had. He wasn't going to live or die based on whether he won or not but it was just the fact that he was doing it. What might be holding him back was the thought of screwing up Chelsea's life and causing him to lose her, to lose contact with her. I never realized how much he was affected by the loss of his father but I think it weighed on him a lot in terms of inspiring him to do something with his life.''

By July it was no secret to many of Clinton's insiders that he would run for the presidency. Bill Bowen was asked if he thought Clinton felt bad that he had Bowen step on as chief of staff and then announced his candidacy for presidency so soon after. ''I didn't feel bad about it. My position was designed to support and implement his plan because he knew he was going to be gone a lot. It was part of the strategy. He took over the Democratic Leadership Conference in 1990 from Nunn. He made a speech in Cleveland on May 6th—now that's my birthday so I remember it. I've read the speech several times. It was a blueprint of what he expected to do. After that speech I left a note with Mike Gaulden saying, 'Number One: Run. Two: Do not resign. Three: I'll help you with money. Four: You've got an outstanding chance to win the nomination.' ''

Woody Bassett remembers, ''When he came to Fayetteville in August of 1991 when he was thinking about running for president they called and asked me to get some folks together. We had about fifty or sixty of his friends and supporters in a private room and I remember him coming in there and saying, 'These are some reasons why I ought to do it and over here are some reasons why I shouldn't do it.' He likes to think out loud and he'll give both sides of an issue or a question. I remember that a lot of people were encouraging him to run but there were some people who thought it would be a mistake for him to run for a variety of reasons. I remember a couple of things that he said during that meeting though. This was when George Bush still was way up in the polls and when people assumed that Cuomo would probably run. I remember somebody asking him 'If you run for president, how do you expect to defeat Cuomo?' His answer was 'Well, if I get in, I'll just play the schedule.' Then I remember him talking about how high Bush was in the polls but there's an undercurrent out there of disenchantment across the nation. He said the Gulf War thing's going to fade and the economy's really what's foremost in people's minds. He said, 'Four or five months is a lifetime in politics. If I do decide to get in this thing and run, I may get my brains beat out. I may get creamed. I might fool around and win the thing. Who knows?' And he just kind of laughed. A few people out in the audience laughed.

"It bothered him and it bothered some people that he had promised not to run. That's one of the things that he talked about. My recollection is that most people felt that he'd had a good session of the legislature in 1991. He got a lot done. Some people were obviously very concerned about his commitment to stay four years but a lot of people felt that his running would be good for the state of Arkansas. Many people thought he probably wouldn't survive the primary but he would do a good job and get his name out there and he would be in good shape in 1996. A lot of people thought he'd be back in Arkansas soon after the primaries were over."

Sheffield Nelson wonders why Clinton didn't run a poll. "You know this is the funniest thing, and this is what I said at the time. He will always run a poll on anything and everything but he didn't want the people to find out if most wanted to release him from his promise not to run for president. In fact, I raised that issue publicly. I said, 'Why didn't he run a poll? He polls about everything else.' Finally somebody did run one and it said what I said.

"You know, the one difference, if I can really differentiate between Bill and myself is that Bill will tell the people anything they want to hear and he does not hesitate to lie. I was watching an interesting thing on television last night about how the most successful liars are those who can do it without any twinge of conscience and they said politicians seem to be that way and the better they are at doing it the better politicians they are. I've watched him. He is the ultimate. He is the consummate politician based on that criteria."

James Merriweather says, "He became angry when we were pressing him about his pledge to serve for a four-year term. He argued for weeks that he had never made an ironclad promise and then I think it was the Associated Press who pulled out the quote that said he had pledged not to run. So he went throughout the state with this dog-and-pony show. He said, 'Well, let me ask the people of Arkansas' so he rigged up this statewide tour. He would be here today and there tomorrow asking the voters what they thought and as it turned out, a bunch of these things were arranged in advance with his supporters in the audience. He went to great pains that the press would not be eyewitnesses to his soul-searching as he made the rounds of the state. He did not invite the press to these meetings. He'd say, 'This person was here and this person was here and all of them wanted me to run.' That is now he justified backing out on his promise to stay.''

James Walters recalls one of those meetings—and the uninvited press. ''We had a meeting at the Harvest Restaurant and we had between 250 and 300 people there. These were supposed to be private meetings but the media came anyway which was fine. I told them at the time, I said, 'Look, this is supposed to be a private meeting. I can't tell you to come in here until the governor gets here. If he's comfortable with it, and I think he will be, you can stay. But when he got there, I had channel 4, channel 5, I had channel 9 TV. I had the Rogers paper. I had the Bentonville paper. Had the Bella Vista paper standing there. I had the *Arkansas Gazette*. I had the *Arkansas Democrat*. Again I said, 'This was supposed to have been private. I think it will be okay but you're going to have to get off my back.' Bill arrived, got out of the car and I said, 'Well, Bill, I told them that when you got here you would decide if they should stay.' He said, 'I don't have any problem with that at all. Tell them let's go.' He turned around and they even got inside the building. This was about 6:30 in the morning. He first discussed the things that he felt needed to be addressed if he were to become a candidate. Then he threw it open.''

Referring to Clinton's promise in the 1990 campaign, Walters says, ''Things change. Conditions change. Issues change. Personalities change.'' Cal Ledbetter says, ''Circumstances had changed. I'd give him the benefit of the doubt and say the circumstances had changed so he changed.''

Knox Nelson recalls how Clinton agonized over whether to run for president. ''He'd ask my opinion and I'd encouraged him for two reasons. First was his desire to run for that office and I thought he would make a good candidate. You had Tsongas and Kerrey. Out of all those candidates, I think Clinton was the best candidate and he happened to hit at a time when Bush was as low as out. Six months before, Bush had a 90 percent approval rating and now the man was down to a 39 percent rating. Clinton would ask us if he should. 'Would I get criticism here at home for leaving after saying I would not run?' I said, 'Well, Governor, only a fool never changes his mind. I would just be up front with the people and say "Look, I have changed my mind. I come to you and ask you to support me." ' And he did."

Longtime State Representative John Miller feels that "there's nothing wrong with changing your mind. I just believe that people need to exercise the best talents they've got as long as they have the talents."

Jimmie Lou Fisher had been campaigning for Clinton since 1978, and in October 1991, when he announced that he would run for president, she introduced him. Here she recalls those early days on the campaign trail and, for her, one more recent and truly unforgettable day, "We would get up and get to campaign headquarters by seven or seven-thirty because we were dealing with a lot of farmers. Some of them will tell you that I was at their farms at six-thirty and seven and stayed past ten-thirty or eleven o'clock at night which sounds a lot like the presidential campaign. But he was tireless and just outworked us all. He made several speeches a day and was always on the telephone. And that was before the days of mobile phones. Bill Clinton always tries to squeeze in one more conversation, one more handshake, one more stop at his little grocery store where he used to stop and pick up his messages which meant that he had to make more phone calls. We were always looking for a pay phone and there are parts of Arkansas in which you can't find pay phones. I remember standing off to the side of the road at some pay phone and handing him dimes. He never had dimes. That was another thing I wanted to get to in this interview. Bill Clinton never had any money. Someone asked if Bill Clinton ever did anything for you that you really remember? And one of my most vivid memories was when he was out of office he and his family lived not too far from me and I saw them every once in a while. I was recovering from surgery and he and Chelsea were going out for a walk and stopped by to see if I needed anything. I said, 'Yes, I need a quart of milk.' And he bought a 69-cent quart of milk and that's the only time I've ever known the man to have any money in his pocket. But you know, I say that in jest.

"I have never seen anyone that can literally talk on the phone, write notes, and pay attention to what you're saying all at the same time. He literally can do three things at once.

"I had the honor and privilege of introducing him when he announced he would run for president. I had been to Hot Springs the day before and I was staying at my apartment here in Little Rock. I got a call about 11:30 the night before the announcement. They said, 'Well, Jimmie Lou, we want you to either read some letters or introduce the governor.' And I said 'What?' They said, 'Well, you might need to be thinking about some things to say.' And I said, 'Now wait a minute. I'm an early riser, but it's time for me to go to bed. I'll think about this in the morning. Y'all just let me know and I'll meet you at 5:30 in the morning.' They said, 'Do you want us to come over now?' and I said, 'No, I've gotta' get some sleep.' So I went to sleep, got up early the next day and they had jotted down some things and I had jotted down some things and until I got there I wasn't sure that I really would get to introduce him. It was quite a thrill for me. It's a day I'll never forget. I looked out over that crowd and I saw a lot of the same faces that I saw on that dark, dreary day in November of 1980 when he lost that election. The same people were all there, some holding signs, 'Bill Clinton for President.' We all were very excited about that race.''

3

The Making of a President

Washington Post political reporter Juan Williams first saw Bill Clinton at the National Democratic Convention in San Francisco in 1984. "There, at the convention, I remember having a strange thought which was that he looked lonely. Before and afterward, he didn't look like part of the crowd. I don't know if you've spent much time with politicians, but I have and politicians tend to be the boys on the bus. I mean, they're rubbing shoulders, and they're back slapping, they're smoking. They're joking. Clinton, for some reason at that convention, looked like a novice, looked like a guy that was trying to be one of the guys and looking to get in the magic circle but not quite in it. He had people telling reporters, 'That's Governor Clinton of Arkansas. You want to talk to him and he's going to be delivering this speech' and all that kind of thing. I remember going over to say hello. I think he was clearly trying to spread his name around and hoping that his speech would have impact. What's unusual about that is in most cases, the reporters are hungry to get to know the politicans and so you don't have to introduce yourself. Typically, they know who you are."

Eleanor Clift met Bill Clinton six years later. He was no longer a party outsider. "My first exposure to Bill Clinton was really at

209

a dinner party at the home of Esther Coopersmith in early 1990. I sat across from Clinton and everybody went around and introduced themselves and then they gave him the cake. It was a replica of the White House, which was obviously a tip-off to those who hadn't picked up on it already that this was sort of new talent that was being showcased. He handled himself exceedingly well on a range of topics. He was endearingly charming and I walked out of there thinking 'This is somebody the Democratic party needs.' Shortly after that, I proposed to do a piece for *Newsweek* with the headline ''Desperately Seeking Southerners.'' I talked about Clinton and Gore as the party's two rising stars. I said that Gore was more well positioned in terms of the Gulf War and talked about Clinton's positioning on domestic issues as sort of the responsibility theme. Now, this would have been a very impressive article except for the kicker where I proclaimed that the true southerner and perhaps the fastest rising star in the Democratic party was Doug Wilder, and the three of them were pictured, but anyway I felt kind of proud that I had spotted them early. That was my first exposure to Bill Clinton.''

Max Brantley remembers ''a cattle show at the Democratic National Committee meeting at Los Angeles in October of 1990. That was when Clinton really broke out of the pack as a potential Democratic candidate. I was floored by meeting a rancher from Wyoming and a small politico from New Hampshire and a businessman from Iowa and businesspeople and lawyers from California who all felt like they knew Bill Clinton from events that went back fifteen years or more but had identified him even then as a comer. They shared only their Democratic party ties and their connection to Bill Clinton. It was interesting. Looking back, maybe there was some calculation in how that all came to pass. For years, he and Hillary have been building this data base of names that's legendary. They've formed these networks of people who were there for them when they ran for office.''

Former senior editor at *Newsweek* Peter Goldman considers Clinton's timing, his luck, and his guts. ''I think had Al Gore run or if he had gotten in early, Clinton would never have gotten in the race. There was kind of an established hierarchy among young southern moderates and Gore was at the head of the class. I think if Mario Cuomo had gotten in, it would have been a very interesting fight. I don't know who would have won that. He was lucky in that the competition was not very strong. On the other hand, is it luck if you're bold enough to get in at the point when Bush still was looking unbeatable? If you're brave enough to do it at that point, then you've got to say, well, maybe it's not luck, maybe it's luck plus guts. Hillary at that early stage felt that maybe Bush was unbeatable. Her stance was do this for practice and then we'll run seriously the next time. We'll learn our way around. We'll get to go around the country and talk about our issues. Probably that was in Clinton's mind, too, although I think Clinton is more result-oriented.''

Luck, guts, and friends. Political consultant Skip Rutherford says, "The first critical development (in Clinton's campaign) was our ability in Arkansas on December 16, 1991 to raise $90,000 at a state fund-raiser which was at that point, the most money raised by a Democratic presidential candidate in a single event to date. There was a lull in the polls. There was a rap that you couldn't raise money from Arkansans. A lot of the national donors were not doing anything because they were waiting to see if we could raise money here, and nine days before Christmas, we did. A lot of money.''

Peter Goldman shares thoughts about Clinton's campaign. "One, it was a tactically, strategically brilliant campaign. On the other hand, an unencumbered Democrat could have won just by showing up, could have almost phoned it in. Clinton was not an unencumbered Democrat. He had taken more blows to the solar plexus than any candidate probably in history and survived them. The Flowers scandal. The draft problem. Some of the pounding that he took was fair, but a lot of it was unfair like the stuff about personal finances that Jerry Brown called the scandal of the week. He was very damaged goods and there came a point when he and his team were at a kind of a do-or-die showdown. Perot then looked like a possible winner. Clinton's strategic team got together and in a series of meetings and memo exchanges that they called the Manhattan Project, figured out how to make his message coherent, powerful, and dynamic. It had been kind of sloppy until then. So I think strategically, the campaign was brilliant because they had a damaged guy and they had to make him a hero in a situation complicated by the presence of Perot. I've been told by a Republican pollster that absent Perot, Clinton probably would have won 60/40 and totally on a change dynamic but with Perot in the way, there was a possibility that Bush might beat Clinton. I think Clinton owes a lot of the five-point difference to his strategic team. He himself is very strategically smart. Hillary is very smart and put together as an entity, they ran a strategically good campaign."

Eleanor Clift says, "I thought he was going to win in New Hampshire because you just couldn't look at the field and take anybody else very seriously. I don't think Paul Tsongas was ever real. I mean his health would have interfered. I always thought that the race was Bill Clinton against himself and whether the good Clinton with the ideas would prevail or the bad Clinton with the private life that people didn't exactly sanction would prevail was the battle all along. I don't think he ever had a real opponent."

Flies in the Ointment

America is a nation fascinated with sin, its consequences and its details. It is probably fair to say that Bill Clinton, during the 1992 presidential campaign, at times acted like a repentant sinner. It is to his credit that he decided there were certain things he would not discuss, personal things that fell within a zone of privacy claimed by him and his wife.

Of course, the Gennifer Flowers affair shook up the campaign, but people in Arkansas were aware of rumors—there were always rumors—about Bill Clinton. For the most part, local reporters did not care to pursue these rumors—most claim they thought Clinton's alleged affairs were private matters that did not affect his public performance. That is a convenient and disingenuous story, for while smoke billowed around Clinton, no one—until the dubious Ms. Flowers—ever came up with any evidence that the governor was a philanderer. There were also rumors about most of Clinton's gubernatorial opponents, most TV reporters, and most of the state's high-profile businesspeople. Arkansas is a small state, and people consider themselves discreet when they keep their gossip out of the newspaper. But even in Arkansas, the volume of rumors surrounding Clinton's love life is astounding.

Still, Clinton's appearance on *60 Minutes* in the early days of the 1992 campaign, and his subsequent admission that he had "caused pain" in his marriage begs the question of outside affairs. In Arkansas, Clinton's friends usually politely decline to comment on such matters; his critics, however, are not always so polite.

KARK-TV reporter Alan Kelley flew with Clinton before he

announced his candidacy. "It was a real hectic schedule and they had kind of squirreled away some boxed lunches for us and so we were all kind of eating this chicken out of boxes in somewhat cramped quarters in this little aircraft. We were telling jokes and shooting the breeze. We did talk a little about presidential politics which we were all nervously dancing around without actually asking him because he had been exploring the options at that point with those exploratory committees. He never specifically talked about running but we did talk about the womanizing issue. He didn't say a whole lot. He was letting other people throw their opinions around and there was some sentiment that the public had tired of the media always looking for skeletons of that nature in people's closets. I think he agreed that if Gary Hart had handled it better it wouldn't have been the completely destructive issue that it was."

Rumors of womanizing would haunt Clinton's campaign. In 1990 government employee Larry Nichols claimed that he had been fired from his job because he knew, he alleged, of the governor's affairs with five women. His claims were aired on Bill Powell's call-in radio show. Bill Powell states, "I did not read the Larry Nichols lawsuit. It was read on my air, but I did not read it. A caller read it. Larry Nichols had called a news conference and said that he was going to tell all. So, he has this news conference and the fellow who is in charge of the Associated Press here in town is reputed to have turned around to the media that was here, small as it was, and said, 'This is not a story.' So it was ignored. I woke up Sunday morning expecting to see something about Nichols in the newspaper and it wasn't even covered. So Monday morning I went on the air and I was talking about it. I wondered what he'd said. And a guy called and said, 'You want to know what he said?' I said, 'Yes.' And he said, 'Well, I got it right here.' He read it and I was so aghast at what was being said, the allegations that were being made, that I put my bunny on idle and listened instead of shutting him off before he started to name names. The names got out over the air which resulted in a lawsuit being filed against the station and me. I was working under the miscomprehension that once it was made public, it was public knowledge. A lawyer for Gennifer Flowers sued and they kept us quiet for a year. By the time the statue of limitations ran out on it, in this area, it was old news. We all breathed a sigh of relief that it was behind us and shortly thereafter, Gennifer went public. Nichols talked a good game but when it came time to fish or cut bait, he kind of backed off. His case is a travesty if what he says is correct. The way it was handled through the courts and everything else, a travesty.''

Jerry Russell comments on Larry Nichols. ''He did about fifteen jingles for me during a period of time in the 1990 election cycle. He's really a good producer, an excellent musician, and he did a fine job on the jingles but as a consequence of that I was privy to a lot of that other bullshit about his lawsuit.''

John Hanchette was managing editor for the *Arkansas Gazette* when he ''would go and take supper at the Capitol Club. They had a lounge singer there who I thought was quite good and who would come over and talk to the customers. I probably had maybe two or three conversations with her. It was Gennifer Flowers. She was a brunette then, her hair was very dark. It did strike me that she was always very interested in current events covering the state government. She used to ask a lot of questions about what was going on at the state Capitol and what was going to be in the news and all that sort of stuff. There had been rumors that Clinton had been a skirt-chaser in his early days as governor but the citizens of Arkansas seemed to have made their peace with that. The general feeling I got was that they all believed he had stopped womanizing several years earlier. They seemed to be pretty protective of him. Both major papers pursued the lawsuits and pursued the complaints about Larry Nichols but they didn't get into the charges that he later made. I remember the *Gazette* broke that story about how he made all these phone calls to Central America and when we asked him about it, he claimed that he was just looking at the ad for the CIA. He never liked us because that's one of the things that got him in trouble—making those calls on state phones. During the 1992 campaign, in the primaries when Clinton was getting hammered daily and there was all that tabloid stuff about Gennifer Flowers, from everything that I can put together in my own mind, I'm very convinced that he knew her and they possibly were friends but I still am not convinced that the evidence was strong enough to have accused him of having an affair with her.''

Bob Steele recalls the turmoil in Clinton's camp when the Flowers story broke. ''The very first day the story broke, operatives in the campaign were panicked. They wanted to know what the network had and what the network was going with and were we going to show pictures? I said, 'No, no. We're just going to tell a story. There won't be any video. Just the graphic.' And then they said, 'Are you going to run the tapes?' They really just panicked because I didn't even know about the existence of tapes. Later another operative called me wanting to know if I had heard whether or not Gennifer Flowers had been paid for the story and I told him, 'Yeah, but by the *National Enquirer.*' And they wanted to know how much, and then I heard it out of the candidate's mouth. That afternoon, on the campaign trail, Clinton said, 'I understand this woman's been paid.' ''

Reporter Scott Charton finds the tapes puzzling. ''I was perplexed when I heard the entire Gennifer Flowers tape. There's a point on the tape where Clinton calls Flowers, 'Baby' and I remember watching Sam Donaldson asking Hillary about this when he taped this interview with her in Denver, why did he refer to Gennifer Flowers as 'Baby,' and I believe her response was to say 'that it didn't happen' and Donaldson let it go and that to me is a very good question. I always wondered about Gennifer Flowers. By the way—this may show how out of the loop I am—but I had never heard of Gennifer Flowers the whole time I covered him. I had heard lots of other names in many other rumors but I'd never heard of Gennifer Flowers.''

Nor had Guy Reel. ''I must admit, I'd never heard of Gennifer Flowers when I was covering Clinton. That's one thing that he pulled over on me. I thought it was real strange how it was covered so intensely and then the national press just dropped it. He's on the tapes and he talks to her in such a way that you wouldn't talk to somebody unless she was a lover. As far as I'm concerned, those tapes prove that, but the press never touched the tapes and they could have had a field day with them.''

Dick Herget, Clinton's gubernatorial campaign manager of 1980, says, ''Clinton and I spent an awful lot of time together and really got to know each other very personally. I was astonished when the Gennifer Flowers thing came up because during the time period that she gave, Clinton and I had a great relationship. The Flowers events were supposed to have happened the same time that we were working on all these campaigns and I had never heard her name mentioned.''

Paul Berry suspects political chicanery. ''For Bill and Hillary, there wasn't any subject that came up in that campaign that they hadn't talked about and that they weren't ready for, although I'm sure there were specific names and nuances that surprised them. I'm sure they were shocked by the clandestine shopping by elements outside of the formal Republican machinery that were actually offering money to people to say things. I can't prove that. I've heard that many places and I have no doubt of it whatsoever.''

John King, chief political correspondent for the Associated Press, says, ''When Gennifer Flowers first came up, my understanding is that George Stephanopoulos and Clinton had a sit-down in a hotel in New Hampshire and George said, 'You've got to tell me. I've got to be prepared to defend you so you've got to tell me what went on.' I don't know what Clinton told him but I know that conversation took place. I don't know that either George Stephanopoulos or James Carville had the luxury of trying to step back and think whether or not they believed it. They were just trying to do their job. Do I believe it? I know for a fact that there were a lot of holes in her story. Do I think there's something odd that tapes exist of these phone conversations and does that lead me to believe they had some sort of relationship? It does. My gut feeling is that there was some kind of relationship. Do I have any evidence that it was a sexual relationship? I don't. It's not my call to say what they had but obviously they had some form of a relationship. The personal tone of the conversations led you to believe that they knew each other very well. There are so many conflicting statements that I don't know what to believe.''

Deborah Mathis, a White House correspondent for the Gannett News Service, had been linked to Clinton in rumors. ''Of course the rumors were disturbing. It can't help but be disturbing except that I see now in hindsight I was blessed by it but at the time I felt cursed. I don't know when it started. The first time I heard of it was right before the election. I was floored by it. I had heard all kinds of rumors about Clinton and you name the woman. If a woman was prominent at all or attractive, her name got in there. Some of it sounded so flimsy, you just kind of said, 'Oh, come on.' And it was almost like the crying-wolf syndrome where you've heard it too much and you just started wondering if any of the rumors were true, but I had never heard my name connected to it. I don't know if other people had heard my name swirling around for years or what, but I hadn't heard it until right before the gubernatorial election in 1990. My first reaction to it was to laugh because I thought the person who called to tell me about it was joking. My second reaction was to my family and tell them, 'Here's the thing that's being said. I just want you to know so you won't be blindsided.' I even told my little children about it. They don't understand what affairs mean really but they got the drift well enough so they asked, 'Mama, what are you going to do?' Well, I subscribed to the old adage that you don't answer a critic unless he's right, unless he's telling the truth.''

Anne Jansen was also featured in rumors about Clinton's womanizing. ''There have always been rumors about Clinton. There will always be rumors. Personally, I've never had any woman come up to me and say, 'I was with him.' It's always, 'My friend. My daughter.' I've even heard that I was with him. I made an appearance at a mall once where a friend of mine worked. A coworker said to her, 'Have you heard who's going to be here today?' My friend said, 'Yeah, Anne Jansen.' He said, 'Well, you know who she's dating, don't you?' and my friend was thrilled that I was dating someone and said, 'No, who?' and he said, 'The governor.' She called me over and asked about it and the fact that people have said that about me—that I was one of the rumors—made me really question how much of it was true. That's not to say that I don't think some of that went on. I think there's probably some truth to it but as far as my ever having firsthand knowledge of it from anyone else, no.''

Campaign staffer Kathy Ford does not believe that Flowers had an affair with Clinton. ''There wasn't any evidence. There's probably about 500 women in Arkansas who would like you to believe they were with the governor. I don't know where it comes from. I guess their lives are so narrow that this is the most famous person they're ever going to know. People were just trying to dig up anything and everything.''

A reporter who wishes to remain anonymous places more stock in the rumors. ''This young attorney who had been a journalist was working at the *Democrat*. She had a very nice body and made sure everybody knew she had a nice body. She was divorced at the time and had been for a while. So Clinton comes down the hall and he stops and he talks to me and then he says, 'This woman used to be a journalist, she used to work at the *Democrat*.' I just looked at him and I said, 'I know.' His enthusiasm for the woman seemed to me just really misplaced. Someone told me that on a Monday there had been a ceremony for Martin Luther King and that this woman had shown up in casual clothes, not work clothes, not like she was there for the deal and had had several minutes of private conversation with Clinton. They were out in the open but there was nobody else participating in the conversation. Another person who had worked at the *Democrat* had seen Clinton driving down this particular road in the Lincoln by himself one day in March and it was at the same location as this woman's apartment complex. The person who told me was smart enough to know something was happening but didn't have the other information to put together with the location.''

Democrat Gazette journalist Ed Gray says, ''Everybody has heard the rumors. They were fairly common. In the McRae campaign, we had a source who gave us the phone number of a man who lived in Denver whose marriage, this person said, had been broken up by Bill Clinton. All we had to do was call and get that man to talk, and the source said the man would talk, but we didn't do it. It would have been hard to do. I felt that it was just too low-down for me.''

An anonymous source has been following Clinton's activities, social and otherwise for years. ''I seem to recall he was a whirling dervish on the bar circuit during the years he wasn't governor (1980–82). I remember bumping into him in various spots— Bennigans, Busters. That big red nose of his was unmistakable during the Christmas season. He was always with women, with an entourage, and you never knew whether this was his 'action' or just staff members but he was always with a pack. His wife was never there. I probably saw him half a dozen times and he just seemed to be having a good time like everybody else. He generally would seem to be pretty well lit up and I remember one occasion at Busters. He was working this woman like there was no tomorrow and it was pretty late. We were getting ready to leave and a group of us, a group of guys, were all just laughing our asses off and watching our former governor. I remember talking to the guys I was with about how the mighty had fallen. We were all mimicking what he might have been saying and we all thought it really pretty funny that it was so unabashedly done because this guy was married. His entourage would be around him like Jilly Rizzo around Sinatra, I guess to make it look like he was with a group, but very clearly he was beaming in on one attractive woman. He had good taste. It was always someone with a very attractive body. No question that our former governor was a sport. The time we're talking about he closed the deal and left with her right before we did.''

A Little Rock source states, ''I've heard reports of an open marriage. I don't know if that's true. I do know (through friends) that he had numerous affairs and his wife was aware of them. Finally in 1989 she slammed him with an ultimatum and basically said, 'Look, I'm going to divorce you and your political career is over.' She apparently just laid it on the table. 'Here are the terms.

You have to stop seeing people. You have to stop embarrassing and humiliating me. I will not have affairs. You will not have affairs, and we will work on this marriage and get it together for the sake of our child. For the sake of your career. For the sake of my sanity.' As she is wont to do, she took control and dictated the terms and apparently he swore solemnly that that would be the case. From what I heard, after Hillary gave Bill the ultimatum he was much more restrained and they had a pretty good marriage and apparently things were going very swimmingly.

"However, everybody who follows this little Peyton Place drama feels that Clinton's back on the hammer if you will, and that he broke the vow he made to Hillary.

"A friend of mine who lives in the Heights [a Little Rock suburb] has been having an affair with Clinton for years. She and I have talked about it quite often. To Clinton's credit, he never said 'Hey, I'm going to take you away from all this and we'll get married and you'll be the first lady.' It was very clear that it was an affair. He would say he loved her, but that he wasn't going to get a divorce. He told her a few times that Hillary had talked about divorce.

"I've heard from a very good source (actually someone who lives in Washington and is very close to both of them) that some Secret Service agents are loyal to Hillary and some are loyal to Bill and apparently some of Hillary's Secret Service agents notified her in a rather alarmed manner that the president was having a fling on *Airforce 1*. Hillary grabs a limo and races out and catches him dressing. This was around the time that we started getting reports about the throwing of ashtrays and lamps. She stormed out, went back to the White House, and began throwing a wild tantrum. When he came back, from what I heard, she just went crazy—throwing stuff at him, screaming at him. Shortly after that she left to visit her father because he was ill and she was in Little Rock for twelve days.

"A very good friend of mine who danced with him at some kind of big black-tie gala, is a very attractive busty blonde and bright. She was newly married when Clinton asked her to dance. She was flattered to be dancing with the governor. She said that he was instantly sexually aggressive. She said sometimes a guy, will touch your rear end just to try to get a sense of where you're going to go. But his hands were all over her. He asked her to go to bed with him. He said right then they could just leave. They were in a hotel apparently.''

An anonymous source speaks more specifically. "I know a woman who attended a Democratic party affair one evening at a Ramada Inn in West Memphis. This was not terribly long after Clinton had won back the governorship from Frank White. Hillary was not at the party. Clinton asked this woman to dance and was fairly aggressive, being quite physical. He suggested that state troopers pick her up at 2:00 A.M. and take her back to his hotel room, adding that he thought 'we'd make a pretty good fit.' She said no and nothing happened. What struck her as being particularly offensive about this event was that Clinton knew this woman was recently married because her husband had been working for Clinton at the time. Additionally, her husband was not more than twenty feet away from them when Clinton made that pass at her on the dance floor."

A woman reporter says, "We had a running joke about the Bill Clinton handshake. Every time that you would shake his hand, he would grab your hand, look into your eyes, and you would literally have to pull your hand away because he wouldn't let go. It was like this lingering that always made me think, 'Okay, okay, I'm a little uncomfortable now. Let me pull my hand away.' "

James Merriweather finds the rumors numerous but the proof elusive. "Some people looked into the womanizing rumors more carefully than others. It got to be a hot issue just because of all the allegations coming in from all over. We looked and we were never able to find any kind of a smoking gun. There had been these persistent rumors for years and there were specific names that floated around for years but I don't think anybody definitely pinned any of them down. Gennifer Flowers was one that kept surfacing. I'm still not sure if there's a lot of fire there but they clearly knew each other and talked on several occasions. That's as close as anybody ever came to finding that smoking gun."

Steve Barnes comments. "I'll say this for the record. I have never covered anybody in public life about whom there were as many rumors over such a long period of time. The only way that I can know about an affair is if I participated in it or if I'm in the bedroom and have firsthand knowledge, and I don't. Those rumors were such a common commodity—they were in every strata of Arkansas society, from government, from corporate levels, from political insiders, from people in the small colleges . . . academia. There were so many rumors, I think it was accepted as a given that he was engaging in extramarital liasons. But when it reaches that critical mass, he is in all probability being accused of being with women he had never met.''

Barnes did, however, have sources in the governor's office some years ago who described the distress Clinton's staff felt at appearances that were less than discreet. Evidently, Clinton would come to work and Betsey Wright would repair to his office, slam the door and there would be great shouting. Not only from Betsey, but also from one or two aides, to the effect of 'You've got to worry about appearances. How can you go there and do that or be seen there? Don't you care about appearances?' They weren't suggesting that anything had been consummated only that people were being left with the perception that he behaved improperly.''

A TV newsperson relates what was supposedly going on behind the scenes during the campaign. ''I heard from two people within the Clinton campaign that they hired a private investigator to investigate his past and all or any of these alleged liaisons that occurred. He could not remember every woman with whom he had slept. The Clinton campaign then created a file in the campaign headquarters that was developed through private investigations of their own candidate so that they would know what some of the charges could be if somebody really tried to hurt him. They did their own investigations independently. They wanted it to be thorough as if it were being done for the Republicans. Supposedly they said, 'Don't hold back any of the facts; anything you can find out, we need to know.' They called it the Doomsday File and it was apparently in a file cabinet in the war room that held three full drawers. It wasn't just on Clinton. It was also on Bush and all of the alleged liaisons that he had. So if Bush had gone after Clinton, Clinton would have gone after Bush. It struck me as being a sad commentary on politics in America today.

''Campaign people told me they would quiz him. 'Who's Marie in Hot Springs?' They would ask, and he couldn't tell them. 'What are you talking about?' he'd say. 'She's a nurse,' they'd tell him. Because he couldn't remember. The campaign people were scared to death because he didn't think it was that big of a deal. That's what Arkansas boys do in their spare time I guess. When they would find something out, they would ask him about it and see if he could recall it and how he would defend it and sometimes he knew and sometimes he couldn't remember. Again, I can't prove the truth of any of what I'm telling you.''

As Eleanor Clift sees it, the rumors eventually were superseded by issues. ''Obviously the stories didn't go away. I think the press pursued it and pursued it until the polls said the public was tired of it. At some point, if you don't come up with new information, you can't just keep going over the same ground. My goodness, reporters were stationed in Little Rock looking for new dirt. If they could come up with it, the story would have gone further. I actually am heartened by the fact that the public decided this campaign on issues other than a candidate's private life. With Gary Hart, I thought his womanizing was a bigger window into the man because I thought there was always a feeling among people who knew Gary Hart that he was just a little bit weird whereas that was not the case with Clinton. He seemed like a fairly regular person.''

Maria Henson reported on issues because she felt that rumors without proof are not newsworthy. ''Rumors of womanizing surrounded him for a long time. Until Gary Hart that topic was out of the realm of what we would report on. We were so public policy oriented where I worked. We wrote about the minutia of government and his policy. We would cover every utterance and every movement of a bill but even though everyone suspected that there were probably women there it wasn't really our charge to go after that. There was no proof, proof being photographs of someone credible saying that they actually saw him go off into a room with a woman.''

Nor is it news that Bill Clinton likes women. Maria Henson continues, ''One story comes to mind. I was on the road with Clinton and he was making speeches in late fall of 1986. We were off in some greeting card plant and we looked out into this big room and there were row after row of people sitting side by side folding greeting cards. That meant the press had a long time to stand there because Bill Clinton, as usual, was going to shake every single hand of every person. So this little group of press people stood around and we looked out into the room and we saw this gorgeous blonde sitting there. One of the camera men moved into position and focused right on that blonde. I said, 'What are you doing?' He said, 'Well, let's just see what happens.' We all just sat back and cackled because Clinton in fact did go and shake every hand. When he got to this woman and she shook his hand we looked at each other in astonishment because he didn't pause but kept going. He went to the next person and then he went back to the blonde and shook her hand again. It was great because we'd all predicted that he would do something like that, that he would focus on that blonde.''

Susan Rodman says, "I won't say anything that I don't know for sure. I always thought he was very friendly. I would never go as far as to say that he made a pass. Nothing overt. I think it's in his nature to maybe flirt a little, to be friendly but I've seen him be that way with guys too. Some people thought that the way he looked at women was as if they didn't have any clothes on or that he was undressing them with his eyes ... I don't know. I never really felt uncomfortable. I always thought the flirting was just more his personality. I never knew Gennifer Flowers. Do I believe her story? I won't say I do. I won't say I don't."

George Jernigan thinks that "Clinton was extremely lucky. He was at the right place at the right time. I introduced him in November of 1991 to the Democratic chairs in Chicago. It was the first time they had all met. And then the other candidates came, each candidate had a private breakfast, lunch, or dinner with the chairs and a public presentation with the media and the chairs. Clinton was the last on. He got up there and gave it his all and everyone said, 'Hey, this one is going to win. He's the only one that has a chance to carry this campaign.' It seemed like the one break was Gennifer Flowers. I think that Gennifer Flowers made him a household name."

Kit Seelye of the *Philadelphia Inquirer* shows how the rumor became news. "Gennifer Flowers wasn't really a surprise because there had been rumors about it for months and he and Hillary had in fact tried to dispel those rumors. Gene Sperling has these breakfasts periodically and invites reporters and public officials in the news. At one Sperling breakfast Clinton and his wife were saying, 'We know of these rumors and we just want to say that our private life is private.' They thought by doing this they could put the matter to rest. But during that whole period, reporters were running down to Little Rock to investigate and they never came up with anything. When the Gennifer Flowers stuff first blew up, my paper and the *New York Times* and a few others didn't mention it. We used three paragraphs of an AP story that said there were these allegations but editors here really wanted to stay away from it. The next day, Clinton was holed up in the Mansion because of the Flowers story. The day after that he went to Boston to a Massachusetts state Democratic Committee Meeting. It was his first appearance since the Gennifer Flowers story blew up or since she appeared in the *Star*. There was just an absolute feeding frenzy, a mob of reporters and microphones. He and Carville got off the elevator and there was this surge of camera guys and reporters around them and it sort of separated Carville from Clinton. As people were asking Clinton questions, Carville was saying sort of over the microphone, 'This is democracy, folks. This is democracy in action,' and clearly messing up the sound bites that they were getting from Clinton but also sending a message to people. They were very shrewd to turn it into a press issue as opposed to a Clinton-being-faithful-to-his-wife issue. They filmed *60 Minutes* in Boston that Sunday morning. After *60 Minutes,* for the first time, my newspaper put it on the front page and I wrote the story. It was no longer one of these little buried stories, so in a sense it did make it legitimate news by discussing it on *60 Minutes.''*

John King interviewed the Clintons immediately after their appearance on *60 Minutes.* ''I got to interview both of them in the car from the Ritz-Carlton in Boston where they did the interview for *60 Minutes.* We drove to Logan Airport and then Mrs. Clinton went back to Arkansas to make sure somebody was there to watch it with Chelsea and I got on a small plane with Clinton, Carville, and Stephanopoulos to New Hampshire. Because they did the interview, they were running late for this New Hampshire event so they actually flew even though it was only a twenty-five-minute flight and I spent another fifteen or twenty minutes talking with them on the plane. My questions were pretty similar to the *60 Minutes* stuff because that's what was obviously the issue of the day but they were both pumped up when they came out of the hotel because both thought that they had done a really good job answering the questions. There was a scene during the interview when a light fell. One of the light banks in the room started to fall and Clinton literally lurched across Hillary and grabbed it before it could conk her on the head. They wanted that on television. There were a lot of emotional moments that didn't make the final cut and I think they felt betrayed in the sense that Don Hewitt had egged him on a little bit. He was literally trying to get him to confess to adultery. He had kind of stirred it up to get them to be more emotional and then some of their answers to those questions actually made a better case for the Clintons, which Hewitt wasn't thrilled about. A lot of that stuff didn't make the program which they didn't know at the time. When I was with them, they were really pumped up and there were people outside cheering. We were in a Lincoln Town Car and a couple of people pounded on it and said, 'Go get 'em Bill. Don't worry about it.' And I remember Bill pointed out the window and said, 'See, they understand. If people would just let us explain this to them, they will understand.' They were both very emotional. They seemed to be very encouraged and very happy. When it actually aired they weren't unhappy, but they were disappointed that some of the material that made them look more favorable hadn't been included.''

John King speaks further about the interaction between Clinton and Hillary. ''The day I was with them in the car after the *60 Minutes* interview, she was up front and he was in the back. His arm was up over the seat and she was clutching his forearm. They would finish each other's answers during the interview and I found it to be very genuine. You would see that sometimes at events. There was a time in New Hampshire when part of his line was, 'Buy one, get one free.' People would tell him that saying that was risky. Some thought they should be a little bit more detached but during the bus tours when they were together it seemed like smart politics. I find their interaction genuine. I think they have a very complicated relationship that is based partly on this intellectual attraction that may be difficult for some people to understand. When you see them talking policy on the plane sometimes, they'd play devil's advocate just to keep the argument stimulated and I think that's a great deal of their attraction for one another. I suspect that that intellectual interest in each other is partly what got them through some of their personal difficulties. People say it is political convenience. I don't know that to be the case.''

Robert ''Say'' McIntosh, most often described as a black community activist, is kind of a Little Rock yippie with an aptitude for street theater. Over the years, McIntosh's antics have become so outrageous that a few local news organizations refuse to give him any credence. Yet, when, during the 1992 campaign, McIntosh claimed Bill Clinton fathered an illegitimate child with a black woman, he got everyone's attention.

Bill Powell speaks about Say McIntosh, another potential threat to Clinton's campaign. ''Say McIntosh was a black activist in Arkansas. His son was busted up around Batesville, Arkansas, because he had about four and a half pounds of cocaine in a van. He got fifty years in prison. He just got pardoned which created a stir. After Bill was elected while Tucker was in Washington, D.C., celebrating the election, Jerry Jewell, who is the president pro tem of the state Senate, pardoned McIntosh's son. Caused

quite a flap. McIntosh is the guy who put the flyers out about
Clinton's black child and all that wild stuff. One day he's for
Clinton, the next day he's against him. He sued Clinton at one
point. Said that he owed him money for supporting him and getting black voters for him. He had a restaurant that he lost because
he didn't pay his bills. He's a man with a spotty reputation in my
humble opinion.''

Jerry Russell elaborates on McIntosh and his flyers. "One of
them says, 'One of these days, Bill Clinton's going to look down
and say, "Dick, you kept me from being president of the United
States." ' There's another picture of a black baby with the caption
'This is Clinton's kid.' Then McIntosh, who has never shut up for
anybody in the last ten or fifteen years, all of a sudden vanishes
from the political scene. For years he'd put out flyers about how
Clinton preferred black tail and went after black women and then
all of a sudden, McIntosh is quiet. And then his kid who had
eighteen years before he should have even been considered for
parole, is out of jail. The stories go that Tommy McIntosh didn't
know anything about it. They came down and said, 'Kid, you're
out of here.' And he was gone. He was in jail for fifty years on
drug charges, and, of course, obviously, the only reason he was
in jail was because he was black—the fact that he'd had a pocket
full of marijuana had absolutely nothing to do with it.''

Mara Leveritt says, ''The role that Say McIntosh has played in
this community is that of a fool. I mean that in the traditional
medieval sense, a person who can sometimes tell the greatest
truths and sometimes makes an ass of himself. I wrote a cover
story for our newspaper about Say and his son Tommy and I
interviewed both of them. Say was very explicit in his explanation
of the situation but, on the other hand, the tracts that Say McIntosh
has distributed are disgraceful. They're just libelous. He heralds
himself to no standard of backing up anything. He distributes his
papers all over town and he has never produced any proof of his
charges. He's charged that there's a child and that Clinton loves
black women—this whole range of things, none of which have
ever been substantiated by Say McIntosh or anybody else. So
when he comes out and says, 'My son got out of this deal because
I swung my support to Clinton at a critical moment and I influenced him,' a lot of people, myself included, have a very hard
time swallowing it. Say said his son was pardoned because he
swore his support to Clinton. He said Clinton was behind it and
had made the arrangements with Tucker before he left. If I recall

right, he said that Clinton had intimated to him that it would be taken care of before Clinton left the state to campaign.

"Tommy McIntosh's case is interesting in its own right because it was a very extreme sentence for the conditions of the case. A governor who wanted to could reasonably have looked at that case and said, 'This is an outrageous sentence in a predominantly white county. There are overtones of racism in it. The sentence is way out of line with other similar crimes.' Other prosecutors could argue the opposite but the case could warrant attention just on its own merits, period."

Bob Steele notes, "Some said McIntosh had information about Clinton and some women in eastern Arkansas and made a deal whereby when the governor was out of town, Jewell would pardon the son in exchange for McIntosh staying quiet. The kid was pardoned."

Joe Quinn points out that McIntosh was "a guy who had done a lot of good things early in his life. He had been involved in some programs to feed poor people and he was the paper's "Man of the Year" years ago. He had a sense of the theatric. We had a sheriff here that he did battle with for years. I would be very, very surprised if any kind of deal was cut. His targets came and went and obviously he went through a phase where his target was Bill Clinton. His target before that was Tommy Robinson, a guy who went to Congress, the sheriff I mentioned. I just don't think any deal would have been cut. I think the media finally realized that this guy's not a public figure. He's a private citizen. It might be valid to debate the parole process for Tommy McIntosh. I don't think Jewell handled it right at all and it was a situation that just exploded."

Jerry Russell certainly agrees that it wasn't handled right. "Tucker became governor, the office of lieutenant governor was vacant, so when the governor leaves the state, the president pro tem of the state and Senate is acting governor. A black dentist named Jerry Jewell is president pro tem because of seniority which meant Clinton would be able to say, 'If I win, Jim Guy becomes governor and Jerry Jewell can take care of this' and Tucker went to the inauguration. Jewell pardoned two guys and released two guys. Three of the four are black and you can just hear somebody say, 'Well you better get a white guy too' and they say, 'Well what about this white guy, Jones?' Jewell didn't know anything about it. What was Jones in for? He didn't know. Jewell was asked about this other guy that he pardoned. 'He's been out of jail for eighteen years and now you're finally giving him a pardon? What prompted that?' Jewell said, 'Well, I'm not going to talk about that.' Another guy's in jail because he hit a guy in the head with a baseball bat fifteen years ago and murdered him. Why did you let him out? 'Well, I'm not going to talk about it,' Jewell said. 'You all are picking on me because I'm black.' "

KARK-TV anchor and reporter Sonja Deaner thinks it unlikely that a deal was cut. "The Say McIntosh story was never confirmed. Everyone was kind of batting it around and talking about it but nothing was ever done about it. People saw Say McIntosh as a kind of a nuisance. He's very loud. I don't know how much of what he has to say is true or just pure garbage but he puts flyers on people's cars every week and they're flamboyant flyers. When Bill Clinton was running, McIntosh would have pictures of black children with Chelsea's face imposed on them and the text would say, 'This is Clinton's illegitimate child,' and things like that. He never offered any proof. The story about Tucker never leaving the state could be true but it seems a little farfetched to me that it would be planned that far in advance, that Say McIntosh would have thought through the whole scheme way back when Clinton was running. Say McIntosh speaks at city council meetings and there's a grain of good in what he says but there's all this smoke and mirrors, and people tend to ignore him because he's so irrational and loud."

A Faulkner County marijuana grower offers this take on Bill Clinton's famous statement that he tried marijuana in England but didn't inhale: "I think I can explain that. You see, to this day, in England, a lot of what they smoke isn't simply marijuana rolled up in cigarette paper, but hashish and tobacco. Now, if you're not a tobacco smoker, that stuff will punish you. It's likely that if that's what Clinton got a hold of, he just started coughing—he didn't have a chance to inhale. Or to like it." That's one theory. Others think that a man of Clinton's experience and generation could not have had only a single encounter with illicit substances.

Bob Steele talks about Bill Clinton, his brother Roger Clinton, and drugs. "One story that impressed me says a lot about Clinton and his family. A friend of mine who's a state policeman was doing an undercover investigation on drugs in Hot Springs. He went to the governor and said, 'Hey, your brother is in this.' My friend told me, 'The guy is powerful. He could have told us to lay off and probably gotten away with it but instead he said, "Arrest him." ' That impressed the hell out of me. What impressed me even more was that Clinton was at his brother's trial every day and he was right in the middle of a campaign. He didn't have to do that. He could have sacrificed his brother for his own political well being, but he stood by his brother and he also probably saved his life because he said, 'Arrest him,' and then he followed up. He stayed with him, walking with him, and there were cameras everywhere. He was embarrassed, I'm sure. Roger's a wild man. He's been in a lot of trouble, and Bill has always been right there for him, so that's impressive to me.''

An anonymous source reports further on the former governor's social activities. "I was at a Halloween party with Bill and Roger Clinton. There was a back bedroom that people were going back to. I wandered back with the host and saw several people— including Clinton—milling around a plate of cocaine. There he was, big as life, snorting coke with about six other people! Admittedly they were all people that I think he felt he could trust, but he did not stop when I came in. He seemed to be animated and not at all self-conscious.

"As for the Roger Clinton investigation, I think the police or the FBI or somebody came to Clinton and said, 'Look, we're going to do this thing with your blessing or without it so we better get your blessing,' and that's the best I can reconstruct it. Clearly I don't know the facts."

Pam Strickland notes: "One of the people who got rich off of bonds at a time when the economy was good was Dan Lassiter. Lassiter had been connected with Roger, and in his run for governor in 1986 Frank White was trying to tie Clinton to Dan Lassiter."

Investigative journalist Mel Hanks reported on the Lassiter case for KARK-TV. "A grand jury investigation involved one of Clinton's best friends, Dan Lassiter, who owned a bonding company that got a lot of the state's business. Lassiter was implicated in 1985 in a drug case in Hot Springs involving Clinton's brother. Lassiter was a big contributor to Clinton's campaign and Clinton used to go to parties and to a ski resort that Lassiter owned, so it was pretty big news when there was a drug probe of Lassiter.

"We were the only ones who knew about it because I had a source near the grand jury. We kept reporting and there were quite a lot of threats to us including a man on a motorcycle who kept following me. The motorcycle man himself was so stupid—that's another reason I thought it was a government operation—and so sloppy that he made it obvious after a while that he was following me. So we got him on tape. We used our whole photography staff. I'd go out to draw him out, and we'd have photographers who knew the route I'd take following me. About two or three car lengths behind me was this idiot on a motorcycle. I'd stop and act like I was doing something and he'd stop and take notes on me. Meanwhile our photographers are getting him on tape. We ran the tape on the air that night and people called in, scores of them. They told us the name of the man on the motorcycle and the name of the man he was working for—a private investigator out of Hot Springs who apparently used to be Clinton's state police director. He had hired this motorcycle man to follow me to see who my sources were.

"Our news director told me to bring my wife and son to Little Rock so they could sweep my house to see if it had been bugged. En route to Little Rock, there was a heavily tended limousine that followed my wife and son and then tried to run them off the road and we think that was connected. They seemed to be saying 'Well, you may have found out about us but we can still get you.' At one point they pulled a gun on my wife. The limo was right behind her and somebody leaned out the back window and pulled out a gun. We never did find out who hired the detective agency but I was told later that the order came from the governor's office itself.

"I had heard that Clinton was told about his brother and he said, 'Go ahead,' but I also heard that by the time he was informed, the investigation was so far along, he really couldn't have called it off without giving an appearance of impropriety. I'm sure that he did say, 'Go ahead,' but I think he didn't have much choice.

"I had a lot of drug rumors brought to me during the last few years. In fact, a pretty high-level source said that the FBI had a photograph of Clinton snorting cocaine with Lassiter at a party but I never saw the picture. The person was never able to produce the picture for me so it really never went beyond being just a rumor. That was 1986."

Scott Charton remembers "in 1986 when it was the big rematch of Clinton and Frank White, best two out of three. Bill Simmons was moderator of a debate out of the Holiday Inn sponsored by the AP and I was covering the story for AP. Frank White made his big publicity grab: His grandstand move was going to be challenging Clinton to take a drug test, but Clinton one-upped him by saying, 'Not only have I taken a drug test, my chief of staff has taken one as well, and I challenge you to do so.' That was because White's campaign manager, a guy named Darrell Glascock, was known to be kind of a partier. Simmons was moderating that and he asked him directly about using drugs. Clinton again said he had not.''

Maria Henson asked him the same question. ''It was late fall of 1986 and the press was moving in a pack to ask him to answer the charges Frank White had made so there was this horde of press people there. I asked him whether he had used cocaine and he said, 'No, I wouldn't know it if I saw it.' I thought that was a really interesting answer because a lot of people can say that he at least could describe what cocaine looked like. We all just looked at him like we couldn't believe he had said it but moved on.''

Clinton's responses to questions regarding marijuana during the presidential primary have likewise been cause for incredulity among members of the press. Randy Lilleston is Washington bureau chief of the *Arkansas Democrat-Gazette.* ''I thought the press was more than fair on the drug issue because he did such a song and dance about that. He would say that he had never broken the laws of his own country, which raises the obvious question 'Well, what about the laws of another country?' In fact he told me that once and I didn't follow it up. I should have. But it finally came up during the New York Primary when he was doing a televised debate with Jerry Brown. A local reporter asked him about it and followed up on it and put him on the spot. That's when he gave the 'I never inhaled' answer. And it was such a case of him trying to cut it so fine, to give almost a lawyer-like answer, that it really did reflect badly on him. It cut to a much more important question about veracity and truthfulness and that sort of thing. I sure didn't have much trouble with what they were doing over the drug question and to some degree I didn't have much trouble over the personal life either because I think it is a legitimate issue. It's not really that it was brought out as much as how it was brought out and how the story was advanced that really makes me pause.''

A reporter who wishes not to be named says he, too, would have preferred candor regarding the drug question and the draft. ''There are times when I really started to like him and then there were times when he made me so angry because of his arrogance. He is likeable because he is so full of ideas and goals that he wants to accomplish. Then an issue like the draft would come up and he would just stonewall us and treat us like we were friggin' idiots and pretend it would go away. He would be angry that we even would have the nerve to enquire about subjects like these.

"Clinton would rather say something stupid like 'I didn't inhale' or categorically deny something that was not an absolute than confess. I felt like saying to him, and I've had this conversation with his aides before and have only gotten shrugs, why doesn't he come clean: Why doesn't he just say 'I smoked pot.' Why doesn't he just say, 'Well, I did this thing in the draft. That's what I did.' Why does he have to spin it out over all these months and in so many different ways until we become suspicious of his responses to things? What is it about him?"

Bill Clinton is an artful rhetorician. He's not called "Slick Willie" for nothing. To those who've followed him over the years, this legalistic tendency is often disheartening.

Mark Oswald says, "I think Clinton is always so sharp about the exact use of his words. That's why as a reporter, I learned pretty quickly that you really had to use a tape recorder on him. When he was asked that question about running for president throughout the 1990 campaign, he always left some wiggle room. 'I don't intend to run now.' 'I don't foresee any circumstances in which I can run.' I covered his debate with Sheffield Nelson and neither myself, the opposition, or anybody else reported on what later became 'the pledge' because we'd heard him say it so many times that we didn't pay that much attention to it, but when he started running for president the AP retrieved a tape of the Nelson debate. That time, he hadn't left any wiggle room. He said, 'I will not run for president.' I remember when he was hit with that, he was angry. It was kind of like he had gotten caught.

"He got caught another time by the infamous, 'Have you ever used illegal drugs?' question. When it came up in 1988 Clinton would always give these evasive answers like 'I don't answer "Have you ever" questions,' and the famous response at one point was, 'He had never used illegal drugs as an adult in the state of Arkansas.' I remember when I was the *Gazette*'s state Capitol bureau chief and I'd sent our other reporter, Scott Morris, to interview him, Scott asked him, 'Did you ever smoke marijuana or use illegal drugs in college?' And he thought for a second, and then he said, 'No. That's the answer I'll give to that question.' So later he admitted trying marijuana at Oxford and I'm thinking, 'didn't Scott Morris ask him if he'd ever use marijuana in college?' So

I looked up a definition of college in the dictionary, and *college* is your first four years—graduate school is something else. So he answered it truthfully, but again to me that shows how much he thinks about exactly what he's saying. Actually I was amazed: He didn't lie, he was telling the truth.''

Maria Henson often had problems with Clinton's answers. ''Wherever I went people wanted to know, 'What was it like covering him?' I would say, 'He was in some ways an easy person to cover because he was accessible and he enjoyed the press. He enjoyed talking to us and he made it easy for us to get answers. However, a lot of times we would think for sure he had answered our questions, but when we would come back and play the tape we'd find he didn't really answer the question.' He was known for his long sentences that were all grammatically correct, they would last a paragraph if you typed them out. He's got you so convinced when you're sitting there talking to him eye to eye that you just got your question answered that you have to walk away and play the tape before you realize he left himself an opening.''

Nightline correspondent Chris Burrey says, ''Everybody on the press bus thought that he performed poorest in the morning and that he was kind of sluggish. I don't know if depressed is the right word but he was often off and he didn't really get going until late in the day when he gave his best performances. He's an extraordinary performer and if he was able to mask depression and anger and other emotions which might leave others with a negative perception, I think he did a good job of it. I think he's a masterful politician. I don't think I've ever seen anybody who is as facile and glib as he is.

''I think, though, he's got a terrific problem with the truth and obviously we saw it in all kinds of little ways. I mean, we saw it clearly with the Gennifer Flowers story. We saw it with the draft story. You know, the bit about him not getting a draft notice and then getting a draft notice. He was able to get away with it in Arkansas but only to a certain extent; they were the ones who named him Slick Willie after all. That was my biggest problem with Bill Clinton. He seemed to have a fundamental problem with being entirely honest. Maybe that's a politician's defense mechanism. There is obviously a bullshit factor among all politicians in Washington. With him it seemed a bit more pronounced and it certainly put you on your guard. Having lived through the campaign, I'm a little bit more skeptical.''

John King notes, "During the whole character issue and the draft and Gennifer Flowers, the Clinton campaign was saying that they were being as honest as they possibly could be and I essentially wrote that maybe you can't say that they're lying but they're not giving the entire truth either. With the whole draft thing particularly, they thought that if they just revealed a part of it the entire issue would go away. There were more letters and more contact than he had said, and he can stand up and say, 'Well, I never said there wasn't more contact,' and not be lying but at the same time he's not being truthful when he has been asked open-ended questions for which he didn't volunteer any information. So I wrote a piece about how maybe you can't question his answers but you can question his candor. He was pretty mad about it. He just dropped the story in my lap and said, 'I don't think so.' I talked to him later that day and other days and there were times when I thought I had a pretty good relationship with him throughout the campaign. I got a lot of access to him. At times he would argue about things I had written but never in a way that I found threatening or intimidating. That's his job. I understand that."

Darrell Glascock worked with Clinton promoting tourism in the state of Arkansas. "So I had some nonpolitical contact with him during that time and he's just a very likable guy. He sometimes reminds me of the old adage about the fellow who would climb a telephone pole to tell a lie when he could stand on the ground and tell the truth. He'll tell you whatever you want to hear basically. I don't think that's intentional. He's the type of personality that wants to be accepted by everyone and so if he can find a way to accommodate you and say to you what you want to hear, he'll do that and then if he gets trapped, he'll say he didn't say it.

"It seems that most politicians who have been very successful have an immunity syndrome that kicks in. They think anything they do is acceptable because people will love them anyway. People are all over you when you're the governor. Huey Long didn't want to be a United States senator, he just had to be because he couldn't run for governor again. Being governor is a big deal in the South. It carries with it the groupie mania and Clinton is great with the media. And the media, many contend, was less than hard-nosed with presidential candidate Clinton."

Juan Williams discusses the relationship between Clinton and the press during the 1992 campaign. "Almost right from the start, there were these stories coming out of Little Rock that said, Clinton's not who he appears to be. Some of the people in Arkansas were saying, 'Isn't it interesting that Arkansas's favorite son is not getting kid glove treatment from the Arkansas press?' There also were these crazy stories—Say McIntosh was saying all these crazy things about Clinton. All this stuff was constantly bleeding into the wash but it was peripheral. Everyone was aware of it but no one was giving it big play. He's successful in Arkansas. Maybe these are people who have their own agendas and are backbiting and jealous of his sudden prominence in the national arena, so in a sense I was aware of these problems but I didn't give them any specific attention.

"Why did I think he survived the marijuana thing and Gennifer Flowers? In the case of Gennifer Flowers, I thought it had little to do with him and much to do with the press. This had come on the heels of Willie Smith. It had come on the heels of Clarence Thomas. In political terms it had come on the heels of Gary Hart, and the American people in that case had been pretty clear in saying to the press, 'You guys are way out of bounds. You guys have gone over the falls here and you're out of control.' At my paper, the *Post*, which is a purely political institution, there was a great sense that we don't want to offend people. We reported the story, but unlike our behavior in the Gary Hart situation, where Paul Taylor, one of our political reporters, went on to ask Mr. Hart if he had had an extramarital affair, there was no such pressure in the Clinton situation. On the contrary, the pressure was to do this in a tasteful way so that if people, if they want to know about it, will know about it. Without our hammering at this issue. I think a similar posture was taken by all the other papers except maybe the Arkansas papers and maybe some of the conservative papers. Hard-nosed political reporters saw Hart's indiscretion as a character flaw on Hart's part. With Clinton, a new question arose and the question was, who is going to want to run for president if you're going to flyspeck every aspect of their life? Many reporters, I might add, were just hugely attracted to Bill Clinton. He's of our generation. He's in our age range. He's highly educated and most reporters now, especially people who rise to the top ranks in the political field, are Harvard/Yale type people. The *New Republic* started running a feature about who's done the latest job of kissing up to Clinton and Gore. You could see this when Clinton's travels in the Soviet Union became an issue. All of a sudden you found out who were the other Rhodes scholars in the press corps, because they were standing up and saying, 'Well, gee, Rhodes scholars traveled all around. Sometimes he didn't have any place to stay.

What's the big deal? Why are you making Clinton out to be a
suspicious figure on the basis of that?' You also have to factor in
a huge distaste for George Bush. People were saying, 'Here's this
guy who was a remnant of Ronald Reagan, still in the World War
II generation, and along comes this young charming guy who says
he wants to re-create the Kennedy era.' I think that many people
saw it as time for change, which was exactly Clinton's campaign
phrase. People also saw it as an opportunity to get in with the
new group.''

In Herbie Byrd's opinion, ''Clinton got extremely good treatment from the press during the presidential campaign. I don't think
they were unfair to him at all. The only thing I would say is that
the press made a whole to-do over the Gennifer Flowers affair. I
think that was blown all out of proportion and it's the first time that
I can remember the mainstream media picking up something from a
tabloid. A tabloid story becomes front page news all across the world
and I'm saying, 'What the hell is going on here?' That's the closest
to being unfair to him that I think the media ever came in that
campaign. The rest of the time they treated him extremely well—to
the point, in fact, of him becoming their darling.''

Lottie Shackleford describes some of the personal attacks on
Clinton as ''gruesome,'' and says, ''In a political sense when you
address the issues and you distort the truth on issues, that's one
thing. But I don't think the Clintons thought that people would
go at them in the personal attacks the way they did. And the press
printed it. There were instances of some things that were being
printed, particularly by the mainstream press, that truly were tabloid quality and should have stayed in a tabloid.''

Perhaps the kid gloves the press may or may not have worn
are less significant than the boxing gloves Clinton put on. Gene
Randall observes, ''I really don't think the press treated Clinton
with kid gloves at all. The whole Gennifer Flowers thing and the
ROTC letter came out so early; once Clinton survived that, Bush
was in serious trouble because these issues had been vetted. People
pretty much said, 'Okay, that's it. We're not crazy about him but
who cares about this other stuff?' Once those issues were out there
and taken care of, Clinton really had the rest of the campaign to
recover from it. He did recover and then he controlled the agenda
and once that happened, he basically said, 'Okay, we're going to
fight this battle on my turf and my turf is the economy.' That
really shaped the campaign.''

Running to Win

If Bill Clinton is at his best during a campaign, the protracted and bizarre race for the presidency also allowed him plenty of time to stumble. While Betsey Wright may think his only flaws are his allergies, the American people had plenty of opportunity to observe the vagaries of Clinton's character. He was always most impressive when he was coming back from a disaster, clinging precariously to the dream he'd so long held. Presidential primaries are brutal things, and though Clinton wrapped up his victory fairly early, it was never so clean a win as he might have liked.

Maria Henson tells a story about a visit to a Little Rock elementary school where Betsey Wright, Clinton's chief of staff, was scheduled to speak. "I had the morning off and nothing was going on at the Capitol. I figured why not go and hear what Betsey Wright had to say to a group of elementary school children? She went on and on about how great he was and how smart he was and how many books he read and how reading was so important and then she decided to take a few questions. One perceptive little kid raised his hand and said, 'Well, what I want to know is whether Governor Clinton has any flaws.' Betsey Wright just sat there and paused and thought and thought, and by this time I'm hanging off the edge of the chair wondering what she is going to say. Her reply to that little child was 'Well, yes, of course he does. He has allergies.' And I thought, 'Well, lucky him' "

By the winter of 1992 Clinton had more problems than allergies. And more flaws, it appeared. Virtually all agree the Clinton campaign hit its low during the New Hampshire primary. *Newsweek* reporter Mark Miller was there; he had accompanied the Clinton campaign from its outset. "Although New Hampshire was obviously a dark period for the campaign, I think he never really gave up. I never got any sense that he conceded defeat but there were these huge hills and valleys that the campaign went through. It was either on the verge of collapse or it was about to win either the nomination or the presidency. New Hampshire certainly was a low point. He spent much of the spring in a deep funk. He was actually not that pleasant to be around. He was preoccupied, self-absorbed, and very angry at himself. He felt that a lot of damage had been done by the draft and by Gennifer Flowers. After Paul Tsongas dropped out, Clinton was obviously the sure nominee, but the public wasn't ready to have the race be over and Clinton wasn't really ready for the race to be over. There were still a lot of primaries left to go and so he was sort of a sitting target. When Perot took off I think Clinton felt usurped in his role as the outsider because Perot in some ways was more of a true outsider and the press wasn't paying attention to Clinton anymore. He felt that he was flailing, that his message wasn't very tight, and everything seemed directionless. He sort of slogged through those primaries, each one more anticlimactic than the last, and by the end of the process, with the nomination locked up, most people were discounting him as a serious candidate. Everyone was enamored with Ross Perot and that affected him quite deeply personally. Some elements of his personality were not particularly attractive then because he was self-pitying and he was self-absorbed, preoccupied with what was happening, as you would expect.

"Hillary was really one of the only people who could get him to do something when he didn't want to do it or when he was feeling irritated. I remember one time when they'd had a horrible flight, an overnight flight back from California. They went to visit the riot area in Los Angeles and were flying overnight from L.A. to New York to give a speech before the newspaper publishers association. Thirty minutes after takeoff, the campaign plane broke down. They had to go back and take a commercial jet so no one got any sleep and it was a horrible night of travel. I saw them later that morning in his hotel suite and he had a draft of the speech that Paul Begala had written during the flight. Clinton had stayed up all night when they flew from L.A. to New York and he was really very unsatisfied with the drafts. He was complaining and generally being petulant and annoyed and Hillary said, 'You know, Bill, just put that away. Just throw that away and write down what you want to say. If you don't like what's been written for you, do it yourself.' And he did. He sat down and wrote what was in fact one of his best speeches of the year. It was very compelling. It addressed the issues of race and crime and society and why we were in the fix that we were in. It was a very, very strong speech that he basically wrote in longhand right there."

KATV anchor Gina Kurre covered the New Hampshire primary. "I went to New Hampshire with him back in February of 1991 and I really think those were the darkest days of the campaign. We had a couple of exclusive interviews with him during that time and I was amazed at the good face that the campaign was putting on. They were really hurting. The polls had just gone into a tailspin because of Gennifer Flowers and the draft-dodging stuff and I learned later that he was thinking about pulling out at that point. I heard he had said to George Thomason, 'I think we need to just pull out,' and Thomason said, 'No. You've got 150 Arkansans coming up here who are going door to door for you' and I was really impressed with that. I think those Arkansas Travelers really did a lot to help him.

"I remember running into a businessman from Benton, Arkansas, who had come up with his wife. They went to all of the businesses in every town and really talked him up and I think that did more good than a lot of people think because they worked hard. All of us did. He had scheduled the last day before the primary up there—eleven stops in eleven different towns. Unbelievable. We worked I bet, twenty to twenty-one hours a day and still did not work enough. I've never seen anything like it."

Woody Bassett was among those Arkansas Travelers. "We were in New Hampshire during the campaign, about a week before the election, and things were just falling apart. A bunch of us went up the last week to help him and I'll never forget, we were in this little junior high school gymnasium down in Nashua and they seated the Arkansas Travelers right behind where Bill was going to speak. He came out and they had a band playing and this gym is just packed with people. It's snowing and cold as heck outside but inside it's hot. People are crammed in there. He comes out and what do the Arkansas people do? We call the hogs. In Arkansas calling the hogs is a call to arms and an expression of loyalty and support. He turned around and grinned—it had a profound effect on him. He needed some support from home. Here he was way up in New Hampshire getting treated like a human landfill and all these things were going wrong. They appeared when he most needed them. It's just an example of how people in this state rally around each other. There was fierce wide-ranging support in this state when he ran for president, something you probably wouldn't find in many other states."

Randy Lilleston recalls Clinton's remarkable perseverance even in the face of certain defeat. "I interviewed Clinton just after he did the *60 Minutes* piece. CBS filmed that in a hotel room in Boston. They filmed for an hour but only used about twelve to fifteen minutes of it—only the stuff about his personal life. Then he went to New Hampshire for a campaign rally in Portsmouth. I was at that rally. That rally was the point at which I realized how badly this man wanted that office. Here is a guy who had been forced to attempt to explain aspects of his personal life, some of the most intimate details of his personal life on national television right after the Superbowl. He had gone directly from that to this campaign rally in New Hampshire and he made a great speech there and rallied a bunch of people and then hopped into a van to make more campaign stops.

"Immediately after he did this rally, I hopped in a van with him and rode with him between a couple of campaign stops. First of all, it was a very difficult interview for me to do because I had to ask him about the *60 Minutes* interview and there were a lot of things I personally didn't want to ask him about. It struck me that here was a guy who was willing to deal with this and willing to deal with frankly a certain level of humiliation. I realized that's probably what it takes if you want to win a modern day presidential election; you have to be willing to be humiliated. It was just daily humiliation.

"So in my interview he basically knew which questions were coming. I asked him what he had wanted to accomplish with the *60 Minutes* interview. He said that he wanted to convince people that these weren't the issues, that his personal life wasn't important.

"Historically when these things happen to a political candidate the campaign collapses. He's the first guy that survived this sort of thing. There was no history to indicate that his campaign should have survived. His poll numbers were falling right through the floor. He fell out of first. He was heading for third fast. Third place meant good-bye campaign because his money would dry up on him. He wouldn't be able to get political contributions.

"He was tired. He was sick. He had been sick in New Hampshire for weeks and weeks. He spent about half his time in New Hampshire very hoarse and he did not look good. He had also put on some weight in New Hampshire. He looked bad all the way through the Illinois primary. That's when he started getting in better shape and losing weight. People still kid him about his weight but I have some photos of him from last year and I bet he's lost thirty pounds since then.

"The day before the New Hampshire primary, Clinton knew he'd lost the primary. He also knew that he was within a hair's breadth of finishing third. So what does he do? He campaigns all day long again and then he goes out again that night. Now, there's no reason for him to go out that night. He's not going to get on the local TV newscasts. He's not going to make any difference at that point. He goes to a local restaurant and shakes hands. Goes to a bowling alley and shakes hands and he and the staff and all the reporters go bowling. I remember thinking at that point 'this is a person who will never stop campaigning as long as he can get a pulse up and keep his organization in place; nothing is going to stop this guy.' At that point I thought he had a chance to just grind them down, which is exactly what he wound up doing to his competitors. He just ground them down.''

Sidney Blumenthal says, ''I don't think he ever equaled his performances in New Hampshire. You get a glimpse of it when he sort of improvises in front of a joint session of Congress. I saw him in gymnasiums before crowds of two or three thousand people at the moment when he was fighting for his political life in these overheated gyms in the cold of New Hampshire. He would speak very heatedly and he would get all sweaty and throw his jacket off and then he would take questions from the crowd. People would harass him and then they would yell at each other to shut up. He would answer a question about AIDS and soon would talk about abortion and he would disagree with them. In the background would be the Arkansas Travelers, a couple of hundred people from Arkansas who came to lend him moral support. It was like a combination revival meeting, early Elvis concert, and sideshow.

''I think that the key moment was at the end of the campaign, the end of the primaries. He was very low. He was going to be the Democratic nominee but he was third in the polls. He somehow revived himself between that period and the Democratic Convention and he did so the same way he revived himself in New Hampshire—simply through persistence and perseverance. I think there was a kind of morality play here and the point of it was not the Gennifer Flowers issue. The focus of the play was the person who gets down and, through his own persistence, brings himself up again, and time and again Clinton would do that. In New Hampshire, I think he shook hands and met and touched more than a hundred thousand people. He tried to do the same thing by appearing on as many forums on television and radio as he could. He kept on trying to touch people.''

Adam Pertman recalls two particular days in New Hampshire. ''What impressed me was watching him the day the Gennifer Flowers story hit the press. I was struck by his composure. He walked into a swarm of reporters and was as cool as he could be and answered every question confidently. I've covered politics a long time. I don't know if I've ever seen a pol swim his way through waters that choppy and still look that calm—that's really a striking quality. I don't know if that's good or bad. I don't know if he's impervious to feeling or if he's just able to move through it but it certainly is a dramatic trait. That is one story I've told more than once. It was the day of the Manchester headquarters opening.

"The night before, he had gone bowling. What he really did was throw a couple of balls and talk to all the people in the bowling alley. The following morning, he went to an employment center, a state center, and then we went to a municipal center or junior high where some female students talked about suicide and the pressures on them. On the way to the headquarters opening, one of the houses of Congress passed an extension of the unemployment benefits which he was briefed on while we were all in the same van. He didn't take any notes at any of these stops that I could see and he walked into the headquarters opening where he was supposed to give a rousing speech that would get the troops riled up. This type of speech is usually pretty vacuous. He proceeded to give a ten-minute off-the-cuff speech that incorporated conversations he'd had at the bowling alley complete with names and hometowns, stories he was told by these girls at the school, and he wove in the unemployment benefits extension including all of the exemptions and it all just flowed seamlessly. I couldn't deliver or write that speech given all those elements if you gave me a couple of days and he did it off the top of his head, and it worked. He did it in such a way that he got the troops all riled up and I thought, 'This is a pretty good politician.' Part of it is just memory. He's got an astonishing memory."

Randy Lilleston says, "One thing that stands out in my mind is maybe ten reporters in New Hampshire flew with him to an event in Berlin, New Hampshire. It was in January, it was incredibly cold, and we flew these two little six-seat turbo prop planes over the mountains into this tiny little airport. He went to this event in the paper mill and came back, and while we were waiting for the planes to warm up we sat in this tiny little one-room airport building and Clinton was talking about one time when he went on a skiing vacation with Chelsea and Hillary. He had hurt his leg skiing and kept falling over and falling over and falling over until the instructors couldn't believe that he was still trying and eventually he hurt his knee and couldn't run for like a year. All the reporters were just sitting around shooting the bull with him. I can remember going to a high school and playing basketball after he did an appearance. It was in New Hampshire, and he did a campaign appearance there in a classroom and then afterward he walked over to this gym where some kids were playing basketball. He started playing basketball and all the reporters started shooting hoops too and I couldn't help but think 'If this guy goes somewhere I'm going to remember this for the rest of my life.' At that point it was very early in the campaign, it was November and Clinton had 10 percent support in New Hampshire."

Unquestionably, Clinton strove—and kept coming back, and kept getting better. Regina Blakely says, "When Clinton won the New York primary, I thought he had a chance of winning the nomination, but when he announced his candidacy for the presidency George Bush was incredibly popular. Even people who supported him very closely were saying, 'This is a real good chance for him to get his name out there.' Even with all the turmoil of the campaign—the Gennifer Flowers stories, the marijuana stories, the draft stories—he kept getting better and better. Nobody expected that and that is sort of his own saving trait. He thrives on a challenge and the more people watched him persevere, the more they wanted to support him. Even people who hadn't been supporters began coming over and saying, 'Well, maybe this man isn't going down the drain. Maybe he is going to be able to make it.' But I think when he first started to run, nobody really thought that he could win the primary."

Chris Burrey observes "there were cycles to the coverage of Bill Clinton. Before the first primary, he was sort of celebrated as the hope of the new Democratic party. There were flattering cover stories in the *Republic* and I think *Time* and *Newsweek*. He got extraordinarily positive, some would even say fawning, coverage. Then Gennifer Flowers entered the scene. He was written off. His poll numbers dropped. George Stephanopoulos was widely quoted as saying they were in a free fall. They had emergency meetings. He was written off again when the draft story broke in New Hampshire. They went on *Nightline* where Ted Koppel read the entire letter. This guy has many, many lives. He was hit again and again and he survived all those things.

"Having come in after the Gennifer Flowers episode, I was impressed that he was able to survive the nagging doubts about the draft. He obviously never told the complete truth about the draft and obviously was a master of the fudge factor. Considering the number of times that he came up as a national story, I was surprised that he was able to withstand the onslaught. It turned out that the tenacity—not only Clinton's but also his staff's, people like Carville, Begala, Stephanopoulos, Mandy Grunwald, kept him alive. It was a tough bunch. They knew these things would come up and they were ready and poised to respond and they did. It clearly was one of the things that got Clinton into the White House—his ability to withstand these withering attacks.''

John King on Clinton's resilience: ''His resilience is what stands out the most in my mind particularly in the early part of the campaign when he was in some trouble because of the Gennifer Flowers stuff and the draft stuff. There was one night in New Hampshire. It was the first round of tabloid stories. The Nichols story was in the *Star* and then Fox TV in New York picked up on it. The *Star* picked up the lawsuit, which essentially listed all these allegations of infidelity. The press jumped all over them and you could see there was concern about it. I had dinner with Clinton that night in New Hampshire. He was very relaxed and even joked about it and although a lot of his aides were pretty worried that this was going to take him down, he was much more relaxed and affable and laughing about it than I would have expected. I think in his heart Clinton had some worries, but he didn't let them show.''

CNN political correspondent Gene Randall on Clinton's tenacity: ''His tenaciousness is probably what I found to be the most impressive thing about Clinton. He is very, very tough, his endurance level is very high. Just after the Flowers story broke, all kinds of people were saying that he was through, that he would never recover from both the Gennifer Flowers thing and the ROTC letter. Some people thought he might never come back, he was just going to disappear. I was in a private plane with him and there were eight of us on board. I swear to you he was the calmest person on board, and I thought this is instructive. If this guy can be in the center of this whirlpool and show this kind of mental discipline he may be ready for this race in more ways than a lot of us thought.''

Randy Lilleston recalls, ''After New Hampshire Clinton went immediately to Atlanta and started working the South because he knew that if he was going to turn his campaign around, it would probably hinge on the South and then, two weeks after that, on the Super Tuesday Illinois and Michigan primaries. Meanwhile, Tsongas had won New Hampshire. He was really coming on. His numbers were up all over the place. He started picking up wins in places like Maryland, which is the state Clinton once thought he had, but you could see the gap starting to close primary by primary. Then the week before Super Tuesday—it was just when I started covering him full time again—Clinton won the Georgia primary. He was in Miami when he got the results that he had won the Georgia primary, and you could tell the mood of the campaign was about to shift, that they thought a corner had been turned. Not just because he had won it but because he had won it big."

For Clinton, the Florida campaign became a new ball game. Adam Pertman remarks, "In Georgia and Florida when he criticized Tsongas on the social security issue, I think he was fairly harsh but I don't think he was playing all-out hardball. He wasn't throwing as hard as he could. Plus I would say that it was a test for Tsongas. You got to be able to take hardball, and Clinton certainly did during the course of the campaign in other ways. There's no question that Clinton and his folks turned Tsongas's record inside out at some points. Is that fair game? I'd argue not. I think that in campaigns no one tells the perfect truth at all times. Do I like it? No. Do I understand that virtually all politicians do it? Absolutely. All sides play the game and the one who plays the best wins. I think Tsongas showed he just couldn't take heat very well. And in that respect it was a clever ploy by Clinton to see how far he could push him."

For Sidney Blumenthal the Illinois primary debate revealed a more combative Clinton. "During the Illinois and Michigan primaries—they were taking place at the same time—Clinton was staying in Chicago at the Palmer House. The debate between the Democratic candidates took place in Illinois, and in the debate Jerry Brown angered Clinton by talking about Hillary regarding the Rose Law Firm and Arkansas state bond issues. Clinton moved away from his platform toward Brown and told Brown he didn't want anyone attacking his wife. And from that moment on Brown seemed to shrink in the campaign. That following day Clinton went across the lake to Michigan with Hillary. They spent the day campaigning and got back to the Palmer House after midnight. I was at the Palmer House with some of his advisers and campaign aides when he got off the elevator with Hillary, and he still had the cold air from outside with him. His face was all red and he was very tired but he was very excited, and what he was excited about was that some man in Michigan had told him he should have hit Jerry Brown for picking on his wife. And he said, 'Yeah, yeah.' Clinton was extremely enlivened by this whole idea of physical combat in defense of his wife."

Jerry Jones is a partner at the Rose Law Firm. ''The allegations concerning favoritism toward this firm have come up in the gubernatorial races a couple of times. Frank White, when he ran against Bill Clinton, ran ads that had the front of our building prominently displayed in an ad saying that Bill Clinton had funneled state business to the firm. That was absolutely false. Hillary did not receive compensation for any of the work that other lawyers in the firm did for state agencies. We set up our compensation system in such a manner that she did not get her partnership percentage of any of those things. As a result of that she made less money than she would have otherwise. Both times the charges were made they were made by somewhat desperate political opponents of Bill Clinton. Frank White, in one instance, made them because he thought they were the type of charges that would stick. They were also the type of charges that a lot of people would believe regardless of what the truth was, simply because a lot of people want to believe that there's a dark side to something.''

Darrell Glascock, who ran the 1986 White campaign, contends that ''when you've got a firm that is involved with every single bond issue done with state money, it looks a little fishy and we had the documents on that. The Rose Law Firm participated in every state bond issue that was done.''

Jones continues, ''Jerry Brown raised the charges toward the tail end of his campaign and he intensified them at the very end of his campaign in the Illinois primary, which was absolutely a make-or-break situation. He had Illinois and Michigan, I think, voting at the same time and the race had come down to Bill Clinton and Jerry Brown. Mr. Brown was desperate. He didn't have the money to stay in the race. He didn't have the broad base support to stay in the race so he went on the attack hoping to just throw up some things and provoke Clinton into losing his composure during a debate, which he came close to doing. Clinton turned to him and said, 'Look, don't you dare pick on my wife.' And if you've ever seen a tape of that, you'd see how Bill's just bristling.

''As a law firm we were in a somewhat unique position because we valued our reputation, but as a law firm and institutionally, we could not engage in the political debate. It was kind of hard for us to sit on the sidelines because we all wanted to just march up to Jerry Brown and say 'Look, you are so wrong on this.' When the facts finally came out publicly, the state released some figures showing that our law firm, even though it is one of the largest in the state, certainly the oldest in the state, and by any accounts one of the most respected law firms in the state, was doing a very small portion of state business. We didn't go back to check, although I would strongly suspect that we were doing on a percentage basis a lot less work for the state than we had been, say, in 1970, eight years before Bill Clinton was ever elected as governor. It was a sensitive issue with us because our integrity was besmirched. Hillary didn't like it either, and I think you can tell by her comments how much she valued her professional relationship with the Rose Law Firm. It upset her.''

John Hanchette says, ''By the time that he became headline news not only for being a contender and leading in polls but also due to Gennifer Flowers and all that other stuff, it was already evident that he could figure out what the political tenor of a state was. It didn't take him very long at all to see how depressed New England was at that time and how people were going through a very bad time. They were not in a recession but they were in a severe depression and he put his arm around me and he cried genuine tears when an old lady described her health benefits running out and pleaded with him to do something about it. With each stop, he seemed to be able to hone his politics a little better. I remember another reporter turning to me and saying, 'This guy really learns doesn't he?' He's so quick to absorb the trends of the nation that it lends to the charge of his being a chameleon—that he could adapt his political speeches to his environment.

''I remember him at the Walter Reuther Hall at UAW in Flint, Michigan. It's the one where Reuther started the sit-down strike. Flint, of course, is also in a depression because GM moved a lot of the auto plants out of there, a lot of the engine plants out of there and as you know now, most people in the auto industry are wildly opposed to NAFTA because they think jobs are all going to Mexico. He hadn't been receiving good crowds but his people had put together a big crowd in Flint that was really ready to support him. They'd liked what they'd heard so far until, inexplicably, he started talking about NAFTA. He was wildly in support of NAFTA at the time. I can remember Tim Blanchard, the former governor of Michigan, leaning over and whispering in his ear that he's in the wrong place to give a pro-NAFTA speech. As a reporter I was almost foaming at the mouth in anticipation that, 'Oh boy. We're going to see a little action here. He might get some raucous heckling.' Without a break in stride, without looking awkward, and without looking as if he was doing a 180-degree screeching turn in the middle of a rhetorical street, he managed to slip into another speech about the economy and get away from that NAFTA theme. He was later questioned about it and he did seem to back off a little bit but it struck me that this guy is really fast on his feet. People keep saying, 'What a great campaigner.' And I thought at the time that if he could keep up his stamina he would really give Bush a run for the money. Michigan and Illinois were the states in which he convinced me that he had a pretty good shot. If he had gotten hammered in those states or even come in second or Tsongas had made a good showing, he would have been history.''

Jeff Stinson remembers a blur and then the Illinois-Michigan Super Tuesday campaign. ''I've never been so exhausted as when he was out throughout the South. He would start in Houston at six in the morning and be all over Florida at midday, and stop in Tennessee on the way back to Houston at two in the morning. I was dead. The reporters that were on the plane barely had time to file. Clinton was campaigning like a madman. The guy was ballooning up in weight because he didn't have time to run and everybody balloons up. You stuff in all this junk food. When Super Tuesday arrived somebody had gotten him a new double-breasted suit. He had ballooned up and he had this double-breasted suit that frankly made him look like the Michelin Tire man. Every time his weight goes up I can't help but think of him as the Michelin Tire man, but it was funny. Bill had been carrying the campaign throughout the South but when they hit Chicago, Hillary with her introduction of Bill Clinton that night was basically making her own campaign speech on behalf of her husband.''

Randy Lilleston remembers ''the night of the Illinois primary when Clinton came down into this ballroom at a beautiful Chicago hotel. It had all been carefully planned. They had these big confetti cannons spraying the whole room full of confetti and he could sense that his staff knew that his campaign, that the Democratic nomination was within his grasp. Afterward we sat around talking to his staff until about two in the morning at the bar there. Even after the bar closed we sat around and just kept talking to them, they were so pumped.'' Clinton had come a long way from overheated gyms in New Hampshire.

Randy Lilleston continues. ''By the time he reached California it was all over. The only question was whether Jerry Brown could carry enough votes to embarrass Clinton.

''The thing that always struck me about Clinton at any of these campaign events was how personal he was. Here he was running for president and when you think about someone who's running a presidential campaign you think about the use of mass media to get your message out, which they certainly used quite well. But Clinton also insisted on a constant and endless round of handshaking. He'd meet a crowd and he would just work that crowd silly. And even a lot of his campaign advisers thought it was in many ways a waste of time. But he would constantly go out to these crowds and it would help him more than anything else. He would do it because it recharged his batteries; just shooting the bull with these people helped make him a better campaigner. I can remember half a dozen airports where he would just stand there for hours. And he would just shake hands and shake hands and shake hands and talk to people.''

Reviewing Clinton's campaign, Skip Rutherford enumerates ''seven things that took Clinton to the White House. Number one was our ability on December 16, 1991 to raise $900,000 at a state fund-raiser. The second thing that happened was that one by one a lot of the major Democratic players did not get in the race. The third thing was that he survived New Hampshire. The Comeback Kid. The fourth thing was Perot getting out of the race because it forced people to focus on a two-person race. The fifth thing that happened was the selection of Gore. The sixth thing was the New York convention which people thought would be a bomb, but Harry Thomason orchestrated a media masterpiece. The seventh thing that happened was the bus trip. If you had told me that they would ride in a bus all the way across America, I would have said, 'You're crazy,' but they rode. People liked it.''

Vice presidential candidates are seldom chosen for straightforward reasons. They are picked to mitigate the excesses of the presidential candidate or to balance some facet of background or philosophy. The ideal vice presidential candidate should complement a candidate's strengths and soften any sharp edges. So, according to the convention, Al Gore was an unlikely choice to be Bill Clinton's running mate. Gore was about the same age, from a neighboring state, his resume was significantly different from Clinton's only in that it included military service. Gore was high-profile. In fact, before 1992, he was the better known of the two, and widely considered the more likely to one day be president. It appears that Clinton picked Gore for reasons other than the politically pragmatic; perhaps it was as simple as some contend—that Bill simply liked Al better than the other candidates.

Randy Lilleston says, "Clinton didn't pick Gore for vote attraction reasons. Clinton picked Gore because he liked him. You don't pick a guy from the same region who's also the same age, sort of reemphasizing the fact that you're a southerner and that you're young. You just don't pick him to draw votes. I was surprised that he picked him because it went against conventional wisdom. But this guy beat conventional wisdom all last year, he beat it to the ground."

Adam Pertman agrees. "Clinton absolutely went against conventional wisdom in picking Gore. He chose a reinforcement rather than a complementary running mate. Gore reinforced Clinton's strengths. He bolstered the vision that Americans had of Clinton because Gore was sort of Clinton with some positives where Clinton had negatives. But boy, that day when they trotted out the Gore family on the lawn of the Governor's Mansion, it was just clear as day that Clinton's political instincts were on the money again. It was just clear as day. You saw the Clintons and the Gores standing up there, and you saw a team that could win at a time when you weren't sure that could happen and you felt that it was true that intellectualizing didn't give you the whole story."

Terry Lemons, Washington correspondent for the *Arkansas Democrat-Gazette*, remembers "the day he announced outside the Governor's Mansion that Clinton had picked Al Gore as his running mate. It was a day that just had incredibly high humidity and everybody was standing around in the sun just sweating and soaked with perspiration. When Gore came out and gave his address, he came across much better than I had ever seen him on TV and it seemed that on this just terribly hot day, Gore was helping the Clinton campaign finally catch fire. I think the selection of Gore turned out to be a crucial step in the whole process. That day, the reaction from other politicians and the pundits was almost universally favorable to Clinton and it also seemed to create a spark in the campaign, because suddenly you didn't just have Clinton the young leader, you had Clinton/Gore, the baby-boom ticket. Suddenly it became a campaign not of Bush versus Clinton but New Generation versus Old Generation. They really seemed to pick up on that and really just drive away with it in the weeks and months after that."

Mark Grobmyer introduced Clinton and Gore in the fall of 1987. "It was the first time they'd ever met. We were in the Excelsior

Hotel in the Presidential Suite. Bill was friends with Dukakis, because of the Governors Association but he didn't know Al. He had heard of him and respected his family very much—I mentioned the book I gave him back in 1974 when I was in Fayetteville. I told Al that Bill admired his family and so forth, and so we got this meeting together. My wife, Libby, and I had had this bet a long time ago, that one or the other was going to be president. But Gore had run and Bill hadn't. When those two guys met, and it was just me, Bill, Al, and Bruce Lindsey, there was a powerful, powerful feeling. You just felt this power—it's difficult to describe. I said, 'If you guys could ever figure out a way to get together, nobody could stop you.' And they both laughed. But I think that they knew it too.

"They communicated so well together. They both knew about this, they both knew about that. Gore knew a little bit more about foreign policy and defense. He was on the Armed Services Committee. Clinton knew more about domestic policy—how to get an economy going, education and stuff. Both are so bright and so personable, there was a great conversation. As it happened a couple of months later, I was taking Tipper around Little Rock and I said, 'Tipper, have you ever met Hillary Clinton?' She said, 'No.' I said, 'Well, Hillary's interested in children's issues too.' Tipper was interested in this music labeling issue so she said, 'I'd like to meet her.' I called Hillary and said, 'Hillary, I have Tipper Gore in town and she wants to meet you.' She said, 'Well, I'm in a partners' meeting at the law firm but I'll come out and meet her.' They had a great meeting and they really hit it off. In the next four years I tried to make sure they stayed in some communication together. Of course Gore got into writing his book and he had this terrible tragic thing with his son. It turned out all right but it had a real impact on his life and he decided not to run. I asked him if he would help Bill on some environmental issues and he gave Bill some ideas. When it got down to picking a vice president, Gore was one of the names. I never thought he'd be one of the names that the group would come up with because he's from a neighboring state and he's young. Well, once I knew he was being put in the pot, I had no question but that's who he ought to pick and so I did a ten-point memo to Bill about why he should pick Al Gore. I called out to the Mansion and I said to Nancy Hernreich, 'Is he out there?' And she said 'Yeah, he's getting ready to go somewhere.' I said, 'Well, I'm going to bring a memo for him out there.' So I went out there and drove through the gate and he was coming out and getting in his car.

"I said 'Bill, you've got to pick Al Gore and here are the reasons why. The only reason I did this is so you could give it to other people to see the logic of it.' He said, 'Thanks,' but he didn't really commit. We played golf that Sunday, and I said, 'Bill, you've got to pick Gore' and I went on and on. He said, 'If you stop talking about it, you might be doing some good with your buddy Gore.' I said, 'Well, I'll be quiet.' So I shut up for a couple of holes. But I really got the feeling after that that he would pick him. Then I got worried, 'What if he doesn't accept?' Gore had been saying, 'I'm not seeking the vice presidency,' so it'd be embarrassing if he were to ask him and Al didn't accept. I called Tipper that night, and I said, 'Tipper, I don't know what's going to happen, but what would happen if he did offer it to Al?' And she said, 'Well, I think he'd be very excited.' She didn't say he'd accept it but I took that as an indication, so I got word back to Bill that I thought it would be well received. I believe it was, when they made the final decision. Hillary called me early Wednesday morning and said to come down to the Mansion as the Gores would be there.

"So we went down to the Mansion and the Gores came in. Bill just said, 'Are you happy? Are you happy?' And I said, 'You bet I'm happy. You're going to be happy too.' So they pulled up with their family and we stayed in the living room drinking coffee and everybody was congratulating everybody else. We were the only people in there other than the Gores, the Clintons, and a few staffers. So they said, 'Well, we're going to go out so why don't you go down and get on the front row.' So my family went outside and there's the world press.

"It was a beautiful day. We were out under the balcony, all the world press is behind us and here they come out: Bill and Hillary with Chelsea, Al and Tipper and their kids—it was a powerful, powerful thing. And I knew at that point that he was going to be president and Al was going to be vice president. I thought 'No way could Bush win against them.' It was real. It wasn't just an image made up for TV. They're both real people. Their families are real people and there's nothing phony about them. What you see is what you get.''

Ark Monroe is a longtime friend of Clinton's and Al Gore's cousin. "I thought Clinton and Gore would always be rivals. It was such a natural fit, though. The best thing that ever happened as far as I was concerned was that they got to know each other and like each other. These guys were raised differently but they had the same interests. They have the same beliefs, the same philosophy and I think it was just a natural fit. I mean, Mark went out to the Mansion and told him why he ought to put Al on the ticket and I called him and said, 'I'm selfish about this; I would love to have my cousin on the ticket,' but actually I know Bill better than I do Al to tell you the truth, even though we're related. I've just had more experiences with Bill.''

The sixth thing that won the election, says Skip Rutherford, was the New York convention. Mark Miller shares a behind-the-scenes moment with the Clintons on that occasion. "I remember watching the speeches of Bob Hattoy and Elizabeth Glaser. Bob spoke first. Bob had worked on the campaign and Clinton knew him and had been personally quite moved and touched when he found out that Bob had AIDS. For a period Bob was quite sick with one of the opportunistic infections. As Bob was about to speak we were in the Clinton's suite. Hillary would come in from her day of campaigning and he would be there having worked on his speech and then they would have TV trays pulled up and they would eat dinner and watch the convention. It was amusing because it was like this couple just pulling up their TV trays and dinner to watch this convention but it was about *them*. Anyway we were watching the speeches from the two HIV-positive speakers. Chelsea was in another room with some of her friends and Hillary and Clinton and Stephanopoulos and Lindsey and I were watching. Bill was overcome. He wept at each speech as did Hillary and it was just an amazing moment. Just before Bob began speaking, Bill was talking with Jerry Brown who had been causing problems at the last minute. Brown was on the phone to Clinton at that point, demanding some concession and Clinton said, 'I've got to go. Bob Hattoy is about to speak. I've got to go.' And Jerry just blithely continued on complaining about the treatment he was getting and Clinton said, 'I've got to go,' and hung up on him because he didn't want to miss Bob's speech. It struck me that Jerry Brown, 'Man of the People,' was so concerned about himself and how he was going to be treated, that he wasn't even paying attention to one of the most important speeches of the convention. Clinton hung up on him and watched and when the two speeches were over, Chelsea came in and she had been crying. We were all crying. Chelsea sat down on her father's lap and talked about how sad she was and what a great speech they had given. At the end of the night, I was leaving and he said something like, 'Those were really powerful weren't they?' 'Yeah.' And he said, 'Well, at least I did something right in this convention.' I think he was really proud of that moment.''

The convention barely over, the bus tours began. They figured significantly into Clinton's campaign strategy and, from Chris Burrey's perspective, contributed to his victory in November. ''I guess the moment when I thought that he had a real chance at the election occurred during the first bus tour. The later bus tours became sort of silly media events but the first one was a genuinely brilliant piece of political campaigning. That first week after the Democratic Convention was a master stroke.''

Television anchor Gina Kurre had the opportunity, both on and off the bus, to observe the Clintons closely during the first tour. ''I was on the bus tour, the very first one from New York to St. Louis after I had covered the convention. We were the only local crew allowed on. The campaign needed to use our satellite truck. If, for example, they were on the trail and Larry King wanted to hook up with him live, they would use our satellite truck, so we said, 'Well, let us go with you at least.' So that's how we were able to go along with him. I had an interview with him one day on the bus and it was the best interview I had ever had with him. It turned out to be pretty good. We talked a lot about the fact that back home, there were people who thought he should resign, that he didn't need to be governor and running at the same time. We talked about his frustrations with the Secret Service, which he was not used to. It's been tougher for him than for past presidents because he likes to go where he wants to go and he doesn't like anybody telling him where he can and can't go. The Secret Service people during that first bus tour were just at their wit's end because he was darting off everywhere in the crowds. I think he was frustrated with them and he basically said, 'They're just going to have to put up with it. I understand their job is to protect me but I'm going to do this.' And a couple of times, I got this on tape. A couple of times when he was talking to me, he was waving out the bus at the same time but he didn't miss a beat of the interview. He was definitely on a high. The national media who had covered presidents in the past were worn out and seemed genuinely baffled at the huge crowds at every town. We said, 'Talk to the people that come to these events. They think he's Kennedy. You know, some people drove three hours from little itty-bitty towns to see him. It was very clear they were on a high. I asked Hillary, 'Aren't you just completely worn out?' and she said, 'Yes, I am. I need more sleep than he does but it's very invigorating when you see these crowds.' We were in Utica, Ohio, in the middle of that tour and I bet there were no more than five hundred people who live in that town and yet five thousand showed up that night.

"The events were so incredibly orchestrated; everywhere he went it was televised. It took away a lot of the mystique for me because it was so slick. I had played saxophone growing up in Missouri and I was first chair all state band. I brought that up to him because I knew he was, too, and we talked a little bit about playing the sax and who he liked and who I liked and that kind of thing. That's as personal as it got; he didn't carry on. He wasn't one to do that. Hillary was just the opposite. When I was on the bus tour interviewing him, after I finished, I went to the back of the bus until we got to our next destination and I sat and talked to Hillary. She did not talk about herself like Bill did. We talked about raising children, families. I told her about my sister who was adopted and she said, 'When did your parents tell your sister and you that she was adopted and how did that go?' She was very interested and I felt that she really was genuine about the things that she believed in and she was more self-effacing I think than he was. Other people who know Hillary will tell you that she'll ask about your kids. Bill will remember your child's name but it's for a reason. 'How's Joe?' He's made his connection and then it's on to something else. Hillary will spend time talking about your kids with you. It's hard to figure him out. It's hard to get a real handle on his soul. Hillary, you get a much better feel for."

Adam Pertman found, "his energy level just extraordinary. I'll tell you what was really amazing were the bus trips. The bus trips were just stunning. To watch crowds line up by the thousands in the streets in the middle of nowhere USA and stand there just to glimpse these guys. They were late for everything. This is just legend. I mean, the guy's late for everything. I think it was in Pennsylvania that we wound up in a town square at two or three in the morning, three or four hours late and there are maybe twelve thousand people standing there who had been there the whole time. They were pissed off and cold and frustrated and then he spoke and all was well. They were glad they went."

Randy Lilleston says, "On the first bus trip after the Democratic Convention, I was just floored. We'd go to these towns, we got into York, Pennsylvania, for example, at eleven o'clock at night and there would be three thousand people waiting there. It was like the Beatles had hit town. It was not the kind of reaction that I had seen at political rallies and I'd been to dozens of political rallies that year, hundreds probably. It was this huge outpouring of interest in seeing these people, Clinton and Gore, and their wives were a big drawing card too. These extremely young men out there working the country, going to these towns where presidential candidates never go anymore because there's no reason to. Carville thought the bus tours were a waste of time. If you look at the cities that they were going to, they were mostly small towns. You don't go to small towns because there's no major media market there. You only have this infinite amount of time to campaign before the election and the argument was why waste your time there? He jokes about it now."

Though Clinton was forced, during the presidential race, to campaign on a large scale, he was still at his best in small groups or one on one. Those who watched him work on an intimate basis affirm that the gifts that worked so well in Arkansas had a universal appeal. Gene Randall says, "He loves doing the people-to-people stuff. He does retail politics very well and one of the constant sources of friction in the campaign was that he would want to go into a sandwich shop or an ice-cream shop and do some campaigning and all of a sudden, there would be thirty or forty of us rushing into the restaurant to do some reporting. 'What is he talking about with people? Let's take his picture.' He ended up instituting this rope line. Wherever we went there would be this moving rope line to keep us separated from him to give him breathing space. Anyone who has ever seen the crush of a campaign, understands his being bothered by thinking that we would somehow come between him and the people he wanted to spend time with. Even if it was only walking down the street at a market or walking into a sandwich shop, the first people off the buses were kids with ropes."

Randall remembers a particular day on the 1992 campaign trail. "We were in San Antonio on a day that was as hot as hell and we were behind schedule. He was almost always behind schedule but he made the entire motorcade go to this famous ice-cream shop so he could buy a couple of gallons of ice cream and bring it back to the plane for everyone. He said they had the best pistachio ice cream in the history of ice cream so naturally the dog-and-pony show had to troop in and take pictures of him eating the ice cream. He just seemed to get a real kick out of the fact that he was able to bring a couple of gallons of it back to the plane to share with us.''

Gwen Ifill also remembers the ice cream, if not the pistachio. "We were in San Antonio, Texas. It was extremely hot. It must have been before Super Tuesday and Clinton remembered being in San Antonio running the campaign for McGovern in 1968. He remembered that when he was there he used to go to a hotel in downtown San Antonio and get mango ice cream. He got two or three gallons of the ice cream and carted it to the plane and then served it up to everybody on board. I think I have a picture of it somewhere. That was something that never happened before. It was also at a time when people weren't poking fun at his weight so much so he was allowed to eat ice cream without people running snotty little stories.''

Sol Levine says, "He loved to campaign and I think this was evident when observing his performance in various venues that seemed to turn him on such as black churches or large college audiences. One day we were riding through Philadelphia in the motorcade behind him. We had just done a street walk, which is an absolutely dangerous affair because you have all the traveling press and all the local press flocking to the area. We get in the motorcade and Clinton is riding up with the mayor. We drive about a half dozen blocks when all of a sudden the motorcade comes to a screeching halt. Clinton gets out and goes into a little mom-and-pop coffee shop with the mayor. Mark Halperin and I get in there a few minutes after Clinton. Clinton and the mayor are talking with the guy who is apparently the owner. He's behind the cash register and they're chatting. Clinton accepts what looks like a cup of coffee. He shook a couple of hands and as he's walking out in front of us he smiles and gestures back at the fellow by the cash register and says to us, 'He's the ward boss. The neighborhood ward boss.' And he smiles and walks on. The neighborhood ward boss is like the neighborhood political boss. He was the party's guy in the neighborhood. Halperin and I could only surmise that they were riding up in the mayor's car and the mayor said, 'You know, that's so-and-so's shop there. This is his ward.' And Clinton said, 'Well, why don't we stop in and say hello.' And they did, but he was beaming about it because you felt his energy at that point. Here he was just driving along and they stopped in on this fellow and shook his hand and accomplished something politically by this. It was a small thing but it seemed like an important thing to him. That was one of the fun things about covering Clinton because he clearly enjoyed being able to do things like that.''

The Clinton metabolism was not just capable of consuming large quantities of fast food—the candidate seemed to have boundless energy that often exhausted the media trying to keep up with him. Adam Pertman says, "He had this habit of coming back at the end of the night to wherever it was he had to be the next morning. If that meant that you were going to Seattle, Washington, and the next morning began in Little Rock, well, guess what? You were going to fly some more. It was stunning not just because of its effect on us but in this revelation that Clinton never seems to get tired. We're all falling down in the aisles and he wants to come back and chat some more. A fellow reporter said something smart in this regard. She had just gotten on the trail and she looked at him after a day like this and she said, 'You know what it is?' I said, 'What? Explain this to me.' She said, 'This isn't exhausting to him. It's fuel to him.' And I think that's right. This campaigning process, this political process is like food for him. It nourishes him so he gets stronger. There's no question that he gave a better speech at eleven o'clock at night after a long day of campaigning than he did at eleven in the morning.''

Gene Randall also notes, "Clinton is not a morning person. He doesn't operate well in the morning and doesn't speak well in the morning. As the day goes along, he gets better and better and he gave some of his best speeches at midnight or one in the morning on these bus trips. Partially he was energized by the crowds that showed up at one or two in the morning. It was an incredible thing. As tired as he would get, he would revive late in the day and even late in the campaign. He had this durability.''

For John King, Clinton's durability paved the road to Mall Hell. "A lot of people thought that his wanting to spend so much time talking to people and shaking hands after rallies was kind of conniving politics but I think it helped him more than just politically. I get a sense that he draws energy from that. Part of it is ego—people telling him, 'Go, get 'em. We love you.' That's obviously gratifying and there were times in New Hampshire when he was physically exhausted, but he'd revive himself by going out and shaking hands.

"One day we went to a shopping mall in New Hampshire and

he shook every hand. By the time he was done, everybody, including Hillary, was sitting on benches or on the floor of this shopping mall. Everybody was dead because we had been up for days if not weeks and he just kept shaking hands. We were in a McDonalds with people about forty-five minutes and he would not leave the mall. Hillary kept up with him for a couple of hours and then even she sat down and said, 'I just can't take it anymore.' He just kept going and going and he thrives on that."

During the 1992 campaign, Clinton took pains to distance himself from the old-line Democratic establishment. Clinton repeatedly invoked "the middle class" in his stump speeches and offered himself as a "New Democrat." Jeff Stinson comments: "In Cleveland at the Democratic Leadership Conference in May of 1991 Clinton basically outlined the major theme that he would take and run on. Frankly, it was a pretty good speech and it was fairly well received. I remember talking to him later that night. This guy could stay up all night, and I was tired and I'd had a couple of beers. It was getting to be one in the morning and he still wanted to talk. I finally had to tell him 'Governor, I'm tired. I'm beat. I've got to be up early.' Basically he wanted to know, 'How did it come across? What did you see in people's faces?' When he speaks, he watches people's faces very closely to monitor their reaction. I told him quite frankly what appeared to get the best response was when he struck the chord of individual responsibility in society which is something that politicians have not touched on for a very long time. It's basically a hallmark theme with DLC. It's one that plays very well—that with rights and privileges in this nation come responsibility and that people have to start assuming responsibility for their actions and for their families and for each other and their community. It's a theme that people had not heard from the Democratic party in a long time and I recall telling him that I thought that was where he came across the most. He absorbed it. He nodded and took it in. I think throughout the course of the campaign, Bill Clinton did best when he stuck to the themes that he had in the DLC. When he strayed from them he got into trouble. Those themes played everywhere; welfare reform played just as well in black churches in inner-city Cleveland as it did in suburbia."

Stinson also remembers talking with Carville before the mock debate in Kansas City. "He was walking out of one of the stations in his nervous little fret, and he's twitching as Carville's wont to do, and he didn't much want to talk about it. I ended up following him into a bookstore and asking him, 'How's he going to do and what is it that you have to do?' As I recall, he shrugged it off and said, 'Well, you just don't lose.' But you could tell by the way his brow was furrowing that they were indeed concerned about it going in.''

Carville's concern may not have been misplaced. George Bush's last chance to be reelected lay in a series of debates scheduled in the late summer. The addition of the bomb-throwing Ross Perot intensified the danger to the Clinton candidacy. As the front-runner, Clinton had the most to lose in the debates.

Mark Miller attended the Kansas City mock debates, which were staged behind closed doors to prep Clinton for the real thing. ''The first debate was an unmitigated disaster. Clinton was awful. It was like there was no emotion. It wasn't one of his dazzling performances where he shows this enormous command of material and a way of sythesizing it that makes sense to people and draws their experience into whatever issue he's discussing. He was stumbling around. He knew the material but he was answering it wrong. He was missing the emotional essence of the questions that were being asked. Perot, who was being played by Oklahoma congressman Mike Synar, won the first debate hands-down and it really threw them because they didn't know up until that point, how the dynamic of the debate would be changed by a third-party candidate like Ross Perot. There was some structural changes in how the debate format had been set up. It seems to me that it meant that Perot got the last word or it affected how the rebuttals were done so they just had to rethink their whole strategy. They had thought through the order of the questions and the order of the answers. They had to go back and rethink it because the presence of Ross Perot changed the dynamic because of his potential for throwing a bomb into the net. Anyway, it was really a disastrous debate but we didn't understand why. In fact Carville probably should have realized this—and maybe George Stephanopoulos should have as well—that it wasn't unusual for an initial debate to be not particularly good. They were concerned. Tom Donnally, who was the debate coordinator, told them, 'Don't worry about this. This is the first one. We're just getting started.' No one actually ever said to Clinton, 'You did a terrible job and we think you're going to lose all the debates and this election's over.' But it obviously bothered him that it wasn't a success.

"There were a couple of things that were interesting about how people related to him. One of them is that both he and Hillary have an air of . . . it certainly wasn't royalty because they didn't consider themselves superior to people. There was nothing of that, but they had that sort of confidence and that air that comes from always being surrounded by many people for a long period of time. You know he was governor at twenty-eight. He was used to having staff attend to him. It wasn't that people treated him gently and tried not to bruise his ego. It was more that they liked him and considered his feelings. For instance, they didn't want to tell him that he did a terrible job in the first debate because they didn't want to scare him. They felt like they had to appear up so that they wouldn't alarm him and further scare or depress him. It was akin to how trainers treat an athlete or a prize horse that they wanted to protect and sort of show to best advantage. He did want to debate. He very much wanted to debate because he really felt that he could. He was very confident in his ability to both communicate and explain something and also of his own understanding of what he wanted to do and what needed to be done.

"Hillary was very concerned that we not lose sight of the fact that Perot was doing well and that we focus attention on how to deal with Perot. She wanted him taken down by some means because Perot's perception was that he was some truth-teller when in fact, he wasn't. His ability to portray himself as a plain-speaking trustee was what concerned Hillary along with his ability to throw off the dynamics of the debate, of a traditional debate, because he was such an unconventional candidate. Clinton's performance improved when Hillary was there.

"I always thought that they rehearsed him too much, that when he was too scripted, he wasn't as effective as he was when he was speaking spontaneously and that to make him too scripted made him sound artificial and less trustworthy. I thought it played into the qualities that people found troubling about him, that he was too calculating, that he was too political. He also thought that there could be a factor of too much preparation. I had seen that in several speeches. His best speeches were not those that were big, planned, tightly scripted speeches but those speeches that allowed him to be spontaneous and natural, and I think, in terms of the debate that was also a problem. At the same time, he needed to do those kinds of serious preparations because the debates were so complex and the subject matter was so broad that he really did need to practice and try to predict how Perot would interact. The key was trying to find some way of practicing and giving him what they call, 'Moments.' They had several things that they planned. For example, they thought that Bush would raise the issue of Vietnam and the protest. David Pryor, who at that point was working for Gephart, had found something that Prescott Bush, a senator, had said along the lines that it was an American tradition to be able to protest and not to criticize those who protested. They planned to spring that on Bush should he raise the issue himself. He did, of course, and Clinton delivered the line and it was quite effective. It seemed to really goad Bush and throw him off. Most of the things that they predicted actually happened and Clinton delivered his moments as planned, and they were effective. Some people thought that they sounded too scripted but generally they allowed him to dominate Bush.

"By the time of the actual first debate in St. Louis, he was sick, quite sick actually. His voice had been fine up until the first of the practice sessions and then at the end they were really worried at one point that he wasn't going to be able to croak out his answers. He was nervous. The morning of the debate, he said something like, 'I hope I don't embarrass you. I'll try not to screw up.' He also said he knew how Trotsky felt before his debates. He said he hoped he fared better than Trotsky.

"After the initial debate, they were all quite pleased with his performance. They were actually quite pleased with all three debates although they still worried about Perot. They felt that Perot was really connecting, particularly in that first debate. At the same time that they were watching the debates, Stan Greenberg had a dial group going. (Members of dial groups are given electronic dials and they turn the dial toward a hundred when they hear something they like and toward zero when they hear something they don't like. Answers in the seventies and eighties and nineties are considered homeruns.) It was like feeding heroin to an addict for these political consultants to be getting these immediate responses to the debate. Stan was on the phone calling out the numbers that each answer was hitting for each of the three candidates: Bush was doing disastrously and scoring in the sixties but Perot was actually scoring quite well and that alarmed them. Clinton was doing well but Perot was surprisingly strong. They were definitely concerned about him. There were lots of studies and polling and that sort of thing about what kind of an effect Perot would have on the election. They were nervous about him."

Like most of those who followed the debates, John Hanchette

thinks that "Perot did very well in the first debate. I thought that Clinton did very well in the second and I thought that Bush won in the third but by then it was too late. I didn't like Carol Simpson's job in moderating the format where the public got to ask questions. I think the public always asks decent questions—the best questions come from the gadflies that are out there."

From the onset, the Bush campaign was too late. Peter Goldman says, "Bush delayed any effort to put together the campaign. He said, 'It's a sprint that begins on Labor Day. I'm just not going to worry about this.'" By Labor Day, the Clinton campaign had for weeks been off and running.

For Sheffield Nelson the debates reflected the same failure of Republican strategy evidenced throughout a campaign that was poorly managed and poorly run. Its strategists and tacticians also ignored his council. "There was a breakdown at the top. I don't think they ever feared Clinton enough, they never really appreciated the type of campaigner he is, and I think they felt that he wouldn't be able to pop back from the difficulties he was having in the primary. They just never feared him enough to run the type of campaign they needed to run. To wait for Clinton's third hour, or eleventh hour depending on how you want to put it, to attack his record in Arkansas was a terrible mistake. At that point it looked like a desperate tactic, when back from day one they should have been saying, 'No, he didn't rank first here and third there, he ranked forty-eighth here and forty-second there.' I thought that was a very distinct tactical error. But things happen in a campaign that nobody can foresee. A lot of the big guns got out and a lot of the ones who were supposed to be the big guns fizzled. Kerrey, as an example, ran the poorest campaign I've ever seen a national candidate of his stature run. Clinton was in the right place at the right time. Had you been able to keep Perot out of the race, George Bush would be president again. I think Perot knows that and got back in with that in mind. He disliked Bush more than he disliked the idea of a Clinton advantage and he was fortunate enough to be in the right place at the right time. I still think that a lot of it fell to the Republicans not running a proper campaign. If we'd gone after Clinton's record earlier, there could have been a different outcome. You don't have to change but 250,000 votes in selective service states to have had George Bush win the electorial college. A lot of people never realized it was that close a victory, but it was. The changes were minor in terms of the states that had made a difference. As I remember 250,000 votes would have changed the electoral college to a majority for George Bush.

"Clinton's got a terrible temper and throws almost childlike tantrums. And I'd get him furious. His veins would stand out and his face would turn red when I would say, 'Bill, you're gonna' run for president and you're gonna' raise taxes.' He's thrown tantrums all over the state. This is typical of Bill and people who know him know this. Somebody in a recent publication said that Bill would explode and then settle back down. He simply blows his cool. And I told the Bush people to take advantage of it. I said, 'Challenge him on his rankings face to face and say, "Governor, you're lying. You're not telling the people the truth. Tell the people how you can say you rank third when this report says you ranked forty-second and this one says you ranked forty-fifth."' The water quality was ranked forty-eighth or forty-ninth and he was saying we've got the cleanest water in the country. Just things of this nature. The one thing that he really could do some talking about was this number-one ranking industrially. I told Bush's people to ask him what happened the previous ten years, make him defend his decade of progress in the country. If he wants to talk about a decade as governor, don't let him take one year which was a hybrid where he got to compress 1991 and 1992 statistics and showed a super year out. I also said to challenge the fact that it's easy to hypothetically add a hundred jobs in a state where you have only a thousand and show a tremendous increase, yet a hundred jobs where you've got ten thousand jobs is not nearly so impressive. The smallness of Arkansas and our small labor base lets any improvement show up real well. They never caught on to that, they never really used it. And the one or two times that the president tried to say it you could tell he hadn't really been coached on what he was trying to get to. He tried to go for the jugular but he had not been told properly what to go for. He let Bill come off looking like he had done a tremendous job here in Arkansas that the facts simply don't bear out."

Bill Clinton's temper was no secret in Arkansas. Members of his staff and state legislators alike had been observing or experiencing it for years. During the presidential campaign, so did some members of the national press corps.

Longtime Clinton supporter George Frazier says, "His temper is explosive. He gets angriest at what he perceives to be ineffi-

ciency or someone making a decision for him that he should have made himself. Some weeks ago they were going out for a photo op and some of his staff had just kind of brushed the mayor of Washington, D.C., aside and would not let her in the picture. He was furious. He also gets angry if he feels that somebody is being hurt or being looked down upon. I think that comes from his own backyard which was so meager. After all these years, he still feels a kinship for those less fortunate than others.''

Little Rock reporter Joan Duffy recalls, ''Once I said something to him that really pissed him off. It had something to do with blacks and the Republican party. I said something like, 'Well, if I was a black guy, I think I'd join the Republican party just because I'd be such a standout that I could be influential really quick,' and he turned around and started lecturing me about how the Republican party had done nothing for the blacks and he started shaking his finger at me and I said, 'Get that finger out of my face.' That was the first time I'd ever seen his temper but it was a real popper-offer. I had been talking off the top of my head, so I said, 'Hey, get over it.' ''

Kay Kelley Arnold worked on Governor Clinton's staff. ''He didn't hurt my feelings but he was very direct with his staff. If you wrote a letter or drafted something that he didn't like or if he felt you were either ignoring someone or mistreating someone then he'd mark with his big black pen along the side of the letter with a big X through it. If he felt you were not tending to your business and not being fair, equitable, and sensitive to people he let you know it, but he was not ugly about it. He never made you feel like you were less of a person, he never made you feel personally like you were a bad person. Some people will make you feel personally like you're not worthy. He never did that, he would just say, 'You missed the point.' It was not ever a personal attack. He would take my thoughts into consideration but without exception his work was better. He had the ability to pull things together in a way that I didn't, unfortunately. Like I said, he let you know but he was never ugly about it. He does have a temper and people do see his temper, but if the temper is not directed at you as an individual then you can understand it. It was very rare that I saw his temper and it was always justified. In five minutes you're on to the next thing because he didn't have time to be mad. Anger is not what he's all about. I don't see anger, revenge or any of those emotions as part of his makeup.''

Former state legislator Preston Bynum recounts, ''Clinton was

warm and friendly, a hands-on governor. When he had an issue that was being decided in a legislative committee or by either House or Senate, it wasn't unusual for the governor to walk right in and be one of the participants and to try to influence members to vote his position. So you know, you sat around in friendly conversation and bantered with the governor while these matters were being considered. And of course, it was also very social and if you were a member of the legislature, you'd be invited to the Governor's Mansion prior to the legislative sessions and during the Christmas holidays. So he was very open, friendly, and warm. But in the heat of battle, you could become very impassioned and that included Governor Clinton. So this particular morning, my dad happened to be here and I took him to the legislature with me. We were debating a particularly intense issue; emotions were running very high and the governor's were to. To make a long story short, after an hour or so of debate, the committee sustained my position and voted against Clinton's. The governor, of course, at that point, was very flustered, and he spoke his mind very graphically. Afterward I was visiting with some of the other legislators and my father tugged on my coattail and I could tell that he was quite excited. He said, 'Son, son, I think the governor called you a son of a bitch.' So, I hastened to tell him that in politics that doesn't mean the same as it does in the mountains of northwest Arkansas. In the mountains, you just don't call someone that but in politics it's a different story.''

Staffer Bobby Roberts has been on the receiving end of the governor's temper. ''We were good friends. I believe Clinton had a lot of respect for my judgment. Even so he got mad at me a lot. I've had him grab me up by the lapels and holler at me. He's got a bad temper. People don't realize that. I can't remember the exact details but we were trying to get the sales tax passed. The bill specifies when the thing takes place and if we didn't get the thing approved by the Senate, it was going to go over the date when it takes place and then we wouldn't be able to collect enough money on the front end to build some buildings for education. We got this thing passed by the House and I was working the Senate, and the Senate had adjourned. Bill came running in and said, 'Oh, great. We've got this thing passed. We've got our money now. All we've got to do is take it down to the Senate and they can sign off on it.' And I said, 'Well, that's gonna' be a problem.' He said, 'What do you mean?' I said, 'Well, they adjourned about thirty minutes ago.' Of course, I was the person

who told him that so naturally I was the one that allowed it to happen. He grabbed me by the lapels, and yelled, 'I can't believe you let that kind of shit . . .' I said, 'Hey, I can't stop them from going home. What am I gonna' do about it?' I just kind of laughed about it. I'm thick-skinned myself. He said, 'Well, what *are* we gonna' do about it?' I said, 'We might be able to round up a quorum and if nobody challenges it we'll just go ahead and vote it through.' So we probably found ten or twelve of them still around. I said, 'Let's call the state police. We'll just run 'em down if you want 'em back here.' So we did and got enough of them to come back.

"He's got a bad temper, but it dissipates very quickly. He gets very red in the face. He goes after the first person who happens to be there and doesn't really care who it is and then five minutes later he understands what's happened and he's fine. One of the things that I think administrators have difficulty understanding, is that just dreaming up and passing the law, doesn't make it happen. You have to go through the bureaucratic steps of bids and it takes time. He gets frustrated because he wants things to be done immediately. When he goes off at me, I just come right back at him, just about as hard as he does at me. The nice thing about him is, he doesn't take any of that personally. Some politicians, if you disagree with them, will cut you off from access. Bill will never do that. You can disagree with him as long as you don't do it publicly and no one should do that, I think. You can have any kind of fight you want to have with him and the next day he's still going to value your opinion. As long as people understand that I think he gets good information."

Bobby Roberts had his problems. If it wasn't a quorum it was an inferior cigar. Scott Charton reports, "Lilburn Carlyle was in the front passenger side and Clinton and I piled into the backseat and we were heading up to the town of Danville where State Representative Lloyd George was hosting a political gathering and a big feast. On the way up there we did an interview part of the way and then Clinton wanted to know if we were off the record so he could do business. He'd say, 'Are we going to work the whole way up there?' and after I was done with my interview, I said, 'No, I've got everything I need.' As we were leaving the parking lot at channel 7, Clinton wanted a cigar and Bobby Roberts or Lib handed him a cigar. I guess it wasn't to his liking because he threw a little tantrum right there. 'I've got some good ones back at the office. Dammit. Dammit. Dammit.' He let loose with a little stream of profanity and I was kind of taken aback. He was quite livid but in a few minutes, it was gone.''

Chris Burrey says, ''Maybe the most under-reported or unreported story of the campaign is Clinton's temper. He has a terrific temper and just occasionally we'd see flashes of it. Sometimes the cameraman had a much better sense of it because they'd see him on the side of the stage chewing somebody's ass or grabbing somebody by the lapel and shaking them. You know, there's a real angry side to Bill Clinton which I think has pretty much gone unnoticed. One of the more telling episodes of that was during the New York primary, and it was actually caught by *Nightline*. There was a rally on Wall Street and *Nightline* was doing one of those day-in-the-life stories and they had some special access that day. Clinton came out and the crowd was hostile. It was a noon-time crowd of bond traders and stock brokers and commodity brokers and before he even began to speak, there was booing and hissing in the crowd. Clinton grabbed this guy, Garabella was his name. He was the trip planner. Clinton gave him a look that could kill and said, 'How could you do this to me? You really screwed up!' There was pure rage in his eyes. He couldn't believe that he had to go out and speak before this crowd. As it turned out, the film coverage of this worked fine for him because his staff was able to sort of spin it off as Clinton in the lion's den. Here's the Democrat who's not afraid to go to Wall Street and handle a few boos and catcalls. It worked out to his advantage in the end but he was just livid and ready to kill this guy. In fact, I think that Garabella was demoted after that and eventually left the campaign.''

Former KARK-TV news director Ron Blome recalls a similar episode. ''Clinton's splashes of anger over the years were always fairly well hidden and for the most part occurred in the office. I had heard from some of the people who worked around him that he had quite a temper but it was like his smoking cigars and occasionally wearing reading glasses. It was just something you never saw in public. At a news conference in 1989 there were some fairly loaded questions asking Clinton about some controversy we were digging up, and the question blindsided Clinton. In a very adroit style, he said, 'I've never heard of that. I don't know the answer but if you stick around till after the news conference I'll find out.' Someone left the door open and so we saw Clinton in there in somebody's face and saying 'Don't you ever let me be surprised by that. I'm the governor. I'm supposed to know about these things.'

"He wasn't really yelling but was very intense. He blamed the aide because he had been blindsided by a question." Kit Seelye asked the right question at the wrong time, evidently. "I started right in the beginning before the Gennifer Flowers story broke, before all of that. The first time I met him was at a small factory in a town called Berlin. He was sitting around a table with about eight or ten workers from the factory and he was talking and he is very articulate, very personable. They were really concerned that he was from a right to work state because there were union guys in the factory and the factory was going down and they were concerned about his stance on labor. Afterward, I talked to two of the guys, the guy who had sat on his left and the guy who had sat across from him. The one who'd sat on his left staid, 'Well, I thought he was great. He's for right to work,' and the guy who'd sat right across from him who heard the exact same conversation said, 'No, actually he was against it.' My story included this little transcription of their disagreement about what he had just said so I went up to him. I introduced myself. He was very personable and I told him I was from the *Philadelphia Inquirer* and he immediately had good words to say about the paper. So I said, 'So, these guys come away from talking with you with two different messages. Where do you stand on right to work?' and he blew up and said, 'That's what's wrong with reporting. You're just trying to make a political argument out of this.' and he went off about, 'I just want good jobs with high wages,' and, of course, he completely avoided answering the question. It was a very interesting first meeting in that, I think, it encapsulated a lot of things about him in that one little session."

"He does have a temper," says Sol Levine, "You could see that side of him in a number of different sorts of circumstances and one was whenever the question of the draft came up. I thought it was legitimate to question the whole draft issue. He usually would start out by ignoring it but then if you caught him when he was tired or keyed up it would just set off a spark. One Labor Day on the way into Independence, Missouri, we stopped at a fire station. Clinton went in, petted the dalmation and shook all the hands of the firemen there. Susan Feeney, who is with the *Dallas Morning News*, asked him really sort of an innocent open question about the draft. I think there had been a break in the story a couple of days earlier and we had taken a couple of whacks at it and got nowhere. Susan asked him something like, 'Is there anything about this draft that you want to tell us that we haven't asked you about or that we don't know about?' He went nuts. He went absolutely nuts. He was on top of her the way baseball managers get on top of umpires. In the face and gesturing, pointing with his finger. Susan said that she wanted to see the tape because she wasn't sure if he wasn't jabbing at her with his finger. We got the tape and looked at it and it was shot too tightly to tell but he was definitely jabbing his finger and definitely very close to her and he was definitely enraged.''

Gene Randall was standing in the wrong place at a very inopportune moment. "I recall one time when he was on the air live with Bernard Shaw. This was the night that he had won the Georgia primary and he was in Florida and I happened to be in the room when Shaw was interviewing him. He and Shaw had some kind of disagreement on the air where Clinton either misinterpreted or took offense at something Shaw said. I think Clinton felt that Shaw was trying to denigrate the importance of the primary win in Georgia which in fact was a very impressive win. When Clinton got off the air, he just read me the riot act and recited a litany of what he found to be CNN's unfair treatment of his campaign. Now, neither he nor his aides had ever accused me of being unfair. I don't think I was but the fact was, I was an easy target and he lit into me with people watching. Campaign people. He just laced into me like there was no tomorrow. I thought number one, I was the wrong target but number two, from his viewpoint, why is he doing this? Why is he making such a public display when presidential temperment is something that people should be and are concerned with?''

Gwen Ifill believes that CNN *may* have been unfair. "I thought it was outrageous that CNN broadcast Gennifer Flowers's news conference live. They had no idea what she was going to say. To broadcast something like that live based on almost nothing was really quite amazing. Clinton was justified in being furious about it because I really thought they gave her a legitimacy that she hadn't proved that she deserved yet. I mean, who knows how much of what she said was true and how much of what she said was exaggerated? You had to do the reporting to find out whether it was true rather than just running it live, which is what they did.

"He lost his temper at members of his staff when he thought that he had been ill served and not given proper information. He lost his temper at me or at other reporters when we asked questions that he thought were inappropriate. We were in Houston, Texas, on the night of the State of the Union speech and he threw on a little response press conference where he was going to respond to and trash Bush. It was fairly late that evening after the State of the Union speech and after he made his opening statement, the first question was about Gennifer Flowers because this was when he had called and apologized to Mario Cuomo for what he had said to her about Cuomo. Yet up until that point he had not confirmed that it was his voice on the tape. By apologizing to Cuomo, he left it open to question that he was apologizing for something he claimed never to have done so I asked him that. He lost his temper at me and he yelled.

"His anger is explosive at the time and then he gets over it. He is red-faced, with veins standing out on his neck, for as long as it takes to make his point and the next time he sees you, he's fine. I've covered a lot of politicians who go around carrying grudges and eyeing you suspiciously because of whatever falling out you've had, but he's not like that. I've never had that experience. I've covered a lot of people like him, which is to say powerful men, who believe that they are out there by themselves. In the end, if Bill Clinton fell, his reputation would be the only one that would be irreparably ruined so the people who worked for him owed it to him to make sure that they gave him as much support as possible. His anger was about the fact that he'd been left swinging. I wasn't surprised to see it. I would have been surprised if I saw him build up grudges and then fire people and have tantrums but I never saw what I thought was a tantrum. I saw very focused, very specific anger and it reached a point where anybody that had watched him a while could tell the difference between his true anger and his mock anger, which he used for effect. During the transition, there was an episode where he was asked about diversity in the cabinet and he came out and said he wasn't going to be a bean counter and many people who didn't know him very well took that to be an angry Bill Clinton but people who did know him took that to be anger for effect and it achieved what he wanted. It wasn't genuine anger."

The misinformation and rumor that sometimes threatened to swamp Clinton's campaign may have been stemmed in part by behind-the-scenes operations like Betsey Wright's "Scandal Control," which for a time occupied Kathy Ford. "During my time on the campaign I had a really dirty job. I worked very closely with Betsey. We called ourselves Scandal Control. I don't think anybody besides Betsey and I will ever know how hard the Republicans tried to destroy him. We were trying our best to stay on top of all of the many rumors they started. There was the Sheffield Nelson stuff. There were just really files of stuff, all totally untrue, so we spent a lot of time just clearing stuff up with reporters as well as working on the legitimate things that were in the press, things like Vietnam and Gennifer Flowers, and trying to get to the bottom of them by collecting facts and piecing things together. I don't think any of us had any idea that it was going to get as down and dirty as it did.''

The attempt to control scandal became an attempt to control the press, as Kit Seelye sees it. ''He made a real attempt to control everything the press did. Campaigns always try to do that but this one—hiring Betsey Wright as this sort of cloak-and-dagger person to range all over Little Rock and report sightings of reporters and what documents they were looking at—took it to an extreme. She had spies out all over the place and a lot of people who were interviewed were told to report back to her.''

Controlling the candidate sometimes posed as much of a problem to Clinton's staff as controlling the press. Mark Miller talks about one of Clinton's favorite games. ''He would play a sort of game of 'Gotcha!' with the press. James Carville actually complained to him about it because Clinton often seemed unable to resist an open microphone or a question from a reporter. He would work himself deeper and deeper into problems on things like the draft by first giving technically correct answers that were carefully worded and then engaging in some give-and-take with the press, which is basically a 'Gotcha!' in which the press was laying traps for him. He loved the game of trying to evade those traps, and he boasted about it to Carville. That's when Carville said, 'You're going to get caught one day,' and he said, 'Yeah, but they haven't caught me yet.' Well, eventually, of course, he did get caught.''

Clinton's spirit of gamesmanship with the press declined in the course of the campaign. John King feels it ended in a breakdown of trust. ''One day at the back of the plane we had a fascinating conversation about abortion. It was off the record so I don't really want to get into the details of what he was saying but essentially it was at the end of a very long day and he came back and talked to us for a while on the record and then we were all just shooting the breeze and you had him and some staff people and reporters essentially in this running debate about abortion, kind of touching on all the arguments about the subject. It was interesting to watch him. He would say, 'Okay. How do you defend that?' He would play devil's advocate and argue against his own position and that stuff was always interesting just to learn how he ticks. In the middle of it, somebody asked a stupid question about something else and Clinton just glared at this person and then a couple of seconds later he went up to the front of the plane. He doesn't have patience for people he thinks are unprepared or just trying to take advantage—many people in my line of work don't necessarily think about the best question, they think about asking the question that will garner the most attention. He doesn't have much patience for that and he'll tell you so.

"Over the course of the campaign what struck me about him was how much he lost trust in us as an institution. He would come back on the plane and be having a conversation with five or six of us who had been traveling with him since the very beginning and with whom he felt comfortable and then others would walk up and you would see his eyes scanning the crowd and at some point he would cut it off and go back up to the front because he didn't trust these people and there were some reasons for that. I think he got a little paranoid about the press being critical but there were occasions when his mistrust was justified. There was a case where he had talked to Gene Randall of CNN and me for about fifteen or twenty minutes, just talking about the issue of the day. It was a welfare day and it was midnight and there was no place to get away to at 30,000 feet and the last thing we wanted to do was keep working. He had a book in his hand so I asked him, 'What are you reading?' and we started talking about *The Prince of Tides*. Somebody walked in late to this conversation and in an analysis of Clinton written in the *New York Times* two days later, said that Clinton was so afraid that all he would talk about were innocuous subjects like books. It was a really cheap shot. I felt awful. We had had conversations in which I asked, 'Why don't you trust us anymore? Why have you become less accessible to us? You know, it helps you and it helps us during the campaign and when we talk we understand each other better.' After that cheap shot he came back and he said, 'See? This is what I mean.' And I had to agree with him in that case."

The press comments on Clinton the candidate. Joan Duffy: "Well, he's unfocused. He lives life on the edge and that's why he's always late. He loves the banter. He loves the interaction and the discussions. He loves to sit around and talk and to leave the details to other people, which sometimes didn't serve him too well in the state government but, as we used to say around here, 'Boy, he's suited to be president because that's what a president does; comes up with a big idea and then leaves the implementation to other people.' But that's why he needs a good strong chief of staff and somebody to keep him on an agenda and keep him from going off on all these tangents like he does. He's the best politician I've ever seen in my life. He never ceases to amaze me. There's nobody who can work a crowd like he can. It's just silly for anybody to try to compete with it because there's just nobody better, and it's genuine when he's campaigning. He loves to campaign.''

Guy Reel: ''Everybody knows he's the consummate politician, a born-and-raised politician. He was elected in a year when supposedly the voters were anti-politician but they ended up electing the most consummate politician in the history of the United States probably.''

Bill Douglass: ''He's a patriot. He honestly believes in this country. He believes in the system and he believes in his home state. That's the one thing I like about him, I guess, as much as anything—his love for the state. He was proud to be an Arkansan. And what's good about the Arkansan? Well, one thing, you don't have a role to play. A Texan has to be a Texan twenty-four hours a day.''

Gene Lyons: ''I think in general he is a quite sincere politician.''

Philip Martin: ''This is more a feeling than anything else, but I think that there is not a thing he does, there is not a gesture he makes, there's not a word choice he makes that is not at some level calculated. That's not altogether bad but I really think that he made a conscious decision to turn himself into an electable candidate first and secondly into sort of a super governor who'd be recognized all over the country for these ambitious programs. Right now he's trying to define himself as a president. I'm not sure he thought very much about what kind of president he was going to be, but he had enough confidence in himself to know, 'Hey, I'll do it when I get there.' ''

Mark Miller: ''If I had to describe him in three words? Driven. Enigmatic. Decent.''

Scott Charton: ''I think there is some natural arrogance with Clinton. This is a man who moves easily among—what's the phrase that's in vogue now?—the meritocracy.''

Gene Randall: "Arrogance: That's such a judgmental thing, whether it's arrogance or hyper self-confidence. I think every politician who runs for that high an office has a degree of arrogance. It comes with the turf."

Chris Burrey: "I think that there are many Bill Clintons. There's Bill Clinton the boring policy wonk who can drone on forever about the most mundane details. There's Bill Clinton the rousing inspirational speaker. If you see Bill Clinton work in a black Baptist church, you can't imagine he's the same guy as the policy wonk. He's a different, moving, eloquent speaker. When he was in the South, he would sound like Joe Cornpone. He would use phrases like, 'Till the last dog dies' and 'George Bush don't know "come here" from "sic 'em." ' In New York talking to the foreign policy association he'd be the Oxford scholar and the Yale grad. Bill Clinton puts on many different faces and obviously those faces change with his audience. Who is the real Bill Clinton? That was one of the most frequently asked questions during the campaign and I'm not sure anybody got the definitive take on it. What you see pretty much is what you get."

Sol Levine: "When I first started covering him, I remember thinking, 'I don't see the regular guy. I don't see the guy underneath the facade. Where's the man behind the politician?' But they're really all one and the same."

Adam Pertman: "For Clinton I don't think that there is an 'off guard.' He's the most seamless pol/person you could meet. It's not like some politicians who turn it off and on—at eleven at night their public face drops and their human face starts to show. With Clinton it's a fascinating mix where it's all part of the same person so there's nothing to drop."

John King: "We were in a room in New Hampshire when Clinton was going through the Gennifer Flowers stuff and we were just drinking coffee at the end of yet another incredibly exhausting day. It was about midnight and Clinton was in this town hall meeting with Hillary. It was not long after the *60 Minutes* thing, and Carville looked at me and said, 'This is the toughest son of a bitch I have ever met in my entire life.' "

4

Moving On

The Clinton campaign was running down to the wire. Jimmie Lou Fisher remembers speaking on behalf of Clinton at a final big rally in Fayetteville. "One of the highlights of the campaign for me came in late October, when he came to Fayetteville. They called me and said, 'Jimmie Lou, we need a woman to go to Fayetteville. Can you go?' I flew up there and was on the stage with them and they asked me to say a few words and I thought, 'Gosh, what am I going to say before the next president of the United States comes down?' And I thought of an old saying that goes, 'Would've, could've, should've.' So I got up and I was saying that George Bush had been nothing but a woulda', coulda', shoulda' president, giving us all these excuses why he woulda' done this and coulda' done that and shoulda' done the other. And I was all fired up; I mean, you can't be around Bill Clinton and that atmosphere and at that point in the campaign and not just be electrified. And there were probably twelve to fifteen thousand people in all and it was a beautiful fall day and I got up there and, man, I was giving 'em this and they were hollering and responding and I felt so good and so proud of myself. I walked back and he gave a little hoot and said, 'Well, you're all fired up today, aren't ya? You got them all fired up.' I said, 'That's what

I'm supposed to do.' I kind of felt like one of the 'Uh-huh' girls. That's what I feel my part in the campaign was. You know the three girls that stand behind Ray Charles? I was Bill Clinton's uh-huh girl.''

Sonja Deaner was running, too, that beautiful October day. ''My favorite interview was two days before the election, when he was in Fayetteville. He had given his speech, he had even started playing the saxophone, and the mass media just attempted to rush him. It was fun for me. It was a challenge. It was kind of like running an obstacle course. You saw your target. You saw your goal but there were Secret Service agents and police lines and everything in between so for you even to get close to him was the challenge. I remember running after him. My photographer and I were trying to get to him and we got the bright idea of running up through the bleachers, through the band, and we're running and we're running and dropping things and trying to get close to him and all of a sudden, there he was, just right in front of me. No other members of the media were there and no Secret Service people were around and so it kind of threw me but I ran up to him and I forgot I had this long boom mike and I hit him right in the chest. I said, 'God, I'm sorry,' and I just felt like a fool. I asked him something about the polls—how did he think he was doing?—and he answered me and it was fine and he left. Then my photographer said, 'I don't think I got that,' so we had to do it all over. But he did stop. And we did do it again. Which saved me.''

Mark Oswald was covering Clinton on November 1, Election Day. ''A friend of mine from the *Arkansas Gazette*, Ann Ferris, was married to Chad Ferris, who was diagnosed with cancer in the spring of 1992. Chad was kind of a political guy. He worked for a labor law firm but I don't think he was particularly close to Clinton. Ann had covered Clinton and was doing some stringing for the *New York Times* on Clinton. Clinton's polling place was the school that Ann and Chad's daughter attended. They had the kids lined up watching him go in to vote. No one expected him to stop but he stopped and signaled out Ann and Chad's daughter and said, 'I hope your daddy gets better.' I thought that was pretty impressive on the day he's getting elected president that he had time to stop and talk to that little girl. He also called Ann on election night and spoke to her. I just thought that was really a great thing for him to do.''

Clinton's neighbor and sometime jogging companion Robert Johnston remembers Center Street on the night of the election.

"This story choked me up at the time and it still chokes me up. On election night, there was a party over there and the intent for most of us was to go over there for a little bit and then go down to the Old State House for the acceptance speech. There's a brick wall facing the Governor's Mansion. When the Clintons came home on election day after a twenty-eight hour marathon, there was a sign on the wall saying, 'Welcome home, Bill and Hillary. The neighbors' which was a nice touch. At midnight, Earl Jones said to me and I think to one or two others, 'Come over. We've got to turn the sign over,' and I said, 'What are you talking about, Earl?' Luckily he had been farsighted enough. We went out there at midnight on a clear cool night and turned the sign over and it said, 'Welcome home, Mr. President.' "

Steve Buel by chance lost his pencil and caught a particularly intimate moment on election night. "I was working for UPI on election night and came up behind the Old State House in a van containing four reporters and twenty or so camera people. I always sat at the back of the van and let everyone kind of run out ahead of me because everyone always runs. So everyone ran ahead of me and I got out of the van and it was dark. Clinton had already arrived and had been squirreled away to wherever he was going. The reporters were off running after him, and right as I got out of the van I dropped my pencil. I had to stop and grope around on the ground in the dark looking for what was my only writing implement and I did that for about a minute before I realized I wasn't going to find it and that if I didn't get moving soon, I was going to be completely separated from the reporters. I ran without knowing where I was going. Usually, there's a little narrow passageway that you run through and then the Service cordons it off. I ran fifteen hundred yards or so. I had no clue where I was going at this point and I looked up and Bingo! There's Bill right in front of me.

"He is standing by himself although there are Secret Service people and campaign aides around. A vehicle pulls up to the right and out of that steps Al Gore. It is evidently the first time the two of them have seen one another in four days and it's the first time they have seen one another on election day. I realized any movement on my part would alert people to my presence so I just kind of stood there mutely and watched as Al Gore got out of the car and kind of walked over to Bill and they hugged one another, but it's not too syrupy, and Al looked into Bill's eyes and said, 'Hi, pal. You look good.' It was an interesting thing to watch because it gave me a sense of what their real relationship must be like. It was friendly and heartfelt and yet it wasn't the way that one would speak to one's best friend. Little six-year-old Al, Jr., had popped out of the car as well and was standing next to Gore and Bill's response was not to the vice president but to his son. He looked down at him and said something like, 'Albert, are you proud of your father?' And it was touching and a good thing to watch.

"About this time, Hillary arrived in a separate vehicle and she walked up and was extremely distressed. She wasn't making a scene but you could tell from her face that she was very distressed. She had obviously lost some piece of paper and she was just frantic about it. It seemed apparent to me that she was telling this aide that she had lost Bill's acceptance speech. About that time I was discovered and kind of shunted away with all the other reporters. Of course the speech was eventually found. Unlike my pencil."

Victory celebrations among Clinton's long-loyal high school friends ran most of election night in Hot Springs. One of them resumed at Carolyn Staley's house the following morning, as David Leopoulos reports. "You saw the picture. It was in every newspaper in the country. [It is also on the cover of this book.] We were all over at Carolyn's house, just some old Hot Springs friends and some of his Georgetown friends that we had gotten to know the night before at this party—real nice people. All of his close friends and regular people. Not too many rich tycoons and billionaires. It was just an impromptu deal. At three in the morning we said, 'Let's go over to your house tomorrow morning, Carolyn, and have a party, get to know each other better.' So we all showed up about ten in the morning after getting all of three or four hours of sleep. We brought a bunch of food over there to celebrate Bill's victory. And Carolyn had told them—Bill and Hillary—about it. We didn't expect them to come; I mean, he's now president of the United States, and he was up till four or five in the morning. So we're in the kitchen at Carolyn's house and I look out the window and there's all these black limousines and here he comes. He spent two and a half hours just shooting the breeze, just having a ball, talking and laughing. We came out on the front porch when they were getting ready to leave and Jerry, Carolyn's husband, is a photographer, and he wanted to take a picture of all of us on the front porch. Well, of course here's the news media, about twenty cameras across the street all taking pictures of him taking pictures of us. And that made the AP. It had to have been on over

90 percent of the newspapers' front pages. It was a wonderful picture. In fact Bill has that picture on his credenza in the oval office. That's what his friends mean to him.''

Also on the day after the election Kay Kelley Arnold received a telephone call from President-elect Clinton: ''It was just me congratulating him and him thanking me for supporting him; it was just a conversation of a personal nature—how's my dad, how's my mom, he always asked about my family, what's Richard doing—I'm sure he made thousands of phone calls like that that day, but I don't care about the thousands he made, I care about the one he made to me.''

Kay Kelley Arnold had supported Clinton for sixteen years. She recalls that ''When he ran for attorney general in 1976 he needed some people to go talk to in my home county so I tried to set up some meetings for him and I remember that he met with my dad. At this time Clinton was still very young, really young, and my father's very conservative. After Bill goes by his office—he's got a little office on Main Street—my father calls me and says, 'Why did you want me to see this guy?' And I said, 'Daddy, he's going to be president some day.' And he said, 'You're crazy.' ''

In January former Governor Clinton would be leaving the Governor's Mansion on Center Street in Little Rock for 1600 Pennsylvania Avenue in the nation's capital. Before then there were good-byes to be said—and farewell golf games to be played. Walter Patterson recalls, ''The last time that we played was a week before he had to leave for his inauguration. It was drizzling but it didn't start raining until we got to the eighth and ninth holes. He was complaining all along that he had so much to do and he probably shouldn't be out here and I said, 'Well, do you just want to play nine holes?' He said, 'Oh, no. We're going to play eighteen. We're going to finish. I might not get to play a game for five or six months.' By the time we got to the eighteenth hole, it had rained so hard that we were soaked. My gloves were wet. All my grips were wet. I tried to hit a drive on the eighteenth hole and I think my driver went further than the ball, just flew right out of my hand. We laughed, but it was starting to get cold and when we finished we were grabbing coffee and shivering because it was freezing. I thought he'd get sick but he didn't.

''We used to play by Governor's Rules, which means anything he wants to do. You have to understand that he doesn't get out very often and so if he wants to hit a few extra balls here and there because he doesn't get a chance to practice, I think it's absolutely great. Now we play by President's Rules."

Mark Grobmyer, too, remembers that golf game. "We went out one day and it was sleeting and we were the only people on the golf course. Us and however many Secret Service people there were. Bill was driving the golf cart and he'd get it stuck up on the curb or something and we'd have to get out and let the Secret Service push us off. We tried to get 'em to help us find balls too, but they wouldn't do that. Bill hated to lose a ball; he would search and search for balls. He'd just driven. 'I know it's here. It's gotta' be here somewhere.' And he'd be rootin' around, rootin' around. I'd say, 'Bill, there are leaves everywhere. I mean, you'll never find it.' Sometimes, I'd drop a ball and say, 'Here it is' just so we could continue to play."

Mark Grobmyer has been playing golf with Clinton for years. "One time, three or four years ago, I'd gotten one of those exploding golf balls. Bill always hits the ball very, very hard, so I said, 'Bill, you won't believe this ball I've got, they say it'll go forever. It's lighter than a regular ball and real powerful. But you have to hit it as hard as you can. That's all there is to it.' So he said, 'Okay.' I teed it up for him and said, 'Just swing as hard as you can. I bet it might go over the green.' He looked over at me and I think he was a little bit suspicious, but he reared back and just laid into this ball and of course it just went, 'Poosh.' Exploded in a cloud of dust and he looked over at me. Everybody was laughing and I said, 'My God, how hard did you hit that ball?' And he just shook his head.

"Another time, one Memorial Day a couple of years ago, we were playing with Rett Tucker. On the eighteenth tee, all of a sudden Rett's back went out and he could hardly bend back up. He put his ball down and slipped a disc or something. Bill professed to be an expert on how to fix backs and he told Rett what to do and Rett said, 'I can't do that.' So finally Bill convinced Rett to lie on the ground and he said, 'Let me walk on your back.' And Bill started taking his golf shoes off. I said, 'What are you doing? You're gonna' kill him.' And he said, 'No, no, I know what I'm doing.' So he started trying to walk on his back but Rett couldn't stand it so we had to quit. Bill's doctor prescribed some medicine for Rett and we got him on home, but Bill was disappointed that he couldn't fix him up—he really thought he knew something about backs."

Ernest Cunningham had a last visit with Clinton in his office at the Governor's Mansion. "I visited with Bill about two weeks before the inauguration. He was here in Little Rock and invited some of us to come into his office and I went in and stayed a little while and visited with him. There were probably five or six of us and we talked about the campaign. We talked about some of the experiences we'd all enjoyed together, laughed a little bit about some of the sessions, some of the highlights of those. But I'll tell you what kind of person I think Bill Clinton is. He turned to me when he was leaving. He said, 'Don't ever let me forget the Belt,' and he put his arms around me and he said, 'I want always to be conscious of that,' because he has a deep commitment to that area and to the whole state but especially to the areas that are really impoverished. Of course I won't ever let him forget about it, but that meant a lot to me because I think it shows not only Bill's caring, but that he just has a deep commitment to people."

That office in the Governor's Mansion as it was before Bill Clinton left in January 1993 belongs now to memories. Rex Nelson remembered the books: "I would think that Bill was probably proudest of his collection of books about Arkansas, which shows his deep roots." And Kay Kelley Arnold agrees. "Absolutely. There's no question about it. I have been over there with people and heard him say, 'Let me show this to you;' and 'Look at this book, this is a book that's very hard to find, it's been out of print for fifty years.' He is very well acquainted with the collection. It wasn't just 'Oh well somebody just sent me this book' and he put it on the bookshelf. He was proud of it. That and his button collection. He has a great collection of political buttons. He had some of the same stuff in his office in the Governor's Mansion that he's got in the White House now. He had great stuff, personal mementos. It may have been in his first term, I can't remember, the staff and cabinet got together and bought him an inkwell and he still has that. He has a wonderful picture of Hillary and Chelsea that was there as long as Hillary and Chelsea were, great pictures of his mom, his brother, some other family pictures, some things that people in Arkansas have made for him, beautiful little pieces of folk art."

Bill Bowen recalls "a Lincoln head and one of Theodore Roosevelt. He had some animals that stand up erect, they kind of look like otters, and they were on the mantle of his fireplace. In the office, he also had three bits of writing that tell a lot about him.

One was Lincoln's famous observation that 'If I do right, I'll get credit. If I don't, all the angels in heaven sounding my praises can't make a difference.' And not far from his grandfather's picture—his grandfather made a great impression on his life—a plaque said 'It never hurt a really good man to take a few unfair lickin's.' (I remember one day we had a French media person in there and he said 'Leekin, leekin. What is a leekin?') On the north wall, just off his desk, he had in an oval frame some language from an early speech of his own that said, 'The way to save your life is through public service.' He had pictures, too, of Sam Walton, whom he admired greatly, and one or two other people.''

David Edwards and Clinton said good-bye over breakfast. Edwards speaks of a particularly thoughtful gesture on Clinton's part. ''Back in 1968 it was kind of a funny period and for some crazy reason I had bought a floppy hat but like a snap bill hat in the front. You know, if you can imagine the hats they wear in the English countryside, you can imagine what kind of hat it was. So that's what I was wearing when I met him. When he left town to go to Washington to become president twenty-five years later he came to my apartment for breakfast and he had had made for me a cap that looked just like the cap that I was wearing the first night we met. During his campaign, he had come to know a man who made caps and he made a cap for Hillary, which Bill liked. He told the guy about my hat which the guy made for me. Bill gave it to me before he left town but it really illustrates this fellow's sense of kindness. He is a great friend. Over the past twenty-five years he has been my closest friend next to my brother.''

Clinton offered the local media people a final press conference before leaving for Washington, and the local press wangled some of their own souvenirs. Sonja Deaner was there. ''He was always pretty fair with the local media until the last days and then he knew who was going to get him the most coverage. After he was elected president, he did have one last round table discussion just for members of the local press and I was there for that. It was kind of a courteous thing just to keep in our good graces, but after we did the interview all these newspaper people who were normally so professional were walking up to him asking him to sign their press passes. I thought, 'Here are these journalists, so called unbiased journalists, some of whom I know didn't even like him, asking him to sign their press passes,' so of course I did too. I just followed the pack. I guess whether you liked him or not, he was the president.''

A few days after the election, on a Sunday morning, AP political correspondent John King took a walk with the President-elect. ''Right after the election, I had a forty-minute conversation with him. He went to the McDonalds in Little Rock because he wanted to talk to the local people inside and we were kind of watching him through the windows. He came out and he saw me and he waved and he said, 'Come on over.' He said, 'Hi Johnny,' and I said, 'Hi, Governor. How are you? Or should I say Mr. President?' He said 'You can call me anything you want.' Then he said, 'Come on over,' and the Service let me through. I thought he was just going to talk to me as he walked to the car but we walked all the way back to the Mansion. The Secret Service were behind us walking along. The good thing for me is my family got to see my picture—a picture of me walking with him was in every paper in the country. He was talking about how his mother reacted and how proud he was in that sense that he had made his mother proud and he talked about having friends over. I think he just wanted to have a couple of days to laugh and celebrate and be happy about it because he knew—you don't know exactly what's coming—but he knew there was a lot of work to do. But at that point I think he felt that 'now I've got a couple of days to relax and then the real world begins.' He was very lighthearted about the whole thing. Then I asked him just what it was like and what he was going to do now. He thought about it and said, 'I'm gonna' have to figure that part out.' ''

INDEX